THIS IS OUR YEAR

A Season on the Inside of a Football Championship

DECLAN BOGUE

Ballpoint Press

To the memory of four people that were lost too early from our family, and the GAA in this parish and beyond.

Paul Bogue
Orla Bogue
Hugh O'Connor
Sharon Campbell

RIP

Published in 2011 by Ballpoint Press
4 Wyndham Park, Bray, Co Wicklow, Republic of Ireland.
Telephone: 086 8217631
Email: ballpointpress1@gmail.com

ISBN 9780955029851

Book design and production by Elly Design

Printed and bound by GraphyCems

CONTENTS

ACKNOWLEDGEMENTS

FIRST up on the thanking podium are my parents. My mother, Veronica, brought me as a child around all the schools in the county where she coached camogie. It was a busman's holiday for her and she spent her free time on the sidelines of football fields and the annual trips to Clones for sunburnt Ulster finals. It nurtured a love for sport that grew into an obsession. What a wonderful gift to give, along with her love and patience.

My father Seán is, simply, my best friend and I am glad to have inherited the majority of his traits and am proud when I'm told that I'm just like him and his father before. It won't be long before we are out on the bikes again. Thank you for always counting to ten before doling out advice, and for the squatter's rights of the sofa that the majority of this book was written on, the peace of 'The Good Room' and the cups of coffee.

Then, there is my beloved girlfriend Ciara. Too modest to want to be in here, but this book would have ended up just another good idea without all the backing, interest, support and selflessness you have shown me and the focus you give me. This is as much your creation as it is mine. I've done my share of taking over the past while, now it's time to give a lot back, beauty!

To my elder brother Niall, for the most significant moment of my working life, when he introduced me to Kieran Shannon. This would never have happened without that. My younger brother Ronan, my sisters Edel and the family pet Eilís, for all the fun and slagging and inspiration.

Others to fire my youthful mind with a love of the GAA were my uncle and Godfather Peter Bogue who collected me every Sunday to watch him touch the ball twice in a match but never fail to pick up a goal! And another uncle Vincie Corrigan, I'll grow into those togs yet.

Almost a year ago I had a number of ideas kicking around in my head, and Kieran Shannon was kind enough to pick out the best of them. He ended up being the editor for this project, but more than that, he has been my most trusted adviser in journalism for the last ten years and a major influence in my life. Must be the Fermanagh in him.

He never makes a bad call and it was a privilege to be pointed in the direction of PJ Cunningham at Ballpoint Press. They took a chance and have been incredible with the level of detail, care and feedback. A big thank you to PJ and designer, Joe Coyle for their expertise, and also to Rosemary and all the Cunninghams for their wonderful hospitality as I brought this baby home.

I must thank Michael Foley and Christy O'Connor, two gents who have been cheering me on through the last several months. Their advice is much valued and they are top men.

My colleagues at *Gaelic Life*, Ciaran Woods, Ronan Scott and especially John Hughes with his appreciation of aesthetics, have to be mentioned here for their toleration of Tuesday night stories and inaccurate regional accents that I inflict upon them.

The true glory of this story belongs to the men out there who sacrifice their lives to display their character and represent the places they come from. To me, everyone featured here are real, living heroes. I selected these people in pursuit of a wide spread of storylines and starting points. None of them turned me down and all of them gave me incredible access and time. The lasting legacy will be the friendships forged.

My sincerest admiration and thanks goes to Paddy Cunningham, Stevie McDonnell, Val Andrews, Terry Hyland, Mickey Conlan, Kevin Cassidy, Aidan Carr, Barry Owens, Dick Clerkin and Ryan McMenamin.

Additional gratitude is extended to Adrian McGuckin, Danny Devlin, Ross Carr and Benny Tierney. There was so much that couldn't be shoehorned in, but I want to thank Geoffrey McGonigle, Barry McGowan, Noel McGinley and Tony Blake nonetheless.

All of these people helped in some way, so they should also be named, but in no particular order; Cahair O'Kane, Jarlath Burns, Johnny Kelly, Joe Brolly, Brendan Devenney, Denise Watson, Tommy Niblock, Colm Bradley, Paul Fitzpatrick, Stephen and Brian Jackson, Shane O'Neill and finally Shane Breen for reminding me that no matter how hard you think you are working, there's always somebody that bit extra. John Morrison also for his quote that, 'Ideas are like rabbits, keep two of them together and soon they will be coming out of everywhere.'

To the friends that I ignored for the last year, I'm going to namecheck you - Mickey, Salad, Big 'Pound for Pound The Biggest Hitter In Ulster Football' Steve, Langer, Aidy Mac, Phairytale, The Rab, Derminator,

ACKNOWLEDGEMENTS

Blocks, Sanchez, Hands, P and Rony Gunn, Big Pitt, Lugs, Rory, Spaddow, Visage au Chocolat... We all have a lot of catching up to do.

And finally, to everyone at Tempo Maguires football club, Lisbellaw St Patrick's hurling club and anyone that ever brought me to a match.

Declan Bogue,
Garvary,
Tempo
September 2011

The fight is won or lost far away from witnesses –
behind the lines, in the gym, and out there on the road,
long before I dance under those lights.
MUHAMMAD ALI

An Arc Like
A Rainbow

ANOTHER kick and the ball takes off through the air. It dances and dips on the gentle breeze ushered in from the wild Atlantic and passes between the posts. Point.

Two telegraph poles sprout jauntily in slightly different directions out of the ground behind the goalposts. They are linked by an expanse of tangled and tatty fishing nets that have served their purpose with admirable stoicism through the years. But the way the player is connecting with the ball today, they are rendered pointless.

Another kick and the ball soars. It clears the goalstop and hits concrete with a smack, kicking up a small plume of dust. It continues towards the new pitch being created by the bulldozers, tractors and diggers in the near horizon.

The club are proud. They are hosting Peile na Gaeltachta – an annual football tournament for Irish-speaking clubs – in 2012 and the new pitch is all part of the plan. The patch they stand out on now will be relegated to the role of training field, one containing a well of memories of battles fought and won and lost. There is no need for gates or security here. The player pushes his run harder and takes a ball on the move. The coach shouts 'RIGHT!' The player alters his position and strikes the ball with his right foot. As soon as he hears the noise, he doesn't have to look. He just knows.

Another kick but this time he grimaces. Just as he gathered the ball, the coach shouted 'LEFT'. He was on the left wing and he tried to catch it on the outside of his left boot. It skews and spins and slices away from goal. Again it lands on the concrete and begins hopping away. Its journey is halted by a holidaymaker, who kicks it back over the wall. Being on vacation, he stops to idle the next hour away, fetching balls, returning them with kicks.

The player and the coach are glad. It means they can work faster and get more done, intense shooting practice with the pressure that fatigue brings. The player asks what was wrong with his last shot. The coach counsels him that he lifted his head a fraction too early. And he could do with making the follow-through a bit smoother too.

Another kick and this time the wind has died down. The player catches it flush and it leaves his boot, creating an arc like a rainbow. It hangs almost supernaturally still for a second at the apex of flight, and makes a gentle descent, filling out the fisherman's nets, making that satisfying gentle ripple sound that compares so favourably to the harshness of the concrete slap.

To their left, the aroma of sea salt wafts in from the pier in the middle distance. The player will relish leaping into that water, just as he does twice daily during the summer months. For now he has to get this next kick right. He begins his run-up. The pitch is short so the kicking position is roughly five metres behind the fifty metre mark. The command comes 'LEFT!' He draws back and feels the swing.

Another kick and he never even feels the leather on his foot. It is still rising when it clears the posts and the goalstop. The holidaymaker suspends reverie momentarily and scrambles into action to stop the ball.

Another kick, followed by another kick. Some go wide, most go over. It is a torture and therapy all at the same time. They remain in these roles and the minutes and hours tick by without interruption. How long have they been out? Neither of them have any idea.

The player, Kevin Cassidy, and the coach, Tom 'Beag' Gillespie, are glowing with their toil. Cassidy has reached the magical number of converted shots. His action and swing are working well. They make their way to the holidaymaker. He is from Silverbridge, County Armagh, and had time to kill, so he stopped by.

Cassidy thanks him for doing that and the three men talk about football and Gaoth Dobhair for a while. It's a strange thing but people always seem to arrive and act as ballboys without being asked. A few days before, a middle-aged woman was out walking and fetched footballs for a full two hours. What on earth possessed her?

Cassidy and Gillespie walk off. Two and a half hours is plenty for a non-training day but it will come in handy. Another downpayment made on his talent, because hard work will beat lazy talent.

He knows that now.

• • •

JULY 30th, 2011, CROKE PARK

Marty Morrissey: There's a chance here for Donegal... Rory Kavanagh, he gives it inside... No free given... Lining up is Neil McGee... Here's a chance...

Kevin McStay: HE HAS IT! HE HAS IT!

Marty Morrissey: It's dropping... OVER THE BAR! Kevin Cassidy, has surely put Donegal in the All Ireland semi-final!

CHAPTER ONE

The Draw

ON October 7, 2010, Ulster's provincial secretary Danny Murphy and president Aogan Farrell stood under the sweltering lights and the glare of television cameras in Croke Park to make the annual draw for the 2011 Ulster Senior Gaelic Football Championship.

The names of nine county teams were contained inside hollow balls lying in a glass vase. Whatever order those balls were pulled out would dictate the course of the lives of hundreds of players and backroom staff for the following year. Fans, sitting in bars, clubhouses and frontrooms all over Ireland, would have their dreams and aspirations stirred.

On completion, the annual nationwide debate would ensue. Credit card details would be handed over to betting websites and many brave promises made in and out of drink would be noted down for future reference. The only way to settle it would be the evidence on the scoreboard when the final whistle blew on Ulster final day nine months later.

Of course there is still the backdoor system for teams to pull something from the wreckage. But defeat in the Ulster championship is a form of wreckage. Defeat means a dream – for many the dream – is all over.

An All Ireland title can still be won. Tyrone have managed it twice in the last decade through the backdoor system, but virtually every player in Ulster dreams of mounting the steps of St Tiernach's Park in Clones to accept the Anglo-Celt Cup. No-one dreams of spending July playing on dreary Saturdays trying to scratch out a win over Carlow in Dr Cullen Park, or heading to Ruislip to face London during the qualifiers.

The Ulster Championship has a deep tradition. This would be the 114th time it was to be staged. It retains its straight knockout formula, guaranteeing that every minute of every match carries real meaning.

Players would give anything to look out over a sea of beaming faces from their own county. History shows that the participants can stop short of nothing in the pursuit of that vision. Since the backdoor system was introduced, it has been speculated that the safety net would make for less desperation in the provincial championships. It hasn't worked out like that, especially in Ulster.

The same anxieties and pressures exist as before. The attention the media devotes to these championships have never been greater and with the outlet of social media, every single incident, score, run and strokes both fair and foul, undergo forensic analysis.

So players will cheat, players will try to hurt each other. Managers will lie about injury scares to players. Teammates will let each other down, some will hide when the heat is turned up, some will be carried off on their shields.

Ulster is a land apart. Despite the language of all-inclusiveness, GAA followers in the province see themselves as existing in isolation. They are the only province that will get behind another representative as they progress in the All Ireland series. With the exception of a few years in the last decade when the Armagh and Tyrone rivalry was at its zenith, they want to see Sam Maguire coming home to Ulster.

Generations of wider social persecution in the north has fostered a bunker mentality belief that certain media commentators and journalists are inherently opposed to what they ignorantly refer to as 'northern-style' football. That term has only made its way into the lexicon over the last decade, with the sophistication of Armagh and Tyrone's defensive systems and how their players redefined roles and for a time defined football. Before, when Ulster sides would traipse down to Croke Park for their annual beating in the All Ireland semi-final and weren't seen as a threat, their language was gentler. They would be gently chided with the description of the Ulster Championship as a festival of pulling and dragging.

Now Ulster teams are respected. The province has been responsible for many innovations, fresh thinking and a willingness to dream up different possibilities. The magnificent obsession has led to a stream of superb managers, leaving other provinces playing catch up.

In recent years it's become somewhat fashionable to claim the competitiveness of the Ulster Championship is overplayed and overhyped, but the reality is it still remains the most competitive provincial championship in the GAA.

From 1999 to 2010, the Ulster Championship might have been won by either Armagh or Tyrone but in that time every other county made it to the big dance. At least once, they all had their day in the spotlight of the Ulster final.

That does not happen in other provinces. Carlow and Wicklow simply do not make the Leinster showpiece. Clare and Waterford get slapped down long before they get the scent of a Munster football final.

For all the Anglo-Celt trophies Armagh and Tyrone have annexed over the last dozen years, there is no duopoly in Ulster like there is in Munster. Only Kerry and Cork can foil the other in their own province. In Ulster Tyrone or Armagh are routinely tripped up by the others; it's just that it's been a long time since the two of them were tripped up in the one year.

In 2008 the eventual All Ireland champions Tyrone were beaten by Down in the first round of the Ulster Championship. It was hardly an ambush either; the tie required a replay and extra-time. Down would make it to the last twelve of that year's All Ireland series yet at the end of the season they could only be ranked the sixth best team from their own province, behind Fermanagh and Monaghan and league champions Derry, Ulster champions Armagh and All Ireland champions Tyrone. In what other province could the sixth-best team in a province beat the All Ireland champions? In 2010 Down reached the All Ireland final, even though they hadn't reached their own provincial final since 2003. That's how tough it is to make it to an Ulster final, let alone win one. Since 2003, six different Ulster counties have reached the All Ireland semi-final. Only four Leinster counties have reached that stage during that time; Munster, just two; Connacht, just the one.

In this upcoming 2011 season seven of the nine Ulster counties will play their league football in either Division One or Two. That's seventy-seven percent of the province playing in one of the top two tiers. In Leinster the rate's only thirty-six percent; in Munster, just thirty-three. No other province has Ulster's depth. The province is a land of pitfalls and peril.

In the 2011 Ulster Championship bones will break. Blood will be drawn. Tears will be shed and hearts will be shattered. All for the glory of your county, where you are from, and who you represent.

●　　●　　●

The format of the draw is much the same with most sporting events. Whoever is drawn first has home advantage. Donegal were first out.

When the draw was staged, Kevin Cassidy was oblivious to it. As far as he was concerned, he had done his bit for Donegal. Apart from winning the National League in 2007, his crowning glory was the All Star award he collected after his debut season of 2002. There were some good times in between as part of the party boys set in Donegal, but the last two Championship exits had been too much to stomach. His wife Sarah had bought him a present of a kayak and he intended to make use of it. More pressingly, Sarah was four days away from giving birth to twin girls, Aoife and Nia.

'I was gone at that stage, I had no interest at all in the Ulster draw. I had other things on my mind. A boy down at the local shop told me we got Antrim and that's how I found out. Normally you would be waiting on the news to see who you got. I can remember watching it in 2008 when we got Antrim. The boy in the shop told me it was a chance for revenge.'

Antrim had been paired up with them. It was an identical draw to the 2009 edition, to take place in the same ground; MacCumhail Park, Ballybofey. Back then, precious few Antrim fans made their way to the game. Although their side had won promotion from Division Four, they were poor in the league final against Sligo.

They rocked Donegal to the core and carved out a win with steel and intelligence. Within five weeks Antrim fans would pack out Clones for the Ulster final against Tyrone. Their place among the bottom feeders of football had changed utterly.

Leading them out that day as captain was Paddy Cunningham.

With tight cropped red hair and a slender frame, he looks every inch like the welterweight boxers that Belfast has in abundance. But the GAA has always been Paddy's game. He is the third generation of Paddy Cunningham, after his father and his father before him, to play both football and hurling for Antrim. Naturally, father and son were glued to the television set in Hannahstown, west Belfast.

When they were drawn out, they exhaled. Could have been worse. Could have been a lot better though. 'You're always hoping for a home draw in the Ulster Championship, because it's wild competitive. We were looking for any draw at home, so when Donegal came out of the hat first you were thinking, "Hopefully not us." Not because it's Donegal as such, but because home advantage is so massive.

'They have a new manager and after us beating them up there two years ago they'll be looking for revenge. It's going to be a mammoth task.'

Because there are nine county teams in the province, there has to be a preliminary round. The preliminary round is the graveyard of hope. Only twice in the history of the competition has a team won the Anglo-Celt trophy from that starting point – Cavan in 1945 and Armagh a whole sixty years later when Joe Kernan's great team were arguably at the height of their powers.

The next ball drawn would face the winners of Donegal and Antrim at home. And so it was Cavan.

Things were shaping up remarkably similar to 2009. Once Antrim got out of Ballybofey with that historic win, they were underdogs facing Cavan in the Ulster semi-final, Cavan having just beaten Fermanagh, Ulster finalists the year before. On a sultry Saturday night in Clones though, Cavan could not live with Antrim's verve for the battle.

In the wake of their ignominious defeat, Cavan coach Tommy Carr faced the brickbats. Observers of Cavan football were critical that the county board had a habit of going for outsiders, men with no real family or emotional connection with the county and attributed the team's perceived lack of fight and passion to that.

After their 2010 championship finished with a thrashing on a wet night in Cork, Cavan replaced Carr with another son of Dublin. Instead of revolt, there was a satisfaction that one of their own had come home. Val Andrews was no ordinary outsider. He had taken on the job as Cavan coach when they were in a state of civil war in 1999, the players having ousted Liam Austin from his managerial post. The problem was Andrews was living in Tralee at the time. It was the impossible job but Andrews came close to pulling it off.

'Year one was a disaster. Absolute disaster. Thirty-six thousand miles on the road. Fatigue, the age of the team, and a bad attitude. Met Derry in the Championship and they hammered us [after a replay]. Wasn't a game at all.

'The second year we got promoted to Division One, were unlucky to run into Derry in the Championship, and this time they kept it to thirteen points.

'Then in the third year, well, you always get a chance in Ulster...'

The chance he talks about was getting Cavan to the 2001 Ulster final. They lost that game by two points to Tyrone but were heading in the right direction. Andrews placed his trust in selector Terry Hyland and his knowledge of what he called 'honest gasuns'. They had a vision.

Andrews seemed all set to secure another term, but instead of being a mere formality at a county board meeting, it turned into a farce. A club delegate proposed a vote of no confidence. It was seconded by another club that felt aggrieved at their lack of representation on the county panel. It went to a vote and Andrews won comfortably but sickened by the lack of support he walked on a point of principle.

Now Andrews and Hyland are back in the role, this time as a joint ticket, while Hyland has the added responsibility of looking after the talented crop of U-21 footballers in the county.

Val caught a glimpse of the draw. He made a few calls about it but his picture of Cavan 2011 at that stage was a blank canvas. 'At that point we hadn't a clue of where we were at, what talent was in Cavan. You know what Donegal are doing and you know Antrim are a good outfit. We're going to be underdogs no matter who we play. We're more about getting the fellas ready for the league, getting geared for the McKenna Cup first.'

Derry were drawn next. Always fancied to do something big at the start of each year, they've routinely flattered to deceive. Although they've reached two All Ireland semi-finals since 2004 and contested two national league finals in the past three seasons their last Ulster final appearance was in 2000. In fact since that appearance they've failed to put two Championship wins together in the Ulster cauldron. They possess wonderful talent but can never pull things together for long enough to mount a sustained challenge. Problems created by the fractious club scene have caused some of their failings, but it would be unfair to say that has been the root cause of their failure. They remain a great enigma.

Following a heavy beating from Kildare at home in the 2010 qualifiers, their manager Damian Cassidy stood down. The mood within the county was that the present day squad could be written off as shapers and fakes. Cassidy was supposed to bring the best backroom team, a higher class of tactical awareness and foster team unity. Instead they left the stage without baring their teeth in the semi-final against Tyrone in 2009 and Armagh in 2010.

Mickey Conlan was a goalkeeper with his club Ballinderry Shamrocks who won an All Ireland club title in 2002. His last county game was in 2003 so he was hardly on tenterhooks to see who Derry would land. New manager John Brennan though brought his own ideas to the job.

'I didn't even see the draw,' said Conlan, 'until John called me to tell me he wanted me to join the panel. Then I started looking into it and considering if I would go back or not. These are the things you have to think about. You look at the draw and see is there a chance could we do something.'

At thirty-three years of age and with three children under the age of three, he had a bit of soul searching to do. It took a matter of hours before he signed up to become the last line of defence. Hand on heart, his decision was already made before the deliberations started.

Derry were at home and the team drawn to travel to meet them at Celtic Park? Fermanagh.

Derry and Conlan were happy enough at that. While Fermanagh's championship record in the noughties stood up to anyone's outside of the big two of Tyrone and Armagh, something has been sick at the heart of Fermanagh football for some time. The line can be traced right back to the moment in the 2008 Ulster final replay, when substitute Barry Owens planted his foot in the Clones turf, went to turn sharply and heard a snap. His cruciate ligament tore, and when he left the field, all hopes of a first Ulster title for Fermanagh went with him. They went from darlings of the nation heading into that Ulster final replay to something of a national joke just a week later when they could barely kick a point against Kildare.

That panel was broken up by manager Malachy O'Rourke. He placed his faith in younger talents, but the overall squad had a lop-sided look to it without the experience of players like Tom Brewster, Shaun Doherty and the retired Raymond Johnston. Owens was ruled out of the following league, and their most valuable player, Ryan McCluskey, gave his first commitment to Portadown in the Irish soccer league. The freefall was only starting. O'Rourke was to take charge of twenty-two more competitive games with Fermanagh in league and championship and they won only four. They dropped like a stone until they reached Division Four.

Owens came back but the same injury occurred during the summer of 2009. Few gave him a chance of ever returning, but he was sitting on his sofa in time for the 2011 draw.

'It's always in the back of your head, the Championship. As soon as the draw was made you would have been texting lads, Eamon Maguire, Mark Little, Chris Breen, asking "What do you think of that?" They were saying back "It's a tough one but we still have a chance." As we've seen the last few years, there's not much between any team in Ulster, it's just all on the day.'

That completed one half of the draw. It would be considered the weaker side of the draw. The serious heavyweights hadn't emerged yet.

Had Stevie McDonnell been watching, he would have good reason to be nervous. Still left in the hat was his Armagh side, Ulster champions Tyrone, a Monaghan team that had humiliated Armagh by twelve points in the first round a matter of a few months previously, and Down, who came agonisingly close to winning the All Ireland final.

McDonnell has won the Ulster title seven times. He is the most decorated player of his generation in this arena, but at times over the last number of years, he has taken on the role of Sisyphus, the King in Greek mythology who was sentenced by the gods to roll a boulder to the top of a hill, only for it to roll back down before he could reach the summit. He was a young substitute for Armagh's first Ulster title in seventeen years in 1999, but by the following year, he was one of the most lethal forwards in Ireland. His consistency has set his standards at frightening levels, and the All Ireland win in 2002 has cast a shadow over Armagh football. As that great team began to break up after the 2006 All Ireland quarter-final and the last of their epic battles with Kerry they have only fleetingly been a force in Ulster and have long departed the thin air of the top tier.

While Armagh share a border with Tyrone, their ancient wars were fought on the other side of the county against Down. And as it transpired, both sides were drawn to square off again in 2011 in the redeveloped Athletic Grounds of Armagh city.

As the balls were pulled out in Croke Park, McDonnell was in Ashbourne, Co Meath, preparing for the International Rules game against Australia. The coach for the series, Anthony Tohill, had given the honour of captaining his country to McDonnell. It was richly deserved, as both he and his good friend, Down's Benny Coulter, have been the standout performers in the exhibition games of the latter part of the last decade.

'There were players all over Ireland there. Myself, Brendan Donaghy and Ciaran McKeever had travelled down together, and once we got back into the dressing room and heard the draw, the three of us each had a smile on our faces. It was the draw we really wanted, because of what Down did last year. If there's any team you want to be meeting in the first round of the Championship, it is the side that played in the All Ireland final of the year before.

'We feel we have the perfect draw. It's going to be our first Championship match in the Athletic Grounds in many a year, it's the best chance for us to stamp our authority on the ground and make our mark.'

Twenty years earlier Armagh and Down played an Ulster championship match in Newry. Ross Carr had been surprisingly switched from his usual role of wing-back because manager Pete McGrath felt he needed the protection of forwards who could tackle. Carr impressed in the new role and stayed there for the rest of that glorious year which culminated in an All Ireland win. Down brought the Sam Maguire Cup to be greeted by bonfires at the border and looking on was his son, Aidan.

Now Aidan is a seasoned county footballer. His pedigree and class ensured he was always going to make it. Aside from the obvious physical similarities between father and son, they both play a remarkably kindred style of football. Aidan may have begun inter-county life as a wing-back, but has featured as a half-forward. Injury kept him out of contention for a starting jersey in Down's heady charge to the 2010 All Ireland final, the first time he has lost his regular place since he was drafted into the panel.

Losing an All Ireland final has been known to cause an ache that never goes away. These things are usually dealt with by a spell of depression and a process of coming to terms with it all. The uncertainty of not being able to contribute though agonised Carr. The financial software company he works for, First Derivatives, provided an ejector seat out of the Newry goldfish bowl with the offer of going over to London to work up until Christmas. He grabbed it.

'I was supporting a financial system for Royal Bank of Scotland, in London, at the time of the draw. The area is Bankside, just across the river from Saint Paul's Cathedral.

'As soon as the football season finished up, I was sent there until four days before Christmas. There is one hundred staff based in London and they have apartments over there. The former Dublin player, Bobby Doyle, his son Ronan started two weeks after me. We got on straight away and he had a spare room in his apartment so I moved in.'

Together, they horsed into the social scene at the weekends. The massive antipodean drinking den, The Church, got a turn. And you can't go to The Church without following it up with a visit to The Walkabout.

'There were a few Mondays that ended up pretty ropey for me. It was great to get over to London, especially after last year. It allowed me to clear my head and forget about it. I went to the gym and that, just to keep myself ticking over. I wouldn't have liked to be still stuck in Newry, talking to the same people about the same stuff. Once the All Ireland final was over, nobody was asking me about football.'

One evening as he was lying in his apartment, his phone hummed with a text message from his sister Fionnuala. 'Did you see the draw?'

'It took me a while to click on to what she was talking about, but once I did I texted back; "No, who did we get?" She just sent back "Armagh. Away." I raised the eyebrows at that.

'It's a good draw, for here [Newry] anyway. The town goes mental for Down and Armagh games, with the city spanning both counties the way it does. You see Down flags and Armagh flags beside each other all the time.'

Another tasty tie was still in the bowl – a repeat of the previous year's final.

Both Tyrone and Monaghan had also met in the 2007 final, a game that Monaghan believe they left behind them.

Home advantage was granted to Tyrone. Players as decorated as Ryan McMenamin tend not to get excited about a first-round draw. It took a few days for the information to get to him.

'I didn't watch it. I wouldn't even be bothered thinking about it. It [Monaghan] has been mentioned a couple of times since but it's more to get the boys going.'

What is bothering McMenamin is the manner of how things were left at the end of 2010. Dublin had been whipping boys at the quarter-final stage for Tyrone in 2008 and then for Kerry in 2009. For 2010 and the All Ireland quarter-final, they learned their lessons and came at Tyrone with ravenous, relentless intensity. Forced to play the game on the back foot, McMenamin and his teammates squandered chances all day long. All over the winter it has stuck in their craw.

'You wouldn't want to leave it like that. When you kick seventeen wides and consider that all we needed was three or four of them to have won it... We kinda knew ourselves that we hadn't played that well but we weren't too far away. People outside the camp, they say we are a right bit away, but I think we know, with the young boys coming in now with a season's experience now, we're close...'

In Tyrone, nothing but an All Ireland is considered a good season.

Monaghan think differently. For them, an Ulster title would mean everything. They would celebrate it for months on end and it would be a lifetime's work bearing fruit. Dick Clerkin has been at the forefront of their efforts, his county career spanning three decades now. His father, the famous Hugo, has his Ulster medals. Dick wants to get his.

'Up until last year, we had won four Ulster Championship games since 2001. That's a dire record. People see the two Ulster final defeats but we lost them. We can beat a lot, but when it comes to the Championship, we flop.

'We need to get that monkey off our back, especially for the lads who have been beaten in the two Ulster finals. We haven't done ourselves justice really. Something that really annoys me is this "You're punching above your weight" bullshit. I don't believe that. We're a Division One team, have been for a couple of years, and we're well entitled to feel we should be up there.'

Clerkin was holidaying in Malta when the draw was made. His aunt Patricia, married to former Monaghan player Ray McCarron, broke the news to him. Tyrone away. Jesus!

'I remember thinking, "Aye, I suppose that's the time to play them." If you're going to get Tyrone you will get them early. You might not have picked them out of the hat, but would you prefer to play them in a final? I tell you what, I couldn't take losing another final to Tyrone.

'Get them now. Especially with the way we lost the Ulster final last year, how distraught we were.

'In '07, we were the new boys a wee bit, and when you come from nowhere like that you tend to earn the patronising comments, the well-dones and the hard-lucks. Then when you're there for a couple of years and you don't actually win things, they start to get nasty and put you down.

'Defeat in the final last year did hurt but if we have aspirations about going further into the summer, we might go this way. There's a lot of balls to be kicked between now in the summer, and even though it's up in Omagh, it can be done.'

It can be done.

In Ulster each county feels that way about their opening Championship game, about even winning the Championship itself. That this could be their year.

CHAPTER TWO

Another Sorrowful Mystery

MONDAY, January 10, 2011 was just the sort of humdrum day Ireland does so well. Wet and miserable. Dark by three in the afternoon. Conditions that inspire dreams of sunshine holidays.

Ryan McMenamin and Maura Kelly, the Tyrone ladies full back, had made the spin up to Belfast to shop around and find some inspiration for their honeymoon. Travelling enthralled them. McMenamin has a fascination with Fidel Castro that goes beyond his facebook profile picture; it once prompted a holiday in Cuba. Together, they toured Ernest Hemmingway's old haunts, cruised about in vintage cars in Old Havana and took a bus trip to Santiago where they visited the scene of Castro's first attempted coup. For a honeymoon though they wanted something less demanding.

He felt his phone go off in his pocket, so out of courtesy he put it on silent while the travel agent suggested locations to them. One option was to combine Mauritius with South Africa. McMenamin thought that Africa might be a bit dangerous for his liking but bit his lip. They finished up by taking a few brochures, thanking the travel agent and leaving.

Once out of the shop, he noticed he had several missed calls. He followed them up and a nightmare descended. Michaela McAreavey, daughter of Mickey Harte, had been discovered dead while on her honeymoon in Mauritius.

Since taking over as Tyrone manager in November 2002, Harte had become an enormous influence on McMenamin. Before he came within Harte's orbit, the Dromore man had been a tearaway wing back with bags of potential but bags of pure rawness as well. Harte took the pocket dynamite and harnessed his aggression into a player that would get inside the heads of his opponents, sticking to them like fly paper, all the while becoming possibly the best ball-playing corner back of his generation. McMenamin was one of the key reasons that Tyrone would gain three All Irelands while Harte was the man to lead them. And where Mickey went, his daughter Michaela followed, his constant companion.

When Harte had taken the Tyrone minor and U-21 teams, he brought his children on the bus to all their games. Their support also extended to training sessions. McMenamin never made it as an underage star so he wasn't as close to Michaela as the group of Stephen O'Neill, Brian McGuigan and others. But when Harte was appointed as senior manager ahead of the 2003 season, she would become a familiar face. An effervescent bubbly character who radiated positivity. Now she was dead and the reality was too horrific to comprehend.

The five stages of grief immediately set in, the first being denial.

'You were wishing it was a rumour,' says McMenamin, 'because you do get these rumours. At the back of your mind though, you knew there was something badly wrong. Too many people were phoning me. I put on the radio coming down the road from Belfast and the bulletins had it. It was true.'

Early reports were speculative. Some had it that there had been a fatal car accident. Later that evening the catastrophic series of events emerged. After lunch, she had gone back to room 1025 of the Legends Hotel to retrieve some biscuits to accompany her tea. She disturbed members of the hotel staff in the process of stealing a small sum of money from her purse that had been left out.

Her husband John waited for his bride to return but grew curious. He went up to the room and found the hotel room locked. After locating a staff member to let him into the room, he came across the grisly discovery of his wife in the hotel bath. She had been killed.

The sheer awfulness of the final act clashed with the wholesome life she had led. The GAA community immediately entered a period of shock and profound grief. Not for the first time, utter devastation had struck the Tyrone GAA family.

Disbelief set in for McMenamin and Maura on the drive home. It felt indecent to be booking a honeymoon. Practicalities were the next thing to occupy the mind with. Tyrone had conducted a brutal training session the day before, so tough in fact that all the players were sent away from it with instructions not to meet up until the Thursday evening.

Now they were gathering again in small groups and over the following few days would head towards Ballygawley with its multitude of makeshift car parks, before being transported up the road in buses to the Harte homestead in Glencull.

It took a while for the remains to be flown home and the next stage was the wake. In that country home on the hill, Tyrone players would make their way up the stairs to Michaela's bedroom. She was laid out in a room lit by a single candle, in her wedding dress. A haunting and unforgettable image.

In Harte's first year, he asked all the panel members to pick songs that made them feel good about themselves. Michaela was in charge of teasing the songs out of the players and compiling the album. McMenamin chose "Just Looking" by The Stereophonics. Two years later they made another album and he opted for "Cannonball" by Damien Rice. 2010 was the last time Michaela got the duty. By then, his tastes had moved on to something by Biffy Clyro.

Any time McMenamin had met her before, Michaela generated happiness. 'She was always remarkably positive anytime you met her, even if we lost. You always seen that after every game she was on the team bus. Michaela was totally into the football.'

It seemed so alien to see her like this in her old bedroom. Elsewhere in the house, he would find her parents, Mickey and Marian. What could he do? What could he say? What could anyone? They knew Michaela had been Mickey's 'little jewel'. Once Harte learnt of her death, he put a call through to his life-long friend, confidant and in later years, assistant manager, Tony Donnelly. He told him that the worst thing had happened. The worst possible thing.

• • •

They're so different from him yet Ryan McMenamin owes Harte and his family so much. Mickey is known for his considered conservatism; McMenamin, as an impulsive beast with an on-field split personality, grinning and sharing a one liner with an opponent one minute, grabbing them by the throat or goading them the next. Mickey is always suitably turned out on the sideline or at functions; McMenamin can happily torture his girlfriend by wearing the beard of a Frontiersman or lounge around in shorts all evening. Yet Harte saw so much of a competitive edge in McMenamin, they were the perfect fit for each other.

McMenamin would have walked away by now, given over the last few years to the club side, only for a perfectly-timed word from Marian Harte, Mickey's wife.

The All Ireland quarter-final defeat to Meath in 2007 had troubled him. He carried an injury into that game and the Tyrone backline were shredded by Brian Farrell and Stephen Bray. The club came good just at the right time for him. Dromore won the Tyrone senior championship for the first time in their history, with McMenamin at centre back, released from the torture of the full-back line.

An Ulster club fixture against Crossmaglen Rangers in Clones was the prize for winning the county. The previous month Oisín McConville in his autobiography "The Gambler" labelled McMenamin a 'mouthpiece' and made particular reference to an ill-tempered league game between Armagh and Tyrone, claiming, 'He [McMenamin] spent the whole time talking about my ma and my sister. Nothing makes you focus better than a genuine hatred and nothing gave me a greater reason for genuine hatred than a couple of their backs.'

Crossmaglen edged home by a single point but McMenamin's performance had been full of energy. At a function later that week he was at the same table as Marian Harte. 'That was the first game where I've seen you buzzing for about two years,' she said. His soul stirred and he knew he was back.

'Up to that I was either going to call it quits on the whole thing or start putting in an effort again. I don't think Marian realised what she said. But she got me thinking again.'

That line of communication has always been open. Between the notorious 'Battle of Omagh' in 2006, the encounter with Paul Galvin in 2009 and a host of other indiscretions, McMenamin was the focus of much controversy and much heat. Through it all, the occasional letter would drop through the letterbox of the McMenamin homestead. It would be from Marian, with the simple message of staying positive, not to let it all drag him down.

That kindness made the visit to the wake house only more emotive.

'It was upsetting to go round there. Seeing Mickey... He always backed me when others were looking to crucify me. He would always be there for me. You were upset for the whole family. It will be tough, and you hurt, but you hurt for Mickey and Marian, because what they put into football and family. Whenever Mickey is with us, I'm sure he's alright, but he's bound to be hurting badly outside of the group.'

With the Harte family awaiting Michaela's remains, Tyrone's Dr McKenna Cup campaign was put on hold until January 23. Even then the game against Donegal was all set to be called off. That Sunday morning McMenamin was eating a bacon sandwich when he got the text the game was going ahead, only it had been switched to Edendork. The players met at Kelly's Inn in Ballygawley.

When they arrived Mickey Harte was waiting there for them, six days after his daughter's funeral.

'I don't think any of us expected it. It was surreal. Mickey spoke to us. He just thanked everyone for being there the whole week and asked us if we could go out and do our best. We all wanted to try and deliver a performance, to get some normality back.'

They went through the team and their tactics in Kelly's before boarding the bus for Dungannon to change into their gear, the dressing room in Edendork having been burned in an arson attack. In the circle before the game, they kept emotion out of it. Tony Donnelly quickly ran over some of the game-plan, then McMenamin repeated key points for emphasis.

At halftime they were a point down and a man down after Colm Cavanagh became entangled with Donegal's Kevin Cassidy. McMenamin had arrived and grabbed Cassidy in a headlock but struggled with the brute strength of Cassidy. For his part in the flare-up, Cavanagh was dismissed.

Harte wasn't taking a back seat for the day. His team needed guidance.

'Once Mickey started speaking, you could see all the boys lifting themselves. He said that being a man down and a point down is nothing to us. He got the hair standing up on the backs of our necks and our performance immediately went up for the first fifteen minutes of the second half. We got the bit between our teeth.

'After all this time, he's still able to do that. Whenever you go out and play for him, he can motivate you, get you up for it. Even at training, he will throw in a one-liner that will make you think about things differently.

'Recently there, myself and Hub [Kevin Hughes] were jogging back from a drill and talking about the U-21s, saying something like "Young boys these days!" Mickey would subtly turn to us and say "Sure youse two are finished, you know that? You're over thirty! It's not me, it's what everyone's saying! So what are you going to do about it?!"

'He laughed then and walked on, so during the next drill you would try and take the head off a young boy, to keep up with them, and he would have a smile on his face. He's subtle like that. He would be thinking two or three steps ahead.'

Tyrone squeezed past Donegal that day, 1-13 to 0-13, but the result was not the important thing. Management told the players they were to relax over the next couple of days but to maintain their gym programmes. In the huddle, Harte once again thanked his players for being the best they could be and delivering a performance. And for being there for him.

'Words can't describe what kind of a man he is,' says McMenamin. 'I don't really see any change in him now. I still see the same driven man, and to be honest, I see an even bigger drive. At the end of the day, he just wants Tyrone to win. I don't know how he does it. He must have phenomenal strength.'

Even in death, life would continue for Tyrone, with everyone a lot more bruised than before. They never make a mission out of their bereavements but a certain shadow would loom large for the year.

CHAPTER THREE

The Last Temptation

FOOTBALL for Kevin Cassidy in 2010 felt like a tide he was fighting against all year. Several times he had to round on teammates as they despaired over the direction that Donegal were heading. Their tactical approach was non-existent, their training was outdated and not specific to their needs. They were a team in name only.

A number of players were prepared to revolt but Cassidy and a couple of other veterans pinned their ears back. Donegal had aired too much dirty laundry in public through the years. To embarrass a decent man like John Joe Doherty, no matter his shortcomings as an inter-county boss, would only disgust a following that had already grown weary of this group.

They went into the Championship like any other team, believing that despite everything they could still win it. They had no alternative: to think anything else would have seen them mown down. In the first round Down came to Ballybofey, Donegal's patch, something, they convinced themselves, which still counted for something.

In the opening twenty minutes they notched two goals and with fifteen minutes to go were still ahead. Some cool heads on the line and on the field would have seen them close the game out. Instead Down's bright young coach James McCartan switched Benny Coulter from full forward to midfield while Dan Gordon made the opposite trip. Blessed with the spring of a top rebounder in basketball, Coulter caught so much leather he almost broke Donegal's willpower.

But they hung in there. Paul Durcan made a dramatic save from a fisted effort from Gordon and in the dying seconds Rory Kavanagh levelled matters to force extra time. There was still time for the Donegal management team to address the problem of Coulter's dominance in midfield.

Most county sides would have had an adviser in the stand wired up to somebody along the line, advising them of positional switches. But there was no man in the stand or no switch made. With four minutes of extra time left, Coulter got on to the end of a flowing movement involving Down's other marquee players Martin Clarke and Danny Hughes, and after rounding Durcan, gently cushioned the ball into the net. The inevitability of it all galled Cassidy.

'We should have beat Down that day but Coulter came out and we never sent a man after him. I don't like to criticise but at that level you should be seeing things like that. But they weren't into things like having a man in the stand so we had to go along with it and get the season over and done with.'

They would draw Armagh away in the qualifiers, a difficult assignment in normal circumstances. Cassidy was the captain and felt a duty to his manager, but privately he wanted out. Armagh stepped over them in Crossmaglen with nine points to spare. As far as the captain was concerned it was hard to leave it all behind but he had to for his sanity.

'I wanted my life back. A lot of players had lost respect for John Joe by that stage. Not as a person, just their belief in his team. As captain I was trying to hold things together. A lot of my friends on the panel were saying to me "This isn't good enough." But the worst thing you can have in any changing room is three or four boys pulling the other way, because once that happens, the whole thing falls apart. My argument would have been "Look, we've put in so much effort, there's no point throwing the dummy out of the pram now. Let's play it out and see how it goes." That's literally how the last few games went for Donegal.

'After that game I told the players, that was it. Over. It would be my last time in the dressing room and I thanked them all for all the years we had been together, for their friendship. I said there was some serious talent in the dressing room and hoped that maybe I would be standing watching the lads win something. The way I saw it, a few of us boys were there long enough, so it was maybe time to give other people a shot. The U-21s were going well, so I thought they should bring them in. I mean, obviously what we were doing wasn't working!

'There were tears that day, yeah. I would be an emotional person anyway. You're nearly ten years with these boys... It was sad.'

In announcing his departure, Cassidy was also making a selfless point. It was an open secret that Jim McGuinness was virtually guaranteed the job of manager for 2011. Cassidy didn't want a situation where the press would make a big deal about him refusing to play for his old teammate. He just wanted to slip out the door quietly and give a few years to his club.

● ● ●

It was no surprise that Cassidy wanted to close one chapter and move on. He sees the bigger picture of life in every working day. His job demands it.

Once he completed his teaching qualifications a few years back, he landed a handy job in the primary school in Gaoth Dobhair. He enjoyed the experience and the school, but when it was suggested to him that he might try a stint at the Little Angels school, an educational facility in Letterkenny for children with learning disabilities, he saw it as the type of challenge to push him out of his comfort zone.

He walked through the doors for the first time after the Easter break, 2010. Fifty-six children were pupils there and each of them presented a unique case. In his previous job the worst case was one child with Attention Deficit Hyperactivity Disorder. Now he was faced with severe cases every day, self-harmers and profoundly handicapped children.

'You have to be on the ball all the time. The day I walked in, it was a shock and they told me "Look, this might not suit you, it doesn't suit everybody. We've had people come in and not come back after a day." But it was great to get that first week in the classroom, because you could see all the different situations and how the teachers were dealing with it. So when I moved into my class, from day one I loved it.

'Hopefully I won't have to move anywhere else. It's so rewarding, it leaves you a happier person, when a wee boy learns to tie his own laces after six weeks. The last school was lovely but you could be dealing with children who are crying because the child beside them has a brand new Man United ball.'

A typical working day for Cassidy is to open the classes with a discussion on what the children did the night before. It's an exercise to improve the pupils' speech. There are two in the class who cannot talk, so they use sign language. Then it could be an art class, or a trip to the swimming pool.

Around the same time that he started in the new school, his wife Sarah was expecting twins. After the initial euphoria passed, he spent hours worrying about the pregnancy. Would she carry full term? Would the twins be alright? It was in his face every day that pregnancies and children are little miracles each in themselves, and he could see the hardships for the parents of the kids he teaches.

In mid-October Sarah gave birth to healthy twins, Aoife and Nia. It was another landmark in their relationship which began as childhood sweethearts. They met when Cassidy left Falcarragh School to come to Sarah's school in Gaoth Dobhair to do the Leaving Certificate and play football. Mainly football.

At seventeen they were going out. With the teaching in school, his Irish improved and he started using it as his preferred language when possible.

Sarah Gallagher was reared in the next townland. Her father, Willie, played for Donegal in his youth, so she understood the pride in the county and what football meant. She just got it.

When Cassidy broke onto the county team in 2002, she had itchy feet and yearned to see a bit of the world, so she went off travelling. Cassidy hung around to play out of his skin in his first full year, earning an All Star. They stayed in touch throughout her travels, her full of enthusiasm for the world at large, him fulfilling his football dreams at home.

On Sarah's first night back, they went out together for a few drinks. A few weeks later, she was on the plane beside him for the All Stars trip to San Diego. Now they are family, living on Sarah's ancestral land. Salt water comes in from the shore to fill out a natural water basin at the back of the house. Thinking he was done with football, Sarah had bought her husband a kayak as a present. He had every intention of using it.

If Cassidy did not play county football, he knows what he could be at. He could finally go on a ski holiday. He could nip down to the Rory Gallagher festival in Ballyshannon, or the Sea Sessions and see the likes of Ziggy Marley in Bundoran. If there was a Six Nations game on, he could go down to the local and have a pint while watching it, or go to a summer wedding that he was invited to. Simple things.

What held him back all those years was a loyalty to the county and a love of testing himself against the best. Then there is the loyalty to Gaoth Dobhair. As a club they are proud of the traditions that they uphold. Before every game the entire senior team go down on their knees and says a decade of the Rosary in Irish. They know where they come from, where they represent, and it is a source of great pride for them when they are represented in any Donegal team.

At times though it has been a mystery to Cassidy just what exactly Donegal were trying to achieve. In 2009 they entertained high hopes despite relegation from a tough Division One. But Antrim came to Ballybofey and turned them over.

After that, Donegal went on the kind of careering run they have become renowned for. Carlow and Clare were lowly teams that Donegal ate up and spat out. Their third game in the qualifiers was against a Derry side who had regained some form, shooting an astonishing 3-16 against Monaghan in the previous round.

In a contest that sat in the lap of the gods throughout, it took extra time for Donegal to finally see daylight, 2-13 to 0-18. Galway were next and a one-point win booked them a place in the quarter-finals against Munster champions Cork. Those wins though were papering over the cracks, and the local newspapers dusted down that famous headline that was last used in another backdoor run in 2003: "Where did it all go right?"

John Joe Doherty and his management team of Tony Boyle and Tommy Ryan weren't ones for overloading players with information. They weren't ones for information at all. Perhaps they felt that Donegal would be better off without complicating the issue too much but that's not how the modern game works.

'Brian McIver had a system where, say we were playing Tyrone, he would go "Right, Kevin, you're nearly six foot, you pair up with Sean Cavanagh." He would always have match-ups. Neil McGee used to be full-back and he wouldn't be used to a player like Colm McCullagh buzzing in and around there, so he would be switched onto somebody else. Just using your strengths and weaknesses, like.

'I said to John Joe about pairing men up against opponents. I had to, because other squad members would be saying it to me. We beat a hot and cold Derry side and we beat Galway but they weren't that good really. People were saying to us "Ah, you're going well", but inside the camp, we knew we weren't.

'At our meetings, we had to bring it up, about pairing players off. You would hate telling a manager what another manager did, so instead of saying "Brian McIver does this...", I would say, "A couple of years ago, we used to do this, John Joe..."'

They returned to Croke Park. The pitch was patched up after a U2 gig the previous weekend but it didn't matter to Cork. They scored 1-27, a tally of points that broke records in championship football at the venue. Cassidy had known Donegal were heading for a fall but the brutality of it still shocked him.

'We were nowhere near that level. It's a funny place to be, a game being over after fifteen minutes, and realising you have another fifty-five minutes to get through.

'The management we had were three very respected men because they were winners and had done a lot with their clubs. It goes back to the old-style manager though. I would still have a wild load of time for the three lads, I text them and meet them now and again. But we went out to play Cork and that was it. No system. They had no time for that. It was fifteen against fifteen. If I was number seven and number ten came over and I wasn't good enough, I shouldn't be there. That was their way of going on.

'Same with kickouts, it was lump it up the middle as hard as you could. No short kickouts, no kicks to the wings, not even a signal. Just kick it as long as you can.

'We knew Cork's signals. They would point to the wing and then bang it down the middle where Pearse O'Neill was. We tried to discuss this in training but they weren't for talking. O'Neill was monstrous and myself and Brendan Boyle started midfield that day like two wee kids. Jesus Christ! But, that was their way, the way it was played in '92, and that was the way they thought they would go.'

The mental scarring from Cork remained throughout 2010 but once that season had ended, Cassidy had made his peace with the fact that he never won an Ulster title or an All Ireland. He had made many friends along the road and that was good enough for him.

● ● ●

A couple of days after Jim McGuinness was ratified as Donegal senior manager by the county board, Cassidy's mobile buzzed. It was Jim. For a millisecond the thought popped into Cassidy's head to let it ring out. He answered.

McGuinness was as direct as ever. "Listen, I'm calling you because I got the job…"

Cassidy stopped him there. He explained that he didn't believe he had the drive to do it at county level anymore. It was over.

'Down through the years I wasn't happy playing midfield. I lost my appetite [so much], I wasn't even playing well for the club. I was too proud of how I would mark men. If we came off the park having won by five points and my man got the better of me, it would sicken me for a whole week.'

On top of everything he couldn't see a situation where he could leave Sarah at home a few nights a week with two wee babies.

McGuinness played along and listened for a while. They made further pleasantries and Cassidy thought he had got away with it. Just as the conversation was ending, McGuinness threw him one line. 'Number seven. That's where I want you playing with me.'

Three days later, McGuinness had another nibble. He called, and they arranged to meet in Letterkenny. Something came up at the last minute and Cassidy couldn't go. After getting the feeling he was being avoided, McGuinness called the house phone. Cassidy answered. Bingo. McGuinness immediately went on the attack. 'Before you give me any answer, I'm just going to lay out this thing to you. Who my backroom team is, how we are going to play, what we are going to do, how you are going to play, what weight you are going to be… everything.'

Knowing how thorough McGuinness can be, Cassidy took the phone upstairs. He knew it was going to be a long haul. It lasted two hours. Cassidy hardly spoke. When he tried to, Jim just talked over the top of him until he shut up.

'He wasn't trying to entice me in by telling me that I could come to one training session a week or anything,' recalls Cassidy. 'He just said "We'll be going five nights a week." He said we would be taking this thing to a completely new level.

'He promised me a couple of things. That I would be back playing the way I was playing when I started county football. He said "That's a promise I am giving you. I'm not saying we will win this or win that. What we will do is be able to compete with the top teams in the country."

'During the conversation I told him I had great respect for him, that I would run through a brick wall for him, but the situation at home was different with the children. That ended up being another conversation and by the end of it he had nannies and cleaners coming when I was away. In fairness, he did everything he could.'

McGuinness got his man.

● ● ●

From the moment Cassidy rejoined the set-up, everything had changed, changed utterly.

For the first session, every player was hooked up to a heart monitor that would record their heartrates during training. The information was fed into a laptop manned by Mark 'Maxi' Curran and the information then transmitted to a hand-held device that Jim had strapped to his wrist. If he noticed a player's heart-rate dipping, he would down tools and name and shame.

The system cost the county board a fair packet but McGuinness insisted on it as one of his terms.

'We did well to compete before, considering what we were working with', says Cassidy. 'Even last year, if you asked me was I training hard, I would tell you I was flying! We used to go back to our clubs, say after Donegal was beaten in July, and we would go for a run with the club training. Me and Neil and Eamon [McGee] would be chatting and we'd be saying "Jesus, we're in poor shape." We passed it off as tiredness but we were nowhere near as fit as we should have been.'

After the second McKenna Cup game, the players arrived for a training session at the Glenfin pitch. An unfamiliar figure was out on the field, laying out cones and preparing for the training session. It was Rory Gallagher.

As a youngster with his native Fermanagh, Gallagher was the leading scorer in the Ulster championship for three consecutive years before opting out in 2003, disillusioned with the structures within his own county.

From then on he gained an unfair reputation as a maverick. Fermanagh reached the quarter-finals of the All Ireland in 2003 without him and the semi-final in 2004. He made a return in 2005 but that championship only lasted two games, ending with Gallagher delivering a dressing down to manager Charlie Mulgrew. He played for Cavan in 2007 but it wasn't a natural fit. When Malachy O'Rourke landed the Fermanagh job for the 2008 season, Gallagher discreetly made enquiries if he could try out for them. The offer was gently turned down.

After Gallagher's string of strong performances for St Gall's in the 2009 Ulster club championship, however, O'Rourke brought him back into the county fold for 2010. It would be a disappointing season for both Gallagher and the team, though he would end up the county's highest scorer for the year. That spring he also landed the All Ireland club title as full forward for St Gall's. Up the other end of the field between the sticks was his brother Ronan, making them the only two Fermanagh men to win a senior All Ireland as players.

John O'Neill took over the Fermanagh job but didn't pursue the brothers. That became Donegal's opportunity. McGuinness would count Martin McHugh as one of his confidants. As coach of Sligo IT, McHugh struck up a close relationship with Gallagher and together they won a Sigerson in 2002 with Gallagher as captain. McHugh always recognised Gallagher's football intelligence and during his years in the wilderness, Gallagher would write a weekly column in *Gaelic Life* and act as the sideline tactical expert for the BBC, forensically articulating the switches and flow of the game. It was an open goal for McGuinness to approach Gallagher. McGuinness had a vision of the kind of inter-county setup that Gallagher always craved as a player.

The integration was seamless, according to Cassidy. 'Some of the boys were asking me who was this boy taking the training. But Rory knew every single player's name, knew what club they came from and made a point of speaking to them all. The U-21s and the seniors train together and there are boys there I didn't even know, yet he knew everyone there. He obviously put in a lot of homework and he won the respect of the boys straight away for it.'

●　●　●

Everybody now knows their place at a Donegal training session. There is no dilly dallying, nobody taking up the role as court jester. Who would have the energy?

'The big difference with our training now is that we start at one hundred miles an hour. We're into Jim's drills, and if it's not one hundred miles an hour, it will be stopped, and repeated again, until it is perfect.

'After that, you go into small game situations, getting tackling drills sorted and little things like that. Jim loves his bit of running too. We're talking four hundred metres and two hundred metres. A big difference from old school though, because in old school, you're talking laps and all the time in the world to do them. Jim has everything recorded and knows what time you are meant to be in within, the recovery you have, and then you're away again.

'There's no drill to hide. There are setups where you could give a wee foot pass here and then go to the back of a line, miss out on a turn and take a wee break. Not here.'

When Tyrone won the All Ireland in 2003, they kept their training sessions short and snappy. McGuinness's sessions could be anything from ninety minutes to three hours long. The workload is huge and so is the travel. Coming across Mount Errigal towards Castlefin takes an hour and fifteen minutes each way. A typical day has Cassidy leaving home at 8am, returning for half an hour after work, and then gone until midnight.

Under Jim he no longer has to hold his own in the midfield area. Instead he has been cajoled and downright bullied to lose weight and become a sleeker shape for his wing-back berth. When other players are lifting weights in Letterkenny gym at 7.30 on a Wednesday morning after the Tuesday night training, Cassidy's responsibility is to get on his trainers and hit the road or the bicycle saddle.

'He's [McGuinness] put me under wild pressure about my weight. During the winter I like to put on a wee bit, so he has me on a running programme. I don't lift any weights now and my target weight for the Championship is thirteen and a half stone. I just put on weight easily. He would see me losing it but then say to me that he still wasn't happy with my weight, talking about shifting it off this and that place.

'I was running for an hour, seven days in a row. McGuinness would come up to me at training and ask me "Well, what did you run last night?" And I would tell him "Nine kilometres." Then Jimmy says "Right, once we get you up to twelve kilometres a night..." Twelve kilometres a night, like!

'Maybe for a month or two there I was training seven days a week. Some days, I would even train twice a day. That's alright for me because I said at the start of the year that if I was going to go back, I wanted to give it everything.'

In those late-night telephone conversations, it was McGuinness' honesty that Cassidy was drawn to most. He's happy he made the right decision but it's strictly a one-year deal.

'I cannot see myself giving this commitment after this year. If the day comes and we're beaten in the first round of the Championship, there won't be a big announcement. It will be nice and quiet and I will leave. You know when people come out and make four or five retirement statements? You don't want to be one of them boys!

'I was saying to Sarah the other day there are very few lads that could stick what Jim wants for three or four years. Not a hope. You're giving so much it's unbelievable.

'Down through the years and at meetings and things like that in the team, I would have been one of the boys giving out, because our standards weren't up to the level of the Tyrones or Armaghs. When I heard stories of what they had and what they were doing, I would always have been the one standing up going "Lads, this isn't good enough." Donegal were never been a big county for training on your own. Brian McIver tried it but not everybody bought into it.'

Everyone is now.

CHAPTER FOUR

Don't Stop Believin'

ALL he can remember is how sore it felt. That and grinding his teeth so hard they might break.

Barry Owens lay prone. Completely still. The Fermanagh team doctor Tom Kiernan told him to. They weren't sure what had happened to him, only a scan would tell them that. All they knew was that his Ulster final was at an end. Once he left the field on a stretcher, the hopes of Fermanagh landing their first Ulster title went with him. Mark Little stood over the stretcher and they exchanged words. Owens can't recall what was said but he remembers the heat and an unrelenting pain pulsing through his body like a current.

He entered the field as a saviour, the man who would strike fear into the hearts of the meanest defence of all and finally bring Fermanagh their first Ulster. Ten minutes later he was being carried from the field. Anyone who had a heart in Clones that day left carrying concerns whether he would ever play football again.

'I done something I wouldn't usually do if I was playing full forward. I would normally stay within a ten yards spot but I made a run out towards the sideline, about forty-five yards out to reach a pass from Shane Goan. It bounced and I went up to jump for it, with Francie [Bellew] jumping too. The ball broke and just as I was landing I put my right foot down to turn and gather the ball. The foot stuck in the ground. I heard a snap and I was in agony. Absolute agony for two minutes.'

On the bus journey home he got talking to Niall Bogue who was out of action with a ruptured cruciate ligament. The symptoms of his pain ticked all the boxes. A scan in a fortnight's time would confirm the suspicions.

The incident was a metaphor for the entire season. While Owens was coming back there was always hope, always a chance that if his teammates could hold the fort, he would drag them over the line.

All year long Fermanagh had enjoyed slices of good fortune. Their two-time All Star full-back came on with the Ulster semi-final against Derry in the balance. The Fermanagh support recognised the emotion and power of the moment and stood to applaud him wildly as he dashed on. Within minutes they entered nirvana when he fisted home the winning goal as a makeshift full-forward. It was just six months after a heart operation had left him withered and reduced. More than his football career had hung in the balance then. His very life had been on the line.

'My first operation was when I was thirteen. I was going in for an operation to clear my sinuses and they found a heart murmur. They ran tests on me and seen I had a blocked artery and my aortic valve was leaking. Two years later they put a balloon up from my groin, an angioplasty it's called, and they blew out an artery. They kept an eye on it for ten years and then said "Look, you've been playing at a high level, and since that your artery has been getting wider and wider." It was stretching and getting weaker.'

The risk lay in the potential of an aortic root aneurysm. If his aortic valve dilated, it could cause a leak from his aortic valve and cause an aneurysm dissection – a life-threatening condition. It manifests itself in the blood flowing through a tear in the inner layer of the aorta, in turn causing the layers to part. Eventually, the arterial wall would burst. It could have been triggered by a hit on the football field, a fall on the training pitch or just loading the bar too much in the gym.

Professor Mark Redmond was the surgeon and he talked Owens through it. He had performed the same procedure on American footballers who returned to the playing fields but Owens wasn't thinking that way. 'I thought "So what if that was it with football, there's more to life than that, I just want to get through this."'

The nine-hour operation was hardly smooth. Twice they had to stop a valve leaking. He went in on the Tuesday morning and regained consciousness on the Thursday night.

As the doctors weaned him off the morphine, his mood darkened. His then fiancée, now wife Caroline, was keeping him company. 'I was really down, telling her that I was finished with the football, it was a load of bollox, I couldn't care less about it and wasn't going through it all again just to get back. I was finished as a footballer, there'd be no more.'

That was only a flavour of the mental pain. The following day, the doctors had to remove two drains that proved stubborn. They wriggled and pulled at them and Owens lay with waves of cold sweat pumping from his body from a pain that came from hell.

'That was the worst ever. The pain when I sneezed or coughed! I was holding pillows against me to stop the stitches opening. Just even moving a few yards was murder, out of breath from it.'

He stayed in hospital for almost a week and before he left the Beacon Clinic in Dublin he was set a task that demonstrated how hard life would be for him. They asked him to walk up a flight of stairs. By the top, he was bent double with the strain and couldn't catch his breath.

The majority of Fermanagh fans never realised the extent of his condition. They had become hardened towards that kind of thing when Marty McGrath – their other All Star of modern times – had open heart surgery. Whenever they thought of Owens, they thought of how long it would take to get him back on the football pitch. His life had been taken for granted but he kept that within his own circle. Six months on from the operation, he lay on another bench feeling nauseous in Clones. He could hear the roars and groans of the crowd outside as he lay in a dressing room, the heat magnified by the closed windows. Again, sweat was lashing off his body.

The mood of people coming and going told him that things were continuing on as the first day. Fermanagh were kicking themselves out of an Ulster title again. Only this time in their hour of greatest need, there was nothing their icon could do about it.

• • •

If heart surgery wasn't going to keep him down, knee injury wasn't either. The following summer Owens was back.

After coming through a nervy preliminary round opener against Down, Fermanagh were struggling against Cavan in Breffni Park when he was summoned from the bench. There was only sixteen minutes left and the instruction was basic. Unleash hell anywhere you can.

He fisted a point and had a shout for a penalty turned down but Fermanagh had left themselves too much of a mountain to climb. They never got to grips with Seanie Johnston and his five points sank them.

Before the backdoor game against Wicklow, negative energy swamped the team. They played a friendly against Donegal in Irvinestown the week before and were slaughtered. A defeat to Wicklow was one of those things they thought they had left behind years ago but they were second best by a distance. In the dressing room afterwards, there was a stink. One player took off his jersey, put a foot on one end and ripped it to shreds in front of everyone. The effort put in over the year was soured as everyone scattered and made for the sanctity of their clubs.

• • •

Back among his people, enjoying football came easy. Teemore Shamrocks were there before anything. When he and elder brother Sean were growing up, they would kick ball at each other along the sideline while his father, John, trained under the shadow of the belching chimneys of the Quinn empire. He played until well into his forties, winning a junior league alongside his son Sean.

Towards the end of the 2009 season Owens felt strong again. He notched up several games and was looking forward to putting manners on Lisnaskea in a tournament match at Donagh.

After three minutes he set off in pursuit of a player and as his opponent cut back infield, Owens went to put the brakes on and planted his foot. His whole weight went over the knee. It didn't feel as bad as the first time because all the nerve endings were gone but already his knee was in ribbons.

He thought it was just the cartilage was damaged so he rested it for a couple of weeks. There was a chance Teemore could make the league semi-finals and he didn't want to miss out on that.

Towards the end of the next game against Enniskillen Gaels he felt a tweak in the knee and was pulled ashore. He even lasted the entire game for the league semi-final. His research on the internet left him to self-diagnose it as a minor problem requiring nothing more than good rest. Something nagged at him though, and he went to the Ulster Independent Clinic to get a scan in mid-October. That weekend he completed a fitness test with the rest of the Fermanagh squad for the 2010 campaign and everything felt alright that Sunday.

The following morning the clinic called. His knee was gone. He travelled up straight away to meet the surgeon and they got a cancellation slot two days later. Just three days after his first fitness test with Fermanagh when he had been full of hope and getting the show on the road for 2010, he was undergoing his second cruciate ligament operation in fifteen months. It would deny him the chance to play league football for the third year running. Before it had even begun 2010 was a complete write-off.

This time his attitude was different to when he had the heart operation. He was now a year married to Caroline and telling her he was finished with football. That only lasted a week. Once he got back involved helping the club minors he figured he'd still play for the club. His county career might have been over alright but Teemore would still have a piece of him.

'Once I got the operation, it was a matter of getting fit again to play for the club. I was always going back to the club.'

He hates the gym but he lived in it over the winter. When he had injured himself in the Ulster final, Malachy O'Rourke had put him in touch with Enda McGinley of Tyrone who had extensive experience in the area. McGinley mapped him out a programme of light weights, squats and everything else.

'At times it would do your head in, doing all the exercises. It's so repetitive, bouncing forward and back on the wobbleboard trying to work on your balance, and it would just be torture running through your head, thinking "Oh, no, not this again tonight!" It's the ballwork and fieldwork you'd miss the most, but you'd just get on with it and say "Feck it, there's no point feeling sorry for myself."'

He made it back in time for the club championship. He was, as they say in Teemore, 'the same old Barry.' He was sent out to mark county players and beat them in the air and across the ground. Some of the old devilment returned, with his trademark dashes upfield launching attacks. If he was up for it, there was more county football in him. Sure what else would he be doing?

After the club season wrapped up, he took a phonecall from an unknown number. It was John O'Neill, telling him he was selected to become part of the Fermanagh panel for 2011. O'Neill had been part of Charlie Mulgrew's backroom management team in the middle part of the previous decade, so both men knew each other. Instantly the new manager's forthright tone was what he noticed.

'What you see is what you get with John. He won't care who you are, you'll get a bollocking whether you're there for your first night or your last night, if you don't do what they want you to do, it's the same. There's no bullshit with him.'

On New Year's Eve, Owens was getting ready to go out and enjoy some socialising when his phone buzzed. It was John O'Neill with a text message, 'Congratulations, you're going to be captain.' His modesty got the better of him and he called up, believing it to be somebody on a wind-up. O'Neill confirmed that he indeed wanted him as his on-field leader, qualifying it with that old-fashioned Fermanagh saying, 'No better man.'

Incredibly, it was the first time Owens had been asked to captain the county. Probably Fermanagh's greatest servant had received what he terms 'the best New Year's present ever.'

The terms of reference have changed. Owens had never started a single league game for O'Rourke in the previous three years. He had seven years of league football before that, all but one spent in Division One. Now, he would face life in Division Four.

'A good year this year would be winning promotion because playing Division Four football and then playing Derry in the first round are worlds apart but hopefully in the next couple of years we won't be far away."

He's not complaining. 'There are a lot of people in worse places than I am. Here I am, able to play football. Through it all, I've always had that to keep me going. What's the point in your knee being alright and not being able to do what you want to do, what you love to do? Playing football. So play football. Play it when you can. I could go out tomorrow and get hit by a car. That could just ruin you altogether.'

●　●　●

At 3am one October night a thirty-three year-old Mickey Conlan got up for his work as the driver of a bread van, then ate his breakfast while he checked his voice messages. There was an interesting one left at 10.30pm from a number he didn't recognise.

'Mickey C, it's John Brennan here. I just want to give you a call in relation to this year's county panel.'

Conlan thought about nothing else until four that morning, and nothing else again until five. He was like a child. As soon as he got a break on the bread run, he called his wife Paula. She noticed the time was only 7.05am.

'We had talked about it before. I was thinking back on the season I had and what if I got back on the panel because I would love to do it again. Paula felt that if the opportunity came and I was asked, I would have to go. We had all the groundwork and all the debate and talking done. I just knew that if it came to it, everything would be okay.'

The next call was to Brennan. 'He said "I believe over these last few years you've been playing well for your club and you deserve a crack at the county team." I said back to him "No bother." I was so proud to be asked.'

Everyone in Derry knows why he was asked back. In the 2010 county championship Brennan was taking his club Lavey for a final fling and desperately wanted to win another championship. In the county semi-final they were drawn against Ballinderry. With thirteen minutes to go Lavey's Kevin McCloy was sent off along with Ballinderry's Enda Muldoon yet as the game entered injury time Lavey were five points up. Ballinderry though somehow managed to conjure up two goals and steal the game.

The local paper, *The County Derry Post*, praised a match that had everything and the effort by the unfancied Lavey yet pondered, *'The here and now for them is a winter of what ifs. What if that Collie Devlin effort had been given wide? What if Kevin McCloy hadn't been sent off? And what if Mickey Conlan hadn't had the game of his life for Ballinderry?*

'When this game is written into the annals of legend, no one should ever forget the contribution of the Ballinderry goalkeeper. Cailean O'Boyle indulged in what can only be described as a one-to-one shootout with the Shamrocks' stopper. The first, high to the 'keeper's left from point blank range, parried away. The second, low but straight at the 'keeper who scrambled it away for a '45. The third, the best of them, hit high and hard but superbly tipped over. Had any of those three chances gone in, Lavey would have been in the county final.'

That county final was a novelty, featuring Eoghan Rua of Coleraine playing in their first-ever final. Coleraine came out of the traps, aiming two rockets towards Conlan's goal, but he kept them out. Two goals in two minutes early in the second half though was enough to secure the newcomers a remarkable breakthrough.

On the Ballinderry coach for the return journey, Conlan sat down beside assistant manager, the revered Adrian McGuckin. They talked about how they were going to make it right with Ballinderry the following year but then Conlan let slip a long-buried ambition.

'We were in the pits,' recalls McGuckin, 'You couldn't go any lower in football, I can tell you. What's more, Mickey C was coming up to another birthday yet he said to me "I wouldn't like to think I'm finished with Derry. I still think there's a couple of years left in me."

'I said "I wouldn't worry about that Mickey C, if we can get another few years out of you for Ballinderry..." But he said "No, I want to play for Derry again."'

That's why, when the call came from John Brennan, Conlan was not that surprised. He may have been the proudest man alive that day but he wasn't shocked.

CHAPTER FIVE

The Changing Man

TEN minutes into Monaghan's second game of the season and Dick Clerkin realises they are in a real battle. It's always the same with Armagh. Doesn't matter how early it is in the year, they are never in the mood for taking any nonsense. Especially when you hammered them 1-18 to 0-9 in the 2010 Championship.

The following scenario is typical of Ulster football: the referee blows for a foul, the player in possession believes he has done nothing wrong and refuses to surrender the ball. An opposing player makes a grab for it and as the tussle progresses, both men apply more and more extreme measures of verbals and violence.

The cavalry bugle is blown. Midfielders, half-forwards, full-backs, it doesn't matter, whoever has the appetite for it gets involved. And everybody has an appetite for this. Players will have their jersey pulled, there might be a sly dig thrown and the crowd shouts out volleys of abuse and encouragement. Then some persistent shrill blowing of the whistle by the referee clears the area. The game is on, nothing to see here.

Only this is not the Armagh side from the last decade. And Monaghan are in the process of changing, no one more so than Dick Clerkin.

He had been expecting the flare up and when it came, he did his bit. He couldn't leave all those raw youngsters to be cowed by powerful men like Charlie Vernon and Ciaran McKeever. He hauled and pulled and dragged like a man who was born to do it, but once it was over, he was glad.

'The fact that it didn't really continue after that was more surprising, especially as we were more dominant as the game progressed. It was always going to be difficult, but we would have felt that we had played the better football and should have came away with two points.'

There was no point in getting too hyped up. Tension has played tricks on him before, causing him to act rashly. It backfired on him eighteen months ago after a nasty day in Derry. Newspapers and radio shows turned his life into a hellish existence. The moment his mother called his phone crying, that's when everything changed.

On May 25, 2009, Derry hosted Monaghan in the first round of the Ulster Championship. The home team had so many slights against their reputations as players and men that motivation was not going to be a problem. They had been beaten in the Championship for two years running by Monaghan but more damaging to them as men, and Derry men, was the tag of being soft-centred.

In the traditions of Derry football, this was new. Was Kieran McKeever soft? Brian McGilligan? Anthony Tohill, was he the type that lay down when the heat came on him? As men wearing the jerseys passed down from these former greats, they had to make a statement. On the training ground in the weeks leading up to the game, they made a pact that they would do whatever it took to win.

The scoreboard at the end had Derry as victors, 1-10 to 0-10, but few neutrals were concerned with that. The game was a mess, an Orwellian vision of war without the shooting. The Ulster Championship has thrown up more than its share of X-rated material but this was particularly gory stuff.

Brian McEniff opined that perhaps Ulster football was truly a unique game and deserved to be refereed by Ulster officials. Writing a column for the following day's *Evening Herald*, former Dublin wing-back Paul Curran responded.

'After looking at yesterday's game between Derry and Monaghan I came away thinking that if that's your game, Brian, you can have it, referees and all. It was a disgraceful affair and an extremely damning advertisement for "our" game. It was one of the worst games I have watched in many years, that's if you want to call it a game. It was nasty and spiteful right from the beginning and it was surprising that only Fergal Doherty received a red card as others certainly stepped over the edge.'

Clerkin and Doherty fought a running battle that day and it would have a lasting impact for Clerkin.

'A line was crossed that day in Derry. Definitely. It played on me for a long time but I have come out of it a better man. Looking back on that game and what followed afterwards, it was the watershed moment. I said to myself "Right, this has to stop." This impression that I'm this kind of man has to stop. All people were ever saying about me was that I was a dog, a workhorse, dirty. At first I took the reputation on board and in many ways played up to it, but after a while it grew a bit tiresome. I'm not one of these players to avoid papers and it was getting me down. I read everything and would always get the paper the day after the match.

'That day... Well, I don't regret anything I done in that game, unlike other games possibly, but in the aftermath people tried to drag me into the mire. I was involved in stuff and I have to take responsibility for what can be perceived following such incidents. It was the way I played and marked and people went away saying that they weren't surprised that I was again involved in stuff.

'I thought about calling up to Fergal. The reality of it was that in the early stages of our careers we would have got on quite well. We're the same age and played on the U-17 Ulster Compromise Rules team, played Freshers football against each other, been out drinking because we would have run in the same circles, so we would have a fairly good relationship up until the [2007 Ulster semi-final] game in Casement Park. I put my hands up, Fergal plays hard, plays fair. I took it to the edge.

'I would have looked at Fergal as being the archetypal midfielder and someone I would have looked up to. But we were so desperate to taste success, for those seventy minutes it was just a case of stopping him playing and getting a result. In a strange way I hoped he could have taken it as a compliment. It's the day you stop getting special attention on the field you need to be more worried about.'

Monaghan fans stood by their man in the face of relentless criticism from Joe Brolly, the former Derry player and well-known pundit and former teammate of Damian Cassidy, the Derry manager. In their next game against Armagh, supporters unfurled a banner with an umbrella depicted on it, alongside the words "Is a tool". The inference was clear.

'Joe Brolly went on a personal crusade to drag me into the gutter. I was raging that I'd allowed myself get implicated in such a mess. I made a decision to say nothing about it in the media when asked. I spoke with my parents because my mother was distraught. She called me twice in tears, after hearing stuff on the radio.

'There was only one altercation at the start of that match that I was booked for, and I didn't instigate anything after that. I knew I had done nothing outside the run of the mill fare for midfielders. There was one incident where I did catch Fergal, but it was not intentional. Joe Brolly went to retrieve every camera at the game, he led Fergal's case in Croke Park, and he went through me in his newspaper columns and on radio chat shows. I held fire all the while, happy that I had no case to answer, and that was what transpired.

'My parents and people close to me found it all very hard to take. It definitely affected my game. Our season fell apart after that game in Derry. There was so much shit being thrown around that people were watching for us. I just said after that "This isn't good enough, I'm not playing like this anymore."'

The sledging didn't end there. In their next game, a tough qualifier against Armagh, Dessie Mone pushed the appropriate buttons with Stevie McDonnell at every chance. McDonnell lashed out and received a red card.

Monaghan scrapped through by a point after extra time and were then drawn against Derry again who had been knocked out of Ulster by Tyrone. The world was expecting a bloodbath of a rematch but something magnificent happened. Fergal Doherty was placed at full-forward and the running battle was put on hold.

Both sides played a thrilling game that ended in Derry's favour, 3-16 to 0-20. Clerkin's head wasn't in the game though. In the lead up to that game he had spent many late nights tormented, pondering what had exactly happened to him as a footballer. Who was this Dick Clerkin?

After perceptive self-examination, he concluded he had yielded too much to management wishes. Seamus 'Banty' McEnaney wanted parts of him, so Clerkin allowed a Frankenstein creation to occupy his body.

'The way I played was part of the job I was given. Seamus would have sent me out to mark Fergal Doherty and that was my job. On hindsight I was too rigid in that. Similarly in games against Darragh O'Sé and Kevin Cassidy. The trash talking crept into my game and it's not something I would be overly-proud of when I look back. I would be chatty enough but maybe in some of those games, especially with some players, I went over the top. It took my mind off the game and it left people thinking I wasn't a footballer at all. Looking back on some of those performances I could hardly blame them.

'That is the impression people were getting off me from the '07, '08 and '09 years. I wasn't playing an open brand of football, and was picking up a booking in nearly every game. Unlike previous years I hadn't been scoring, and the days when I took frees for Monaghan felt a lifetime away. But that's the role Seamus wanted me in. He didn't want me prioritising solo runs up the field and being overly attack-minded. First and foremost he wanted me winning break ball, working back, doing man marking jobs, and getting the ball to the kickers and scorers...

'I fed off his passion and commitment, having grown up around a similar desire for the county jersey. I completely trusted him, so I was willing to sacrifice my natural game and reputation for the good of the team. I have no regrets about that. It's what you do when you are part of a team. But I would be lying if I said I didn't feel like I could have contributed more in some of those games had I been a bit more positive in my play. I don't blame Seamus for that, at the end of the day everyone has to take responsibility for their own actions and performance on the field. Maybe I was a bit naive.'

• • •

People looked at Clerkin and drew unfair conclusions. He's a midfielder that keeps his blonde hair tightly cropped. His biceps are huge and he was a figurehead in a team that evoked the spirit of the Sean McCague Monaghan side of the '80s, characterised by their ruthlessness and steel. As Banty kept reinventing his backroom team, gathering more and more expertise, his footballing philosophy remained rooted in a few core principles. Their aims were to get the ball into the speedy and accurate Tommy Freeman as quick as possible and give nothing away handy. Self-expression gave way to a rigid game-plan and after a few encouraging results in Championship football, they all bought into the belief that Banty's way was restoring pride in the county. They would have run through brick walls if he asked them to but it would only take them so far.

It was little wonder then that so much surprise was expressed when Clerkin made some alterations to his game in the 2010 Ulster Championship. He boomed points over from fifty yards against Armagh and Fermanagh, leading many commentators to describe how he had added another skill to his repertoire. It betrayed his beginnings as a teenage full-forward making his Championship debut, and his early progression as a free-taking wing-forward.

He came from Currin, a tiny outpost that crept into Fermanagh and out of it just as fast. At the time he broke onto the scene, they were deeply unfashionable, but his name and his father's standing as a quality player on McCague's team opened a few doors. When a few junior clubs cobbled together an amalgamation team called Finn Valley, he showed up well in the senior championship. He got a call up for a friendly against Louth at only seventeen.

His parents weren't impressed but he stayed with it, saying a few training sessions wouldn't do any harm. In between revising for his Leaving Certificate he was travelling the roads playing national league on Sunday before taking his seat behind a classroom desk every Monday. He kept a jersey throughout and when they played Fermanagh in the 1999 Championship they were without a full forward, so Jack McCarville slotted him in there. They lost but it was all new and exciting. Playing for Monaghan was just something he did from then on.

Studies would take him to two different universities and work would take him to Finland. His education became a holistic experience and he became interested in all manner of things. Books on politics and the machinations of the economy become his favourites. His family traditionally voted Fianna Fail although he struggles with the concept now. Some day, when all this is over, he will contemplate entering the political landscape. That's a future target. For now, time is taken up with his work as a chemical engineer in Premier Periclase in Drogheda. Leisure time is taken up with the great ambition of an Ulster Championship. He thought he was almost there in 2010. It was the peak before the crash.

• • •

The great passion that Seamus McEnaney brought to the job of county manager dragged Monaghan out of a pit of despair. McEnaney himself was fond of citing the example of going to Carlow to watch his county in a Division Four match when there were only twenty Monaghan spectators present. He came in and brought back traditional values which would propel them through the leagues and into Championship. Some experiments were well-intentioned but ultimately futile. When they approached the 2008 Championship, they sought an edge. 'There were a few boys who were carrying a bit of extra weight, so a dietician was brought in and we went on the Caveman Diet. Basically all you could eat was anything that either ran, swam, flew or grew from the ground. Nothing processed.

'Marty McElkennon pushed it for boys to strip down and lean up that extra bit. Always keen to try anything new, I decided to give it a lash. Rory Woods and Darren Hughes actually lost the guts of a stone at the time. We were training extremely hard and the meals after training had changed. It was just pure protein, fish, lumps of chicken and steamed veg. You knew it could only be good for you, but at times it was horrible.' Sugary snacks were out. Sauces were out. So was gravy and butter. And cooking oils, potatoes and rice. Players would have to load up with grilled meats and steamed fish. They were also expected to drink five litres daily of water infused with several plant extracts. Clerkin compares the taste to what drinking bog water must be like.

'At times you felt better, felt good and I would use it for a day or two if I need to clean the system out now. Trying to balance it with heavy training and studying though, Jesus...

'I was in DCU at the time and when I was studying, the cravings for something like a slice of toast and jam! Or a jaffa cake! There were times I just had to get some sugar. I buckled once at around eleven at night when I had to go out to the vending machine in the courtyard for a Crunchie.' After they were massacred by Tyrone in the 2010 Ulster final, question marks were raised over the level of expertise on the line. Support from club delegates began to wither. While in previous years they were happy to let the county manager sometimes call off rounds of club championship fixtures, a hardening of attitudes evolved.

Paul Curran – no relation to the current pundit or former Dublin star – had just taken over as county board chairman and appeared to back the manager when he said, 'Seamus McEnaney has devoted himself selflessly to the cause of Monaghan football and we will respect whatever decision he arrives at in relation to his future.'

Banty's decision was to request that he remain in the post for a further three years. The shock came at the August county board meeting when club delegates voted 29-19 in favour of seeking nominations for the role. Curran saw the way the wind was changing and later commented, 'As a result of nominations the clubs of Monaghan sent a very clear signal that this management team has got the maximum out of this bunch of players. There is a strong mood for change. That's not trying to be disrespectful. Maybe it's time for a change. Maybe it's time for a fresh voice and a fresh face.' Clerkin was torn, so one evening after that county board meeting he got into the car and went down to McEnaney's pub, The Fiddler's Elbow in Carrickmacross, to speak with him. It wasn't easy.

'Players met and it was agreed to publicly support Seamus. It wasn't the case that we weren't going to play for anyone else. If people got that impression, they were wrong. Seamus knew that I had thoughts on the matter and wanted to discuss things so we met up for a chat.

'I said it to Seamus myself that personally I was open to looking at other interested parties, and that maybe it was time for a change. As a group we had discussed this and some of the players were of the same opinion. There was a lot of chat around the county and it wasn't necessarily anti-Banty, though that's the way some people wanted to paint it. It was more "Y'know, let's see who else might want to take on this job", that it's not just a closed book like it has been for the past six years. Especially as he wanted another three years. I thought, that's the rest of my career. I might play for longer, but with injuries and other things becoming the priority, it's unlikely.

'Monaghan were at a crossroads. We'd had six good years which could maybe even have been better but to me it was fair enough to ponder was there somebody out there that could bring us on that next step? I wasn't against Banty going for it again but I was for opening the floor to see who else might stick their heads up.

'I said to him "If you want to go for it and if you do get it, without question, I will support you as always one hundred per cent." But I also advised him that I would see it very hard for him to go again when he hadn't the support of the county, which the vote indicated. We had huge support in years previous and that was such a huge thing in our regime, that we had everybody with us.'

McEnaney is a forthright character and would have appreciated Clerkin's honesty. Likewise his discretion.

'I made it clear to Banty that I wouldn't be standing in his way, or saying anything publicly, but I had my opinion. My biggest fear was that he would go for a vote and be defeated. I said "Listen, Seamus, you don't deserve that, you've given so much to this county. The people involved in making the decisions in this county seem to want you out. You shouldn't put yourself in this kind of position."

'I had experience of this sort of thing when my father was involved in an acrimonious split from the Cavan management team back in the late nineties. From a personal and family point of view it was not a pleasant experience and it resonated in our house for a long time. I didn't want Seamus to potentially experience that.

'But it dragged on, there's no point in saying anything else. It's unfortunate that Seamus left in such circumstances. Everyone involved with that panel owes him so much considering where we were when he took us over. After the Kildare game such was the emotional tone in the after-match speeches everyone thought it was his last stand. Even though I was a bit miffed at getting substituted in that game I still felt compelled to be the first one up to shake his hand once he finished talking in the dressing room. It was a horrible six days for everyone. It was such a regrettable way for that panel and management team to end its days together.'

• • •

The Monaghan dressing room was going to be a different place in 2011. There was a timely freshness that was needed for a group of men that had been on the road for a long time. Eamonn McEneaney has come in and opened all the windows, letting a bit of air in.   Once the poison was drained from the stand-off between Banty and the board, Eamonn landed the job for his second time. After a few trials, he called his first team meeting and introduced his backroom team. Respected former players Stephen McGinnity and Declan Smyth would be his selectors. Colm O'Hare would be combining his job as a rugby coach in Leinster with the role of physical trainer.

'Eamonn basically outlined the programme for the year, what he would expect. He said a few things that I would have heard before, motivational things and that. Again we have to wait and see how all these things work in practice.

'One thing he is keen on is personal ownership in terms of fitness. You should be fit coming to training and he will not be running you around a field. We will be working with the ball, playing ball, and learning a bit on tactics.' McEneaney gave the squad a target to reach before the season began. They were to be able to run two miles within eleven and a half minutes. When Clerkin heard this, he immediately started calculating the sums in his head, trying to convert the kilometres that are displayed on a treadmill to miles, not liking it one bit. He headed out the following night to a warm gym, busted himself with the effort, and got home in a time of twelve and a half minutes. Running on the road is a whole different task. Propelling your own body weight on tarmac is a lot harder than merely bouncing on a treadmill indoors and that wasn't a reality he could ignore. A couple of nights later, he faced into an icy wind and posted an even longer time. Plenty of work to do!

He was fortunate in that he had five weeks of boxing training done at that stage for a white-collar charity event that eventually fell through. But as he gets older, his appetite is something he curses. Good food is something he enjoys with his girlfriend Alison Coyle, and the evening before the Armagh game he was in Master Deery's, the popular restaurant in Monaghan town. He stuck to steak and vegetables but stole a few chips off his father's plate. Hugo Clerkin was willing to let that one go.

As he approaches the age of thirty, relentless self-discipline is something Dick

Clerkin appreciates and practices but he stops short of making a martyr of himself for an amateur sport.

'Back three or four years ago, I would have gone a bit over the top on the diet thing. To be honest though, I could never match having a really quality diet with good performances. I could equally relax a wee bit and play just as well. That's my approach now.

'I'm not running a marathon nor am I looking to break land-speed records. There's more to football than that, especially when you try to combine football with work and the commute to Drogheda. It's extremely time-consuming and difficult to count every wee calorie. I just try to maintain a healthy balanced diet, plenty of good fresh food, minimise anything processed and keep it sensible.'

During the Banty years, Monaghan always appeared a side that played under a great deal of self-imposed pressure. With a new man and a new setup, seeing how they fare will make interesting viewing.

CHAPTER SIX

Knives Out

ALL week long, he dreaded the letter dropping on the mat, or the phone ringing with bad news.

Instead, he heard nothing. Silence was bliss for Ryan McMenamin. In the Donegal game, a clash with Paddy McGrath brought out the hard edge in his game. His leg was being held and in the struggle to free himself, he stamped down on McGrath's prostrate body on the ground. It was a stamping offence but it was dealt with at the time by the referee, Pat Fox. He showed a yellow card. Michael Murphy had been standing nearby and felt Fox should have shown red. He wasn't shy in telling him that either.

Afterwards, the processes of the GAA's disciplinary system kicked in. The Central Competitions Control Committee [CCCC] had a look at the incident and weren't impressed. They asked Pat Fox to take another look at it on hindsight and see if he would have upgraded the offence to a red card, therefore suspending McMenamin for a month.

Fox declared himself happy with the initial decision and McMenamin escaped further punishment.

'I thought Pat Fox was going to send me off. I was trying to get away and Paddy wouldn't let me. It was a stupid thing I did, I kicked out, but I think he made the most of it and probably Michael Murphy tried his best to get me sent off.'

The citing committee had a deadline of five days within which an objection could be made. After that period, McMenamin knew he was safe. Instead, Pat Fox was the one that was effectively suspended. For the next month he didn't see a minute of action refereeing in the national league.

That could have been the end of it, only for another controversial incident a week later. Dublin forward Eoghan O'Gara struck Kerry's Marc Ó Sé with his head in their league game. A video review of that game by the CCCC resulted in an eight-week suspension for O'Gara, which he did not appeal. For his part in the scuffle, Ó Sé copped a four-week ban.

Pat Spillane was outraged. He waged war in his newspaper column on the perceived double-standards of the two cases. McMenamin wasn't impressed by what he felt was a concerted campaign against him.

'Pat Spillane took a bit of offence, writing three or four weeks in a row about why I wasn't suspended and why Marc was. I don't mind it, but Spillane, I feel sad for him. He just blatantly hates Tyrone, but in a way, if we get under Kerry's skin, and Spillane's, then that suits us.'

It wasn't the first time McMenamin had antagonised Kerry GAA folk. In 2009 at a league game in Omagh, Kerry raced into a halftime lead of 2-8 to 0-3. During the interval, Harte instructed his players to take off their shirts and throw them in the bin as they hadn't fulfilled their obligations to the jerseys. They then went out and reeled Kerry in, holding them to two points in an enthralling second half, but ultimately came up short by three points.

McMenamin got up in Colm Cooper's face for the second half. He also had a bizarre incident with Paul Galvin as he grabbed him in the groin area. At the final whistle, McMenamin and Marc Ó Sé had a set to, with Ó Sé shoving McMenamin in retaliation. The following day's newspaper caught the incident between the two, spittle hanging in the air coming from an enraged McMenamin. It looked bad. It was.

Kerry manager Jack O'Connor was furious and had to be restrained by members of his backroom. There was sulphur in the air and things threatened to turn nasty before stewards intervened. Nowadays, Jack O'Connor's nephew Patrick is dating a first cousin of McMenamin's, who admires and gets on well with the Kerry coach.

McMenamin though was brought to task in the following days. Colm O'Rourke recorded his disgust in his *Sunday Independent* column, writing:

'What Harte won't be happy about was the behaviour of Ryan McMenamin. In total contrast to Harte's own personal discipline, McMenamin was a disgrace, a brat would be the most charitable word used to describe him. McMenamin has strayed over the line many times in the past but last Sunday we were treated to the whole package of in-your-face snarling, sly digs, and open striking...

'McMenamin's continuous mouthing into players' faces is despicable. I thought these new rules were supposed to sort out the likes of that and body checking by flashing a yellow card. Well, last week there was a system failure...

'Marc Ó Sé backed off at the end when McMenamin lashed out. Jack O'Connor should not have become involved either but it must have been very hard to watch the carry-on of McMenamin, especially with a blind eye turned to this spitefulness. The easy yellow cards went to low-profile players, probably deserved too, but McMenamin should have seen red very early on.'

In explaining and defending himself, McMenamin highlights where his critics are literally coming from. It might be the most inevitable and natural defence mechanism in the GAA, raising the matter of a critic's origins, but McMenamin strongly feels O'Rourke and Spillane are compromised in dishing out such criticism of him.

'Colm O'Rourke... look at the Meath team he played on. You kind of think to yourself that they suffer from a selective memory and that there is an anti-northern bias.

'It seemed to be alright when John McDermott did [Peter] Canavan in. I think if you asked Colm about that, he would say it was all part of the game. But when he becomes a columnist for a middle-class newspaper, he has to appeal to the readership. Spillane has to be controversial because that's the hole he has dug himself into.

'It's funny the way the television pundits act too, but they have a responsibility to get viewers watching as well. It's entertainment, and at the end of the day, Pat would be a proud Kerry man who wants to see them winning all the time. He is harping back to the glorious days of no blanket defences and all of that, but I have watched videos of that Kerry team, same as everyone else, and we have all seen Pat Spillane coming from his wing-forward position to help out in defence. He spent an awful amount of time back there.'

In the past, McMenamin appeared out of control on the field. Colm Cooper was flung to the ground in 2003 in the All Ireland semi-final. There were altercations with Conor Mortimor down through the years and the incident when he fell over John McEntee in the Ulster final replay of 2005, sinking his knees into the jaw of the Armagh player. He could have walked for that but Michael Collins awarded a yellow card.

The Central Disciplinary Committee imposed a four week suspension on the player, but Mickey Harte relentlessly pursued alternative justice, and they got one when the Disputes Resolution Authority overturned the decision, freeing McMenamin up to face Dublin in the quarter-final. Remarkably, he has only been sent off once for Tyrone, when he drew a kick across Kevin Bonner from Dublin in the 2006 league game.

That '09 game against Kerry brought a stern rebuke from Harte, however. 'He just warned me. He said "We are going to have less of that crap." He laid it out that I couldn't be doing that again, and I said I hoped that it wouldn't happen again myself. It's one of those things you regret doing, but Mickey warned me, no more of that.'

There's also the part of his game that involves the talk that goes on between him and his direct opponent, as alluded to by O'Rourke in his column. For a lot of people, that kind of 'trash-talking' is unseemly and unsporting but McMenamin has a different take on the issue, feeling people are a bit too precious about it. In terms of introspection, he doesn't feel he needs to go as far as, say, Dick Clerkin. He justifies it and feels no dissonance for what has happened.

'There's verbals in every game. I get a worse reputation for it with Tyrone being successful. I could name three or four players off the top of my head that are ten times worse than me, but they don't get the reputation because they don't play for a successful county. There's a lot of boys, one boy in particular, has come out with a lot of mouthfuls to our boys than I would ever come out with, but it wouldn't be written and wouldn't be documented.

'It does go on, there are some players that are good at it. If you see American sports like basketball, talking is accepted as part of the game. A lot times, I'd say the majority of times, people start on me thinking they're going to get a reaction. Put me off. But I really don't mind. I find most of the times that a lot of the other boys pushing into me, that they're trying to get themselves rised up.'

When he does it, he feels he is in control. He's happy to push it to the edge and sometimes beyond, but he also believes his in-built sensor helps him realise if it's detracting from his overall game.

'If it was affecting my performance or the team in some way, if I was getting in trouble with it or bringing criticism onto the team, Mickey would soon put it to one side. He would put an end to it.

'He backs us one hundred percent and we back him. It comes down to respect. I know myself that he has backed me in more situations, like Galvin and a couple more incidents and he hasn't come out and said anything. He could have got rid of me a couple of times after them, but he stuck with me.'

Hard as it is to believe, the Tyrone fans are growing restless with the league still only in its tentative stages. In their opener in Celtic Park, Derry swept the feet from under them. Thirteen days later the Donegal game was notable not only for the disciplinary scare, but the ease in which the visitors humbled Tyrone, winning 1-10 to 0-6.

The heading on the charge sheet is a familiar one. Harte is once again being accused of blind loyalty to the players that have delivered All Irelands in his charge. Much of the spotlight is being shone in the direction of Conor Gormley. Against Derry, Sean Leo McGoldrick took him on a tour of the field, testing his durability and middle-distance running ability. Against Donegal, Mark McHugh repeated the trick. His impressive engine was ticking nicely and Gormley found it difficult to stay tight to him for the duration. It may not have been the most important factor in the win but it was one of them.

Despite flashes of form from the likes of Niall McKenna and others, the promising All Ireland winning minor team of 2008 remain largely on ice. There is a case to be made that if Tyrone are in a transitional phase it would do no harm to blood some of these youngsters in the early stages of the league but it goes unheeded.

Harte is a master of gauging the mood of Tyrone followers and while he respects their opinion, he knows his own mind. Gormley will stay and build up the minutes on the field he needs to get up to pace. When hot summer days come, his role is rarely out the field now anyway.

Setting all that aside, the chaotic early season endured by everyone in Tyrone football and their manager meant they would always be playing catch-up with other teams that had an uninterrupted build up to the league campaign.

'I think we were a right bit behind in our fitness against Derry and the same applies against Donegal,' reasons McMenamin. 'There has been an improvement and a concentration from everyone, number one to thirty-five. We've been working hard in training and we might play well in patches, only to stop. It probably was our problem last year.

'Conor [Gormley] didn't get much game time in the McKenna Cup and he didn't get much training at that time. Derry were flying. They worked their tactics around hitting Sean Leo [McGoldrick] on the wings. At the same time Conor was feeling poorly at the game, but he is a big enough man to tell you, there are days you play well and days you don't. Once you get over thirty you are too old, and if you play well, the easy thing to say is "That man has great experience."'

Tyrone have a tricky away trip to Sligo in their next game. Their season truly starts here, with Ryan McMenamin, Conor Gormley and all their big names on the field. Time to pin the ears back.

CHAPTER SEVEN
Saturday Night Lights

TONY Poacher doesn't get to that many matches anymore. Married to his Spanish wife Mariluz and living in Switzerland for the past fourteen years can have that effect, but when he looked at the list of national league fixtures for the season, one game jumped out at him. Down versus Armagh. Pairc Esler.

As an underage player with the Ballyholland club and The Abbey Christian Brothers school in Newry, he was part of the tradition and rich rivalry that splits the town: Armagh one side, Down the other. Down would be playing at home but the pitch is in Armagh, another of those quirks of geography along county borders.

This game bursted with more context than just the two league points on offer. It would be a dry run for their Championship game on May 28. And, of course, local bragging rights were at stake, real GAA currency.

There was a time when Tony dreamt of lining out in the red and black of his beloved Down himself. He was a promising player at underage before work took him on another path, to an accountancy job with Hewlett Packard. Life has had other consolations, like the kids, Angelito, Hannah and Daniel, and a comfortable lifestyle in an agreeable country. Yet the little boy in him keeps screaming to be let out, so he follows his heroes through bundles of newspapers posted over from his father, updates on the internet, and the occasional flight home for a match.

On a fresh Saturday night, the February night sky is lit up for miles by the huge floodlights of Pairc Esler. Their luminous bulbs bathe a pitch that looks a little careworn. Hot food stalls belch out the smell of frying meat. Fans of both sides march with a pep to their step, eager to get the best possible vantage point. On a night like this, you relax only when you reach your seat and gaze out across the pitch. Though there's a winter chill in the still evening, it already has the feel and anticipation of a summer game.

This was a hungry young contender in front of his home crowd, seeking to land a crunching blow on a grizzled former champ. The home side are Down. All Ireland finalists five months ago, they enjoy the knock-on effects of their glorious run over the previous summer. Their attendances have soared. The replica jersey is once again a fashionable garment. The county is relishing its rediscovered status as a genuine force and with that tag comes certain responsibilities. Top of that list is to keep the insurgents Armagh in their place.

Their history runs deep but their support grew apathetic during the fallow years of the past decade. In 1960, they arrived like a comet to bring the first Sam Maguire into the northern six counties. Their follow up triumphs in 1961 and 1968 and their distinctive red and black colours leant them a certain mystique. Defeating Kerry on their way to those three All Irelands was another part of the legend.

A generation later, All Ireland titles arrived in 1991 and '94 with a style of play and chutzpah that excited purists and romantics. The player credited with bringing the requisite attitude into the dressing room to trigger the renaissance was James McCartan. 'Wee James' arrived as a cocky teenager with a sense of entitlement that All Ireland medals had to arrive soon. He also provided a sentimental link to the teams of the '60s, his father having been a central figure in the first coming of Down.

Tonight, Wee James is on the sideline, coach of the Down side.

While James inflicted punishment at one end of the pitch during that glorious summer of 1991, Paddy O'Rourke was stopping everything in the backline. By 1991, he had suffered the worst days in the defence for years previous. It all came good for him in his final year when he captained the team that took Sam Maguire back across the border.

The celebrations were boisterous and loud. At 7am on the Tuesday after the final, O'Rourke left the clubrooms of his own club Burren and instead of bringing the cup through the clogged roads, he hopped a fence and went up Burren Hill. As he approached the summit, he turned to see his progress and a crowd had gathered. He grabbed the trophy with both hands and gave it a shake above his head as a lusty roar rumbled up the hill toward him. Immortality was his. As the proudest of Down men, it was a mantle he wore comfortably.

Tonight, O'Rourke is on the sideline, coach of the Armagh side. Sport plays some curious tricks.

Despite winning promotion and beating Down in the Division Two final in his first season with Armagh, O'Rourke has yet to truly win the hearts and minds of a demanding fanbase. He's won the hearts of key senior players though, including the one that basically got him the job.

When former manager Armagh manager Peter McDonnell resigned in 2009, he alluded to some shady forces working against his side and that his management team were 'continually being sabotaged' by other parties within the county. It was widely expected that Paul Grimley, a former player and coach of Armagh's 2002 All Ireland winning team, would finally take the vacant job. He had been overlooked for the job in 2007 but had the support of the clubs this time. He turned it down to join Monaghan's backroom staff and the exhaustive process had to start all over again.

At a players' meeting, they were asked to nominate who they wanted as manager. Stevie McDonnell handed up his scrap of paper with the name of Paddy O'Rourke on it, O'Rourke's only nomination. It would be probably be the last manager McDonnell would have so he wanted this appointment to be the right one. Through his friendship with Down All Star Benny Coulter, McDonnell had learned of the passion and the integrity that O'Rourke had brought to his football when managing Down from 2003 to 2006. Those qualities sounded just like what Armagh needed.

And so just like Pairc Esler itself, a Down man found himself in Armagh tonight, his old rivals now his friends and his old friends now his rivals.

•   •   •

During the day, before the lights have been flicked on to burn brightly for the masses, the Down squad begin their preparations. Father Terry Rafferty says Mass for the squad in the Newry Shamrocks Social Club, a recent tradition that came in during Ross Carr's time as manager.

Barry Clarke takes over then, his laptop and display all in place. Originally from Louth, Clarke is a computer technician in St Colman's College, and lives close to the McCartan homestead, a kind of Kennedy compound in the world of Down football. He takes the team through the statistical analysis from the last game, highlighting some points and playing down others. He mentions what to look out for against this Armagh team, but not too much. Information overload is a stress this side can do without.

James McCartan then addresses his players before trainer Paddy Tally calls the time for everyone to be ready. After that it's up to each individual to get their rubs and strapping completed in time.

Once the team hit the back pitch behind a stand that is filling up early, there is a businesslike briskness to everything. Kicking drills, passing drills, tackling drills, dynamic stretching. All the major muscle groups are loosened out as the heart rate steadily rises.

On their first day out in the league, Down drew with Mayo on a rotten day in Castlebar. Beating a dispirited Galway side then by five points was a decent result but it still left Down wondering where exactly they lay in comparison with the big boys.

Twenty minutes to throw-in.

The Down side go back into the dressing room, put their jerseys on, and receive final instructions from McCartan and selector Brian McIver. Individual goals are being hammered home. Focus on the process and the outcome will follow.

Outside, match day programmes have sold out long ago. Turnstiles click steadily. Nobody expected a crowd like this. The days of 12,000 paying customers to a national league match were meant to be a relic of the Celtic Tiger era.

Fifteen minutes to throw in.

The starting team for Down are playing the substitutes in a warm up game, played across the field. Thumps are flying in. A shooting drill is set up and players flow seamlessly into it. Each player has a few balls to get their eye in immediately before the throw in. Then, the team huddle.

Five minutes to throw in.

The huddle is where the heart of the adrenaline is. But Aidan Carr has no part in it. He makes his way to the stand to sit among the substitutes for the night. His heartrate subsides. This isn't how it should be.

The day before the All Ireland final of 2009, he pulled a hamstring as his club Clonduff won the Kilmacud Sevens tournament. He tried coaxing his body into a few McKenna Cup games the following January but knew things weren't right. The week before the first league match of 2010, the Down panel played an in-house game. He pulled it again. A year of hell had begun.

He got back in time to play the second half of their last league game against Laois. Things felt fine as they travelled to meet Louth at a pitch opening the week after. He took a starting spot and after ten minutes he went over on his ankle, tearing ligaments. He would spend the rest of the year watching Down enjoy their best summer in sixteen years.

'I never had a year like that before,' Carr says. 'You don't get as excited as much when you know you're not going to be involved. As delighted as you are for your friends, for your county, you're watching them and wishing you were out there with them.

'At the minute, because the boys did so well last year, they're in possession of the jersey. You're sitting waiting, coming on as a sub, and you can't really make the kind of impact that would mean you definitely starting the next week. You're really waiting for somebody to play poorly - which is to the team's detriment and you don't want that. Or through an injury, but having been injured last year you definitely wouldn't wish that on anyone. Then you have suspension, but sure...'

While Carr was making the forlorn journey to the bench, his good friend Danny Hughes was doing the captain's handshake with his Armagh counterpart, Steven McDonnell.

Drafted onto the county panel in 1999 as a rail-thin teenager, McDonnell's first season was a period of acclimatisation, a watching brief. Armagh landed their first Ulster title since 1982, providing redemption for warriors such as Jarlath Burns, John Rafferty and Benny Tierney. The boy they came to know as 'Stevie from Killeavey' was kept in cold storage.

He gained a starting jersey in the league during the winter of that year and has never surrendered it since. Put like that, it sounds like the inter-county life has been a charmed one for McDonnell. It hasn't.

In 2008 he was in a funk. Like any attacker in sport experiences at some point, the scores were drying up and the posts were closing in. The great Armagh team of 2002 was fragmenting with huge holes left in the dressing room that used to be occupied by leaders and characters with cast-iron confidence, such as Kieran McGeeney and the McEntee twins. Despite that, a level of expectation remained among the support as they raged against the dying of the light. McDonnell will go down as one of the sharpest and best forwards to ever play the game but that did not satisfy the keyboard warriors.

A popular Armagh website gave a voice to some vile and daft ideas. Measured contributions were drowned out by those with little understanding of the intricacies of the game or the pressure these men are under.

An online poll went up, posing the question, 'Should Stevie McDonnell be dropped?' Benny Tierney, Armagh's goalkeeper in 2002, used his weekly column in *The Irish News* to weigh in on the debate. Under a headline of 'The reasons you don't drop Stevie McDonnell', he spelt things out clearly.

'People have said "He's greedy" but if I had that talent, I'd be greedy too. There was one man who made a complaint to me every time I met him, saying, "He's done, he's finished, useless." Bear in mind Stevie was 26, 27 at the time. He scored 3-6 against Roscommon the week after. I met the same critic coming out of the ground and asked "He's done, he's done, isn't he?" He just said back "He's a greedy bastard."

'I took a bit of flak from people who thought they had the right to say these things. I don't think you have the right to criticise a man who is as good a footballer to ever play for Armagh. People expect him not to be as good as he was but he's doing even better than before. Last year they were depending on him, he was still the main man, consistently churning it out, staying injury-free.

'I'm not in agreement with these discussion boards, I'm not in agreement with Twitter or Facebook where people are being talked about publicly like that. But it's part and parcel of being a county footballer now that people get to analyse you, fifteen or sixteen year olds who know nothing about football putting up crap about you.'

• • •

A roar goes up after the national anthem. The ball is thrown in and both sides go hell for leather. This is Down and Armagh after all.

Conor Laverty strikes the first blow for Down with a point in the opening minute. Danny Hughes tags on another. Armagh's Ciaran McKeever and Charlie Vernon reply during a sizzling opening but there are gaps everywhere. Martin Clarke, the much-admired Down attacker who took time out from a career in

Australian Rules football to come home, curls a beauty over from distance. Hughes and Mark Poland put up more scores to give Down a cushion. Armagh are struggling for air.

McDonnell is seeing little ball, surviving on scraps. He turns provider for the opportunities of teammates but watches their attempts sail wide. His marker, Dan Gordon, is playing brilliant tonight. A little touch here, a hand in there, winning his personal duel.

A high ball in has Down's goalkeeper Brendan McVeigh in trouble. He spills the first catch but recovers to gather it. Tackles fly in and he crumples to the floor. His knee is gone and substitute goalkeeper Cathal Murdock is unexpectedly pressed into action.

As McVeigh is carried over to the sideline, Carr winces. Another man going through his own purgatory. Soon, McVeigh will be spending too much time with team physio Noel Rice.

The halftime score stands at Down 0-8, Armagh 0-6.

Stevie McDonnell is in the portacabin which is acting as a makeshift dressing rooms while the main building is getting a facelift. He takes his time to figure how Armagh can regain their footing. They've already lost their opening game to Dublin but managed to beat Monaghan after a late fluke goal. When they set down their goals at the start of the league campaign, Down came under the bracket of 'winnable' games. Lose this and they're already in the teeth of a relegation battle.

They adapt and survive as the game resumes. Kevin Dyas gets a point and McDonnell taps over a free to draw them level. Rory Grugan converts a dead ball and pushes them in front. The game goes supernova. McDonnell spoons the ball to the marauding Moriarty but Murdock gets down well to make the save.

In the next attack, a ball is played into McDonnell and Gordon contests it. It sticks to the attacker's hands. McDonnell pivots on the spot and lets off a drive like a slingshot but Gordon recovers to dive and block it down. It's a pivotal moment. The home side regain their composure to open up another lead. Armagh rally once more but hit poor wides. In the end, time runs out on the fightback. Armagh players leave the field with their body language upbeat. That's the thing about the league, the game is only important while it's being played. There is plenty of time to put things right.

Individually, it's different. McDonnell will rue the goal chance. 'I had an opportunity and I caught the ball in front of Dan. I thought I had slipped him totally and went to unleash the boot at it. Dan came out of nowhere to block it, it was fantastic, but I was certainly going for goal.'

While nobody is blaming McDonnell, he is taking responsibility for his corner. He scrutinises the little things, the inches that this Armagh side were famous for and he sees the shortcomings.

'I had time with the chances but I need to be more focused in the striking of the ball. Perhaps with the goal chance there was a little bit of sharpness missing. I thought I had done everything to get away from Dan Gordon but obviously he had the time to get back and make a block. Should I have taken an extra bounce or something to get away from him? Perhaps I should have.

'I haven't scored that many goals over the last year or two. That's certainly something I want to improve upon. I set myself a target of getting five goals in the league campaign, I haven't scored any after three games, but I feel I can still make the target. There are four games left to play and I can make up the goals.

'In the Championship I have a goals tally I want to reach as well. I went through last year's Championship and never scored a goal. I missed a penalty in fact, against Fermanagh, so I need to get three to four goals.'

There have been accusations that Armagh are lacking a coherent game-plan. The loss of selector Justin McNulty has been a sore point. Armagh fans watch enviously as he appears to have reinvigorated Laois and sharpened their attack in the opening games of their league campaign. It was noticeable how Armagh played much too rigid against Monaghan, hitting poor ball into Gareth Swift at full-forward while his marker Darren Hughes swallowed up everything.

The evidence is mounting up but McDonnell is not buying it.

'Sometimes you have a game-plan and it can go out the window in the first five minutes and you have to adapt. We adapted against Monaghan and we probably implemented our game-plan in the second half against Down and performed that bit better.

'Down played to a plan, they've been working on it and it did them good last year. We knew their half-forward line would come deep. Perhaps we gave them a bit too much space. They start a lot of their attacks in the halfback line and we need to be putting pressure on them up there. That is what we are trying to get across the board.

'It's fresh and new in our minds, it probably doesn't look like it's much of a plan to outsiders, but I feel it will start to work for us.'

Their new focus has been to push up on players, to go man-for-man and pressurise the ball-carrier high up the field. Against Monaghan, there was a breakdown and some players began thumping the ball in, almost expecting to see the injured Ronan Clarke up there. Old habits still remain but they are in the process of evolving.

'Paddy [O'Rourke] would be a firm believer in consulting with the players and asking their opinions. He would speak to the more senior players and then put it to the whole team. It's about seeing what best suits us and how we want to play.'

● ● ●

After the game, Aidan Carr does not want to face the world. He doesn't want to have to deal with the snipes, the lads out on the town, thinking they're only messing when slagging him. Even the innocents will want to ask him why he didn't get a run. Their way of sympathy, at least to his face, might involve bitching about selection and James McCartan's ability to pick a team. He doesn't need that. He knows James rates him.

When Carr graduated to Queen's University, fate had it that McCartan was their football coach. He immediately asked Carr and three other freshmen onto the Sigerson panel. The quartet was completed with McCartan's younger brother Eoin, who despite health problems preventing him from playing more than half an hour at a time, is currently hanging around the periphery of the Down squad with a view to becoming an impact sub.

For four years Carr was an ever-present on the Queen's side. They lost three Sigerson finals in a row but landed the big prize in his last year against their great rivals University Ulster Jordanstown, 0-15 to 0-14 after extra time. It was a special moment for Wee James who had his brothers Dan and Eoin as key men. Carr was joint top scorer in the final for Queen's with four points.

During that time he fitted in three consecutive years with the county U-21 side and made his starting championship debut for the seniors under his father in 2007. Predictably, some questioned Ross's judgement in picking his son. Happily, the Down support was self-regulating about it.

'Once we were playing Meath in the qualifiers in Newry. I had scored seven points and Down only scored eight points in total. A lot of them were from frees and I had missed a shot from play and a man close by roared out "Fuck sake Ross, take off your fella!"

'My dad heard it and was about to turn around and react but someone else in the crowd reacted instead, sticking up for me.'

After the Armagh game Carr ended up drifting on home. The walls of the front room weren't big enough to hold all his thoughts, so with a bit of persuasion from his friends he eventually went out into Newry for a few drinks. He let himself go and forgot about football for a while. These things will always turn themselves around.

In Stevie McDonnell's world, he's already moved on. This next week will be a crucial one. Scores are a forward's currency and McDonnell lives off it. Practice is vital for him and it's time to get back to the art of kicking the football over the bar. Most people believe this to be a simple process but it is endlessly complex.

'During the months of January and February, and even March, it's not the best of times to be going out kicking balls over the bar, but towards the end of March I would do a lot of kicking up in the pitch in Killeavey. I actually take a young fella on the Armagh minor team, Caolan Trainor, and we'll go up and kick balls over the bar for forty-five minutes or so.'

Caolan is in a privileged position to see the kind of dedicated practice that is required to reach the highest levels. It's a habit that has served McDonnell well from when he was a child.

'I did that at his age but I would have done a lot of it by myself, took balls up and constantly kick balls over the bar. These months are not the best for doing it, so I'm always the first man out on the training pitch for Armagh and I would always be the last to leave. I spend ten to fifteen minutes before and after the sessions working on my kicking.

'I think it's very important for any forward, any footballer really, to do. Kicking balls, getting used to the position you play, getting into good habits. For any player to improve, you always have to go to training with an aim to work on something you're not particularly strong at and that's what I try to do. There were opportunities in the Down game where I could have kicked points and a goal and it's something that I will be working on during the next session.'

The world turns. There's always the next game in the league, but there won't be a next time in the race for the Anglo-Celt Cup if Down come out on top on May 28. It will be dangerous and it will be cut-throat.

Tony Poacher can't wait. He spent the Saturday night in the company of friends and family, in ebullient form, waxing on about the ability of this Down team.

The league is only a taster for what is yet to come.

Championship is ninety-one days and counting.

CHAPTER EIGHT

Staying Home

IT was one of Dublin's rare forays outside the capital. The old town of Clones was a sea of sky blue as the Dubs spread their bonhomie and good nature around. The publicans and shop owners of the town felt blessed while street hawkers thrived as the visitors were spending like it was 2003.

On paper it looked a tricky qualifier for Dublin. A two-point defeat by Laois in the Leinster semi-final had them spooked, and now they were heading into what could be a border ambush. Derry were hurting themselves from a mauling at the hands of Tyrone in Casement Park.

With forty-seven minutes gone, Dublin were up by eight points and coasting. Jason Sherlock had been sprung from the bench to hit 1-3 and then two further goals were put beyond the reach of Derry's young goalkeeper: Michael Conlan to the rest of the planet, Mickey C to those who dwell around the hardcore football area on the fringes of Lough Neagh. Patrick McGuckin, father of Kevin, christened him so when he was just ten and it has stuck forever.

As another point sailed over the bar, a visibly nervous Conlan went to retrieve a stray ball for a kickout. This wasn't like it was with his club, Ballinderry, who would never lose a game in this fashion.

With the Dublin support relaxed and their bloodlust satisfied, they sought alternative diversion. A throaty chant was struck up:

The Derry keeper,
The Derry keeper,
The Derry keeper's going bald!
The Derry keeper's going bald!'

After the match Conlan grabbed his gear and stuffed it into his kitbag. It was his last Championship game for Derry. Seven seasons would go by in the blink of an eye but he never marched behind the band again on the day of inter-county action.

● ● ●

Mickey C, the goalie for Ballinderry. It's been that way forever.

Fifteen years ago on St Patrick's Day, Conlan kept goal as St Pat's Maghera lost the Hogan Cup final to a Killorglin team featuring Mike Frank Russell. Conlan could remember him from an All Ireland Feile na nGael final when the little Kerry wizard collected a winner's medals for Laune Rangers having beaten Ballinderry along the way.

Maghera's manager was Adrian McGuckin whose own two sons, Ronan and Adrian, grew up alongside Conlan. The pair of them regarded Conlan's mum, Mary, a second mother while Conlan went on holidays with the McGuckin family when he was eighteen.

'It was Mickey who coined the phrase about "legends",' explains McGuckin. 'Everything is "Big Legend" with him. He calls everybody it, so he's called it back. You would never get anybody who would ever say a bad word about Mickey C. Friend or foe in any club or county, or anybody who ever met him through school or university.

'He wouldn't have been a great footballer and we would have had loads and loads of young talent about at that time but Mickey C used to hang about and was always part of it. He couldn't have kicked it at all and could never get on a team but then he started going into goals. And he went down to the field every day and would take kickout after kickout. Boys shooting at him for hours. Anything he took a notion to, he would have perfected it.'

The practice began to show gains. He spent his early schooling in St Pius's in Magherafelt and never broke onto the teams there. By the time he graduated to Maghera, he was a different animal and made McGuckin's McRory Cup-winning team.

After that it was onto Jordanstown where he strolled onto the first team and reached a Sigerson Cup final, only for Mike Frank with Tralee IT to deny him again.

The defining year was 2001. Ballinderry Shamrocks managed to beat Bellaghy in the county final at the third time of asking. They kept it going all the way through the winter and into the spring, as far as Thurles and beating Nemo Rangers in the final, securing Mickey C his All Ireland medal at last.

The nucleus of the team was made up of lads who had played on that Feile team against Mike Frank. Enda Muldoon, Adrian McGuckin Junior, Stephen McGeechan, Paul Wilson, Gerard Cassidy and of course the Legend himself, Mickey C: they all came up and grew up together. Along the way, real life entered the equation: marriage, babies, jobs.

Gerard Cassidy is getting married soon, and it seems the only times these lads see each other now is either on the football field or at stag dos and weddings. This weekend the entire fraternity are gearing up, packing away their best shirts and jeans. There are pints to be drunk, sights to be seen, abuse to be fired out.

Cassidy is hosting his stag in London. They're booking a hotel in Covent Garden and all. Standing in his kitchen, Mickey's brother Killian can hardly take the grin off his face as he looks forward to an old-school reunion, but Mickey's not going. His friends are texting, asking why he'd want to be hanging around home and reminding him of all the antics they're likely to get up to.

But Mickey can't go.
Because Mickey's back on the county panel.

• • •

There are only so many hours in a day, which Mickey C has learned at a cost. Early rises in the middle of the night, a working life in the seat of a van, strength and conditioning programmes, team training, raising a young family, team meetings... Something had to give over the spring.

So he handed in his notice at the bakery.

Jobs are desperate hard to come by but he targets a move into the personal training industry. A young entrepreneur from Ardboe has started a gym and can see the upside in having a county footballer hanging around the place, instructing people on exercise and how to look after themselves. The driving job was only meant to be a temporary measure anyway but the main reason he gave it up was for football. Simply put, getting back to the nine-to-five routine will help him win back his place on the Derry team.

'I started the bakery job in the last week of July, 2010, for Genesis in Magherafelt. I had been out of work for maybe thirteen or fourteen weeks before that and I was Mr Daddy Day-Care, with Paula going back to work after having Rionach.'

Conlan had been selling gym equipment and sports nutrition products for a year until the company called, saying they wanted to put more money into their shops and were taking their reps off the road. They said they were sorry and it was just first-in, first-out and all that stuff but Conlan knew the amount of profit they were earning off him at the time and the amount of work that was in the process of paying off.

In the bakery Mondays, Wednesdays and Fridays were the busy days. His working days began at 2.30am when he would rise, grab something to eat and get into the yard for 3am. The van would be fully loaded by 4am when the driving would begin. 'Once I was out in the van, you might not have got back in the yard until 1pm. I would deliver bread to ASDA, Tescos, Sainsbury's and then you would get through all the local shops.

'I was coming home and going straight to the gym because I knew I had that wee window of opportunity when the weans were in the crèche. I'd be doing my programme and get back home for an hour's sleep, then off to lift the weans. Have a couple of hours with them, then straight out to training for a couple of hours in the evening.

'It was all getting too much. I felt it wasn't suiting me, that I needed something with regular hours during the day. A lot of people would say my head's cut, leaving a good job to concentrate on football. But that's me.'

Conlan realised all the unsociable hours, the madness of living your life in the dark, the bad eating habits it encouraged, would cheat him out of this chance. County players who have been out of the picture for almost a decade don't get recalls. He'd never forgive himself if he went into it with a half-assed attempt.

●　　●　　●

Paula Conlan is a saint. No doubt. And she knows the score. Her brother is Paudie O'Neill of Henry Joy McCracken's club in Moneymore, who played for Derry himself under the legendary Eamonn Coleman. Her and Mickey met and started going out in 2000. Mickey can't remember the exact date, only that it coincided with a county final defeat to Bellaghy.

They got married in 2006 and they have three children that are nothing more than steps of stairs. Micheál was three in January, Rionach is the apple of her daddy's eye and will turn two in September, and little Fiachra was born just after Christmas.

'Paula knew I was playing before we met. When we started going out, it was football, football, football so she knew nothing else.

'I'm managing because of Paula, she keeps the children right. I'm out of the house, three, four nights of the week. I would try and do my best from about five o'clock 'til about half-six, help bath them, get them ready for bed and that. You get so little time you have to make use of it because you don't want to be like ships in the night either.'

Given the enormous sacrifices being made, it would be nice if the rewards were coming with it. But they're not at the moment – Mickey has found himself on the bench for the past couple of league games. The Dubs fans might say if he had any hair left he's be pulling it out.

'It's frustrating because you're sorta back now, you've done the rotating keepers thing, you've done everything and to be doing it again feels weird. Coming from a successful enough club and knowing that you're coming to the end of your career and you feel like an influence on other players… That's all stripped off you when you're sitting on a bench, because you don't feel you can do that [provide leadership]; you don't have the right.'

Things began well for Derry with their now annual defeat of Tyrone in the first league fixture. Danny Devlin started in goal and made a string of impressive stops, keeping a clean sheet. Conlan was between the sticks for the next game, another impressive win, this time against Kildare. He stayed there for the aberration that was the Laois game, Derry being crushed 1-7 to 1-21.

The pendulum swung back the direction of Devlin again for the Sligo game as they managed to get back on track with a three-point win.

'John [Brennan] would have always said to us from the start of the year that the third and fourth games of the league are the real season-defining moments. In the third game we were beat and John was preaching to us "This fourth game boys, youse don't realise how important this fourth game is. This is going to be where our season is judged, we have to win at Sligo, there's no other way around this."

'In my eyes the Sligo game was a real dogfight, and to be coming out of it, under lights, at home, was massive. We want a league final to set us up for the Championship. It's only seven or eight weeks away now. We're going good, getting a look at what players can do, getting a system of play going.'

Yet while he puts his emotional investment into playing for Derry, he wrestles with the missed weekends that seem so much more important as you grow older.

'I'm missing Gerard Cassidy's stag-do. It's just so frustrating it's not even funny. They'll be in London partying flat out and sending over wee smiley faces on the mobile.

'People say to me, you always have to think of the bigger picture – that's the picture I'm focusing on now. Everything I do now, should it be the cold, wet nights in Owenbeg, slogging through the muck and all, you're hoping for a good day in Clones in June. You're hoping to be number one, and you're hoping for a performance for yourself and for the team.'

And if he can get that, the decent showing and become the first-choice, then he vows he would never need another stag-do away again. Because the only thing that matters is playing for Derry.

CHAPTER NINE

One Last Big Blowout

'Hail, Hail, the Celts are here /
What the Hell do we care,
what the Hell do we care...'

THE meeting of Derry and Donegal at Celtic Park was to provide a few pointers to the future. The home side ran up a pretty impressive tally of 2-12 but the significant moment came in the fifty-eighth minute when Donegal's young captain Michael Murphy sprang above both Kevin McCloy and Barry McGoldrick to collect the ball before spinning instantly towards goal and driving it past Danny Devlin. Donegal finished with 2-18.

Reporters huddled in close to hear the soft Derry voice of John Brennan after the game. He wasn't impressed. 'If one forward wins a high ball between two defenders and puts it in the net, then there's a problem. I think that we have to look very seriously at that and work on it. It should never have happened and that was the death knell.'

Donegal went home in good form, now unbeaten in all their five league games, but Neil McGee and Kevin Cassidy were particularly buoyant. Straight after the game they showered and changed with alacrity to meet up with a friend, James Sweeney, and catch a boat bound for Glasgow, where their beloved Celtic were to face Rangers in the following day's CIS Cup final at Hampden Park.

The connection with Donegal and Glasgow is a living, breathing one which explains the mad devotion in the county for Celtic. For Cassidy, it's more personal than that. He is a son of Glasgow. Fae Glasgae. It shaped him and hardened him and gave him the street smarts. Donegal might be home but so is Glasgow, and Glaswegians never forget where they come from.

This emigrant's tale began with Sarah 'Sally' Ferry. There wasn't much work for a young girl in the townland of Brinlack in the Donegal Ghaeltacht of Gaoth Dobhair, so she trod a well-worn path to the port city on the west coast of Scotland. While there she met Mickey Carr, a Scotsman with Irish blood well thinned by the generations spent away.

Together they had one boy, named after his father, and daughters Margaret, Mary, Ann and Ellen. Mary made her name as a talented sportswoman and spent her best years playing ladies' soccer in the professional leagues of Italy and Holland as well representing Scotland. She moved back to her mother's homeplace a few years back.

Ann met a young man called Tommy Cassidy, a fellow Glaswegian with half-forgotten roots in Tyrone. He liked his sport but he also enjoyed his pint. He played a bit too and was an apprentice with the Bill Shankly-era Liverpool FC before breaking his leg just as he was threatening the first-team squad. There wasn't much sympathy or rehabilitation back. He was cut adrift to make his own way in life.

Ann and Tommy had two boys, Stephen and Kevin, and a daughter Lorraine, when they traced Sally's steps back home to Donegal. Kevin was only nine but he was delighted. The family initially got on very well, setting up a few sports shops. More girls arrived: Siobhán, Aisling, Cealain and Carol-Ann. The family opened a bar in 1994 just in time for the USA World Cup and all of a sudden they were comfortable.

Before the move, life in Scotland had been hard and over the years they would cast an envious eye at Donegal. Glasgow might have been home but it was rough in Hamilton, ten minutes from the infamous Gorbals area. 'Granny Sally' was part of a close Irish community living in high-rise flats and tenement buildings that expressed themselves and their culture unashamedly in a city troubled by sectarianism. On weekends there would be music and singing and dancing and rebel songs. And drinking. Lots of hard, working-class, Glasgow style drinking where the capacity to hold drink often defined the rank of a man. There was the odd row and fight too. You grew up with your fists mean and your wits keen.

But there was Celtic too. The glory of the Hoops, the songs of the Jungle. Hail, Hail, the Celts are here. What the Hell do we care, what the Hell do we care... Well it's a grand old team to play for, and it's a grand old team to see, AND IF! YOU KNOW! YOUR HISTORY! Well it's enough to make your heart go....

For Cassidy this Cup final would serve two purposes. It was a chance to see Celtic, sure, but it was also the last big blowout before a long hard summer of football with Donegal. The watering hole of choice was The Brazen Head on Cathcart Road. Granny Sally had lived nearby and it is staunchly Celtic inside. The songs are sung all day long on matchday and testosterone takes over. In the company of his cousins and fellow Tims, for Cassidy it's an extension of Parkhead's Paradise.

Other pre-championship blowouts weren't as well timed in the past.

●   ●   ●

Donegal and drink. It's been there from the start of Cassidy's career. Some times it's been a case of giving a dog a bad name, but not always.

Stephen Cassidy was a handy soccer player when he came over from Glasgow. With his size and skill, his coaches threw him into full forward and he flourished, becoming a county player. They did the same with younger brother

Kevin, but while the raw material was there, something was missing. One day, in a move sparked by frustration as much as anything else, Anthony Molloy told him he was going in at wing-back against Down in a minor game. Ronan Murtagh nicked three points off him but he stayed on the field for the entire game for a change.

In 2002 Mickey Moran and John Morrison arrived to take the county team and develop a squad with their holistic approach. An injury to a defender against Offaly led to them slotting Cassidy in at centre back. The next league game was away to Galway and Moran explained that he was starting Raymond Sweeney in that role. After half an hour Cassidy was sent for and he nailed down a place at wing back.

Two months later Cassidy was part of the county U-21 team that lost an Ulster semi-final to Cavan. The next day he was on the road for an overnight stay in Connemara. The seniors had to face All Ireland champions Galway in a pitch opening in Rosmuc.

When they were settled in the hotel, Moran allowed the players to stretch their legs. They walked as far as the crossroads where there was a quaint bar. Curiosity took them inside. Pints started flowing. Moran got wind of it and sent word that they were to return immediately. Some started drifting back in twos and three, but when the disco out the back of the pub struck up, it was too tempting not to stay on.

Cassidy was rooming with two others and they began to make their way back to the hotel at 4.30am. There was no night porter so they spotted an open window and clambered inside. On the other side they couldn't believe their luck.

They had climbed through the window of the bar.

'You couldn't let an opportunity like that pass you by,' recalls Cassidy, 'so we started pouring pints at five in the morning. They were good boys to drink. Our game was at 2.30 in the afternoon.

'The next morning we got the knock on the door for breakfast and headed down. Mickey had called Conall Dunne up to the panel as a teenager and it disgusted Mickey that Conall had seen that. We had a meeting and Mickey said he couldn't understand how a pint could turn into something like that. He didn't know what time we had even got back. If he had we would have been gone off the panel.

'Mickey is an absolute gentleman and I thought I had let him down because he gave me a chance. Although he never identified me as an out-and-out leader of the thing, I felt I let him down. So we went out and played Galway off the field and they had their full side.'

That was the great contradiction of Donegal football. You had a panel of players who were hell-bent on wringing every last bit of guilty pleasure out of the thing but could turn out the following day and flatten the reigning All Ireland champions.

Summer rolled on but the musketeer attitude remained. They muscled past Cavan in the preliminary round of the Ulster Championship. That night a contingent of players went to Letterkenny. On Monday they reconvened, ending their festivities in Derry city. They went on the beer in Sligo on the Tuesday. Come Thursday night they landed back to training without a mention of it.

'This was a common occurrence. We were at college so they just suspected we were busy with exams. [Brendan] Devenney was the first man out. Myself, Brian McLaughlin, Rory Kavanagh, Christy Toye. The rest of the boys, Michael Hegarty, Damien Diver and them, they would have had a few drinks on a Sunday night, but that was enough for them. Not like the north-west boys really.'

They took Down apart in the quarter-final, 3-12 to 1-6. They held firm against Derry in the Ulster semi-final and squeezed through by two points. Waiting in the final would be Armagh, a team that would happily go months without a night out. They were the very antithesis of Donegal and would haunt Donegal over the next number of years.

As they drove up to Clones on Ulster final day, John Morrison threw a tape on of Paul Brady's version of 'Homes of Donegal'. The song reached its crescendo just as the gates opened. The players were hopping and ready to die for the cause after a typical, clever piece of left-field motivation from the fascinating Morrison. Two minutes after the throw-in they got the first body blow.

Diarmuid Marsden took an early shot that fell short and Donegal goalkeeper Tony Blake dashed out to punch it. The bounce caught him out and the ball only went as far as John McEntee who punched to the net. Donegal's full forward line of Devenney, Adrian Sweeney and Brian Roper had amassed 5-27 between them in their three previous games but were held to 0-8 here. Physically, Donegal shipped punishment too.

'At that time Armagh were renowned for being dirty. I was going down for the ball and one of their boys kneed me in the head, just before halftime. In the dressing room at halftime I couldn't remember anything and had blurred vision. I said to Moran "Look, I can't see anything." John Morrison was there and just hit me a dig in the ribs and told me "Just fucking keep it going."

'That was alright, I never really got involved in the game after that, but we were getting close to them, the score was levelling up. I was put straight through from about twenty-five yards out and I don't even know where I put the thing. It wasn't a score anyway...

'We would have felt that we had far better footballers than Armagh had. Pound for pound, we were better. But their system, they were so far ahead. It was a machine they had. We knew what they would do because we played them so many times. We knew that Kieran McGeeney would get on the ball and he would drift out wide to put in a diagonal ball but there was nothing we could do about it. Michael Hegarty was our centre-forward and we knew that McGeeney wouldn't pick him up, but everyone else would do all the covering for McGeeney. They were rugby tackling and getting away with it.

'The thing with Armagh, I'd say over the case of playing them all the time, we would lose at least one player a game to a dirty tackle. Like, they were known for falling on you, with their knees and everything. Fair play to them.'

Donegal rescued the season a fortnight later by beating Meath in a thriller and suddenly found themselves in an All Ireland quarter-final against Dublin on the August Bank Holiday.

It was another corker, with Ray Cosgrove's brace of goals saving the Dubs when Donegal should have swept them aside. But nobody ever talks about the game. It was the aftermath that entered GAA folklore.

'We went to the Camden Court Hotel where the dinner was. We sat there to eat, drinking Ballygowan, and then somebody came up with the idea that the team would be allowed two pints each.

'We shouldn't have accepted them. But sure when do you stop? We were all in our tracksuits, enjoying a couple of Guinness, and the next thing you could see boys after their second pint, going "Jesus Christ boys..." So another boy would get his third pint. And then you would be thinking "Well, if he's getting another pint, so am I..."

'Dinner came and boys chased it down them so they could get back into the bar. The shout came for the bus but by that stage Devenney, Mickey Hegarty, Colm McFadden, Christy Toye, big Brian McLaughlin, we had all decided we were going to hang about. Mickey Moran came out and there was a heap of Donegal bags lying at the foot of the stairs, instead of being on the bus. He asked who owned the bags, so a few of us said "Ah Mickey, I'm staying."

'He knew what was happening so he said to us "Listen boys, there's a game next Saturday week. Youse have a choice of getting on the bus right now." Three people went back on the bus and everyone else stayed.

'You can imagine as a manager, after a performance like that, and you heading back from Croke Park with three people on your bus and the rest of them all back in Dublin...'

The fall out was spectacular once the story got out. Two weeks later they fell badly to Dublin, Cosgrove getting another goal in his dream summer. The margin at the end was ten points and Moran and Morrison had seen enough. Baffled by their attitude, they realised they wouldn't change.

● ● ●

Nobody wanted the Donegal job after that. Mickey Moran was a well-respected figure in coaching circles and those looking in from the outside saw the treatment he got. This bunch of players became toxic.

The county board couldn't identify anyone interested in taking the job so county chairman Brian McEniff took over as a stop-gap who lasted three years. The players realised that McEniff was the architect of every Donegal success but they knew there would be leeway with him. The rollercoaster was off again.

The spring of 2003 was totally forgettable. The most notable losses and wins came from the vicious card schools on the bus. Cassidy and Colm McFadden entered the fray but were taken out by ruthless sharks like Mark Crossan and Brian Roper. Cassidy can recall a few occasions where he was in college in Galway, ringing home to Stephen and asking to be bailed out to pay his rent. 'He knew the craic because he was on the panel himself for years. "Ah, these bastards have cleaned me again. Any chance of a lock of pound?"'

The Championship rolled into vision and they were paired against Fermanagh. They hadn't a clue where they were at as they hit the road from Donegal.

Brian McEniff was still feeling his way back into management. Players knew they weren't subject to the same rigorous training as the top teams but they had loyalty to the gentlemanly McEniff, a fatherly figure to all of them who treats Donegal players like family. Trying to bridge the generation gap was another thing though and McEniff fell into some peculiar ways inspired by his previous years, most notably 1992.

'When we went to play Fermanagh in 2003, we stopped off at Pettigo on our way. There was bunting and banners up and everything, we thought there must have been a festival, but no, it was for us. The bus parked up, and Brian stood at the front and announced "Right boys, we have a wee function to go to here."

'We got off the bus and the song from the 1992 All Ireland "Walking Tall in Donegal" by Margo O'Donnell, was playing through speakers. Women and children were asking us to sign autographs for them. We were only on our way to play a first-round game! Then we went down to Fermanagh and they hammered us off the field...'

During the bus journey home from Enniskillen, some players were answering calls to go out to play in America for the rest of the summer. Cassidy was one of them but John Gildea, the team's veteran midfielder, talked him out of it.

A qualifier game against Longford loomed but Cassidy's head was scattered in every direction.

'I was at a wedding the day before in the Ostan in Gaoth Dobhair. I had men saying to me "What are you doing?" because I was having a few drinks. I wasn't in good form because Fermanagh were after beating us and I wasn't keyed in. No disrespect to Longford or anything, but at that time the back door had just come in. It was seen as a lost cause until you got up to the last few games. It was a stupid move of me. I went and got a bottle of Budweiser and then the disco started and the Fat Frogs came out...

'It's one of the reasons why me and McEniff get on so well. I rang him up when I was loaded that night. I was just asking him how the form was and telling him I was at a wedding and what have you. I know now that I told him I had a few drinks, but I can't actually remember it myself. There were a couple of boys with me and I passed the phone around so they could talk to him too. The night before a qualifier game, boys were mad to chat football with the Donegal manager!

'I went to a party after it that went on to about six or seven in the morning. We weren't playing the match until six in the evening so even at that stage I thought I would be grand. I was lying in the house that day and the next thing the phone went."

It was John Gildea. McEniff and Gildea were close and McEniff knew Gildea and Cassidy would have been close too. Yet Gildea had never phoned him on the morning of a match before. Cassidy knew something was up.

'Well, what's the form?' Gildea began.

'Aye, not so bad," breezed Cassidy. He was fooling no one.

'Listen, you were out fecking about last night.'

'I was John, I was at a wedding down here.'

'Fuck's sake! What kind of shape are you in?'

'I'm grand John, I'll be solid for six.'

That evening as the panel came through the dressing room door McEniff pulled Cassidy aside. 'Kevin, are you alright to play?'

'I thought nothing of it [his escapade] at the time,' winces Cassidy, 'but when I look back now it's embarrassing. All these other boys busting their ass to sit on the bench and me doing what I was doing. Gildea must have been chatting to other boys so McEniff called everyone to attention and said "Sorry, I can't start Kevin today, he was at a wedding last night and he had a few jars." And that was it. He never talked to me again about it or anything.

'I was sitting watching the game and the penny dropped. That's when my season changed. I was thinking to myself "How bloody stupid and immature are you?" Here we are on a real sunny day in Ballybofey, a Championship match against Longford and everybody knew what I was at.

'The boys all went for a few pints after winning the game. I went straight home, got togged out and headed for the beach. I trained until I made myself sick that evening. I just punished myself. I knew what I had done and I knew I hadn't the hunger. I done silly training, running up and down sand dunes. Trying to make myself hurt. I went to training on the Tuesday night and then I was dry until our season was over.'

McEniff had brought Anthony Harkin, trainer to the '92 side, back in. The win over Longford gave them a shove and they rampaged through the qualifiers, one game giving them an extra momentum that they carried into the next. Sligo, the coming team of 2002, were put to bed by five points one Sunday. They stepped over Tipperary in Croke Park with ten points to spare. Down got another trimming, beat by eight points.

A year after their Bank Holiday antics, they faced a Galway side that were fighting the creeping years. Again they drew the first game in Croke Park before the fixture-makers decided the replay would be in Castlebar, a venue Galway would have been well familiar with. McEniff was enraged.

'Brian got a thing going that the whole country was against us and got us riled up for it that way. We actually enjoyed Castlebar, the crowd were close by and there was a great buzz there. McEniff was on every radio station and in every paper, saying we were going on a pilgrimage, as he called it. A pilgrimage to Castlebar! It gelled us as a team and got the whole county behind us. It was a masterstroke by Brian and he was a genius at uniting the county in a cause.'

Donegal would beat Galway that day, making their way through to their first All Ireland semi-final in eleven years.

Facing them were their old nemesis, Armagh, and it would end up pretty much the same old story. As much as Donegal could throw at them, they couldn't make it stick. Oisín McConville and Stevie McDonnell plundered a goal each and Donegal were sunk. Tyrone and Armagh played in the All Ireland final and all the talk was of the two Ulster superpowers. Donegal barely warranted a mention.

● ● ●

There was still enough salvaged from the wreckage of Fermanagh that convinced Donegal they could make a serious go of it in 2004. They made minimal changes to the panel and the players continued to trust in the Godfather of Donegal football. Setting aside the envy of other county setups, they convinced themselves by thinking that perhaps the ultra-clinical approach may never have suited them in any case.

They beat Antrim in the quarter-final and then toppled Tyrone, the reigning All Ireland champions. You know who were there to block the door in the final. The Ulster Council had been expecting a repeat of the previous year's All Ireland final so they set the wheels in motion to use Croke Park for the day. Sixty-two thousand people would turn up expecting a real contest but Armagh would steamroll Donegal, 3-15 to 0-11.

Once they got showered, Cassidy and Colm McFadden decided to split and meet up with their girlfriends.

'We were meant to be on the bus. Sarah was up in Dublin for the weekend and so was Colm's girlfriend. We already had it arranged that after the game we were going for a night out in Dublin or at home, whichever we felt like at the time.

'After the carry on before with Mickey Moran and the empty bus, McEniff was adamant that everybody would be on this bus. There was another game on that day in Croke Park and the bus was parked around the back. Me and McFadden weren't going to sit about so we went up to Quinn's Pub. Not long after, the phones were hopping. Brendan Devenney and these boys were on the bus and we were the only two missing. "Get back here and get on this bus quick, it's about to go."

'We said we wouldn't bother. The women were with us and we didn't want to leave them on their own but the phone went again. McEniff was on the line. "We're waiting five more minutes and then we're going. You better be on this bus. If you don't get off this bus in Donegal town, don't come near us again."

'We thought we would never make the bus because it was parked away round the back of the stadium. We came outside and more boys were ringing us telling us how much we needed to get back down there. My brother Stephen called me, saying "This man's going off his head here."'

An escape hatch opened up. McFadden's father pulled up in his car and they thought they would sort the girls out with a lift and meet the team bus in Virginia in Cavan where a post-match meal was planned.

'Everybody was sitting eating their dinner in Virginia, thinking that we were still pinting down in Dublin. We walked in and everybody went bananas. By the end of the meal though everything was grand and somebody sneaked two cases of beer onto the bus. Oisín McConville had a bar that time in Virginia so we went across the road to it. Men were buying drink, stuffing it up their jumpers and getting back onto the bus.

'It was like a zoo. Men hadn't seen beer in months and they were going mental. Devenney was walking around with a pair of swimming goggles on him. Down the back was mental, there was no stopping us.

'We were singing on the bus and some of us had our tops off. It was a hot day and we were going round like animals.

'I needed to chill out and went up the front to chat to Brian about the game. "Well, what did you think of today, Brian?" And he just sat and talked away to me, giving a serious analysis. Unknown to me, Johnny McCafferty was filming the whole lot.

'That video. It never, ever came out. Thank God Youtube wasn't about in those days. But that was us, that was our mentality. The game was over so it was back to life as normal.

'When we got as far as Donegal town, Brian came half-way down the bus and said to us, "Men, we return with nothing but dented pride."

'He was a brilliant man. Full of lovely sayings. He used to talk about his wife, describing her as "My good friend Caddy."

"Whenever we played Armagh, people used to make such a big deal about the size of them. We were at a hotel before we played them one time and during a meeting Brian said "Kevin, stand up there. Brian McLaughlin, stand up there. They say they have big men in Armagh? Well we know what we're going to do tomorrow. We're going to go at them like the waves of Tory! When they're sick of us, we're just going to keep coming at them!"'

'We had good respect for him but even when he was trying to be serious he would make a comment that would make us scream. He had this saying "Red-Time" that he'd picked up when he was part of the management team against the Australians in the International Rules. When we were flagging he would shout it out and we were to lift our performance by twenty percent for twenty minutes. I don't think it worked but on the bus we used to shout it at each other: "Brian, I think this man's going Red-Time!"

Donegal and McEniff soldiered on for another year but their magic was spent. They loved him like a father and he loved them like sons but he resigned when they went out of the Championship after a second-round qualifier defeat to Cavan.

It wasn't the end of the friendships though. McEniff still keeps an interest and an eye on the boys. On Christmas Day 2010, Cassidy's mobile went off. It was Brian and the first question from him was, 'How are the twins?'

•　　•　　•

The first day that Brian McIver met the Donegal squad, he gave it to them straight. Cassidy can't be sure if he knew about the following tale but he suspects he did.

'Tyrone won the All Ireland in 2005 and myself and Eamon McGee had been up for the celebrations. Brian said we would meet up three weeks later to start preparations. Anyway, we were in Sally O'Brien's in Omagh and we were supposed to head back down the road but we ended up at a party with Joe McMahon's brother, Paddy.

'We were out on the lawn of this house the day after the party, and called a friend of mine to go and hit Dromore drinking. So into this wee bar we went, it must have been only ten in the morning. My friend had to go to work so we went with him, back to Sally's. We were in bad shape at this point but we came up with a loose plan that we would follow the party around the county, drinking in every town in Tyrone.

'We got a taxi to Cookstown. We didn't really know what we were at, drinking all night with no sleep. It certainly wasn't a GAA spot because they had no time for us, so we hopped into a taxi, bound for Ardboe, where Brian [McIver] is from and we were going with the intention of meeting him. We thought he was going to be delighted to see us! It didn't exactly turn out like that. We just went to the pub, forgot the whole idea and got a taxi back to Omagh.

'At this stage everybody was looking for us down home and our phone batteries were dead. I had to call a friend to land up to Omagh and collect us and bring us home to face the music. At the time I was finishing my degree and that was my excuse for it. No doubt it all got back to Brian and I think he had myself and Eamon targeted from day one.

'Brian came into his first meeting and told us his policy on drink. There was going to be no second chances. Training was going well at the start but I would have a routine that I would stick to before the Championship. I have a few pints at a certain time and then cut it off at that point.'

Cassidy's devotion to that routine would become the topic of conversation all over the county and sully his reputation.

'I used to do it on Easter Monday because we would be off school and the local would be good fun. We'd played Westmeath in a league game and I was in good enough shape, scoring three points. We came back that night and went down to the hotel for a meal, Sarah and I, on Easter Sunday night. But I took it easy because the club had a match the following day. In all I'd say I had only about four or five bottles of beer.

'The plan was to play that match for the club, then go up to the bar for the evening. That would be the end of the drinking for the summer. The following day, we had a pool session, togged out, and the next thing Pearse Coyle, a selector from Gaoth Dobhair, approached me and said, "This boy wants to talk to you." I knew what it was about because none of the other boys had been out over the weekend.

'Brian said to me "I have no choice because you went drinking." I told him "Look, it was four or five bottles of beer with my dinner and I went up to the local after a game with the club and had a few pints." But Brian said to me "We're going to have to let you go."'

After that, Cassidy planned to head to America for the summer once his final college exams were over. He had always wanted to do some travelling only for something to crop up but this time everything was falling into place. A little while later McIver rang again.

'Brian asked me to come back up to sort the thing out. I ploughed on regardless. I suppose it's not the sort of thing you should say to a manager, but

I told him I didn't care about a Division Two league title, it was an Ulster Championship I wanted down the line. When I finished the exams, I was off.'

The following year, Cassidy returned and was delighted to play under McIver, and McIver was glad to have him. It was a line that needed to be drawn in the sand and neither side bore ill-will after the incident.

Other county players would occasionally get a glimpse into the partying set of Donegal and be amazed. After the 2007 Inter-Provincial tournament that Ulster won in Croke Park, they were staying at Brian McEniff's Skylon Hotel.

A smattering of Ulster players were gathered at the resident's bar after a night on the tiles when the barman began closing up. Cassidy wasn't amused and called his former manager, who came down from his bedroom in his robes and set a round of beer up for one and all before returning to his room. After that drink, they sought another venue.

One player who landed back to the hotel late found a few of his teammates beginning to gather up and head to bed. He asked where all the Donegal lads were gone too.

'Off to the airport.'

'The airport? Why?'

'Because the bar at the airport doesn't close.'

●　●　●

So that's a history of Donegal through the beer goggles. It was fun when it lasted but it ended when Jim came in. It had to. Drinking is fun and sociable but Cassidy doesn't have to look too far to see the casualties it can claim.

The family bar was a curse. 'Bars are an awkward situation to be in. It's easy to turn to drink. We all helped out with work and we had it until 2001 but by that stage my father had developed a problem with drink.'

Like any alcoholic, Tommy did what he could to get a drink. There were occasions when everybody felt let down. Some of the children were very young when he got up one night and left. It turned into a messy split when he never came back.

Eventually, they would come to realise that it was for the best. Anne was the rock of the family and brought up all the children to expect the very best of things out of their life. She brought them up herself and sent them all to college. Nobody suffered anymore.

When Kevin takes to the field now, he thinks of her strength and how she carried the family. And a game of football is easy with that thought.

●　●　●

Celtic lost in extra time, 2-1 to their old rivals. Cassidy wasn't that upset, the CIS Cup doesn't have enough clout to shed tears over, it wasn't like that night in Seville, 2003.

He got his trip to the Brazen Head and met up with cousins, sang some songs, and had his traditional blowout, a few months ahead of schedule. From here on in, it would be strictly business.

CHAPTER TEN

The Departed

'I would never turn my back on my county, not until I know I'm f***ed.'
Barry Owens, February 2011

IT'S the ides of March and the carcass of Fermanagh football is being picked over as a matter for national discussion. After a promising opening day win over Carlow, fortunes have taken a nosedive. They were dreadful in the home defeat to Longford, improved significantly to draw with Wicklow but a last-minute goal cost them the game away in Roscommon. More significantly they lost James Sherry after he injured ankle ligaments.

The panel had already haemorrhaged the experienced Mark Little after the Wicklow game, along with fringe panellist James Connolly. Now with the chance of promotion blown, a mass exodus has taken place. James and Peter Sherry, Niall Bogue, Tommy McElroy, Fergal Murphy, Shane Lyons and Ciaran Flaherty have all walked, leaving a vacuum of speculation and gossip in their wake.

When a patched-up Fermanagh team took to the field against Leitrim in their next league match it was an unfamiliar team sheet to neutrals. From the fifteen that started the Ulster final three years previously, none remained.

In huge turnover of players, Fermanagh had form. In 2003, they reached an All Ireland quarter-final and were hammered by Tyrone to the tune of nineteen points. It was expected that the retirements of established players such as Paul Brewster, Kieran Gallagher, Raymond Gallagher, Neil Cox and Mickey Lilly would halt the incremental progress of the county. Instead, Barry Owens and Marty McGrath won All Stars and shone alongside newcomers like Little and Eamon Maguire as the county went to an All Ireland semi-final replay against Mayo in 2004.

This kind of clear-out was seen as an overwhelming success, but it also lulled Fermamagh fans into a false sense of security about the strength in depth of players within the county. The county side needed a sustainable pattern of pruning and adding to the panel on a yearly basis, instead of the slash and burn treatment and casting players to the four winds.

The inexperienced side that took to the field against Leitrim in Carrick-on-Shannon went in at halftime up by seven points to one. They ended up losing 0-11 to 0-10. The knife was twisted when they spurned a fourteen-yard free in the dying seconds to draw.

Unattributed quotes formed the basis of stories in the media, casting damning verdicts on manager John O'Neill's leadership. Complaints were made about the lack of physios and medical back-up. One anecdote told of James Sherry being knocked out at training with no doctor present to tend to him. The infrastructure was criticised and O'Neill's ability and inexperience was called into question. A lack of communication from the management team in terms of tactical input and preparation made its way into newsprint. Sources claimed the players had received no direction on a strength and condition programme, or nutritional advice.

For a full week the nation's media gorged upon a drama that had the potential to run. For their part the Fermanagh county board remained practically silent, with one acidic comment to *The Irish Times* dryly observing, 'As of now John is still in charge.'

Counter-allegations followed. As well as a denial that Sherry was knocked unconscious at that particular training session, there was the accusation that players were sharing cars for long-distance travelling to training, only for all the passengers claiming maximum mileage from the county board. The practice of players changing their home address to far-off locations and claiming the added mileage was also cited. With county boards feeling the financial pinch, Fermanagh's arranged for a support staffer to take down the registration plates of cars and record how many emerged from them. The inference was made that with money being tighter than before, players were not as attracted to playing for Fermanagh anymore. Some fans chose to believe that version of events and it became a topic of local conversation.

It was the departure of Niall Bogue, Tommy McElroy and the two Sherry brothers that caused most concern. All had given good service to the county in the past and were seasoned and well-respected players. Claims that some players had bled the system dry in the past and were treating their involvement with the county as a second income could never be levelled at that quartet.

A letter was delivered to the county offices with their four names signed, stating they wanted to play for Fermanagh but not under the management in situ. The Gaelic Players' Association [GPA] were also alerted to the situation and having drafted a document with guidelines in conflict resolution when they were granted recognition by the GAA, immediately pushed for a meeting between players and county board representatives.

In *The Fermanagh Herald* newspaper, Barry Owens granted an interview and stated that while he was disappointed players left, they could be doing with them. In a sentiment echoing Tony Scullion's position in 1994 after the ousting of Eamonn Coleman in Derry, he said, 'There was Fermanagh football before us and there will be Fermanagh football long after we are gone.'

Owens said the departing players never discussed their mood with their captain. Instead he found out through a phonecall from John O'Neill.

• • •

At the time O'Neill landed the Fermanagh job, he unveiled his backroom team of selector Sylvester Mulrone and trainer, Simon Bradley. No clubs raised an objection to this, though there was an element of bitching that O'Neill, while having served as an underage county manager and as selector for Charlie Mulgrew, had never taken a senior team even at club level and had been out of the game for over three years up until his appointment.

Mulrone, along with St Pat's clubman Sean Maguire, had temporarily taken charge of the county side in 2004 before Charlie Mulgrew took over and retained the men as his selectors. Mulrone had trained a number of clubs in the county and had a good knowledge of what was available in the county.

Simon Bradley had been an assistant to O'Neill with the minor team in 2003, bringing them to the Ulster final. It's a damning statistic but that was the last time Fermanagh had won a game in the Ulster minor championship up until this point. Bradley also took over his Enniskillen Gaels club as manager in the middle of the decade, winning a county title in 2006 and running Errigal Ciaran extremely close in the Ulster club campaign. At the time he was hailed by a few county players within the club as a trainer that ranked among the best they had worked with.

For Owens, the matter was a lot less complex than how it was being painted. While the set-up was not as player-centred as it once was, he felt there was a duty of care on the players to try and revive the county's fortunes.

'When things are going wrong, some people pick the easy option and others stick at it. A few of us have been pissed off at the lads leaving. Maybe the older lads, the more experienced lads got us in this position, down in Division Four. The least they could do is try to help us out! If you looked at it, you might think boys are being soft or huffing, but I don't know what's going through their heads.

'James had done ligaments in his ankle and said he wouldn't be back for the Derry game, so his heart wasn't in it. Boguey [Niall Bogue] was in contact with John but I never found out what was up with him.

'Tommy trained on the Tuesday night after Roscommon but something must have happened with Tommy because he didn't train on Friday and that was him gone. Tommy is working in Dublin now and I'd say he has been having a lonely drive up and down the road. Peter wasn't happy about not getting game time. Nobody knows at the end of the day because it's people's own choices, but you would rather see them playing at the end of the day because Fermanagh has a small enough pool to pick from.

'James took a rap in training and there was no doctor. Doctor Tom Kiernan is there for matches, the physio is at training from half six to half seven, but John doesn't want the physio there all night because he doesn't want players in there getting rubs... he wants them out training. He wanted to cut that out.'

From the start of the league James Sherry had been Fermanagh's strongest performer. Coming off the back of a long year when he won his first, richly-deserved club championship, he reported back for duty for the first game of the year against Jordanstown on the Breffni Park 3G pitch. In his youth, he was always seen as a good ball-player and a talented athlete. Maturity had added leadership and the hidden, unglamorous work to his game but life in Division Four was a trauma for everyone. He made his excuses and left the panel.

His brother Peter had been struggling with form and injury, as had Niall Bogue. The performances of John Woods and Michael Jones in their positions meanwhile were of a decent standard, with Woods' handling of Leighton Glynn against Wicklow earning praise.

With the team struggling, Owens feels that the muck-raking from outside influences were damaging the soul of the county.

'Everyone has been against John from the start. I have had no troubles with him. Apart from a kick of the ball either way in some of our matches, we would be top of the table. The training's been as good this year as any other year. The intensity is there, Simon is good at the sessions, he gets you going, everything is with the ball.

'I feel sorry for John in a way. People must just think there is going to be money falling out of the trees to get the likes of Mick O'Dwyer in to take the job. People need to get realistic, this is Fermanagh, and there are not many out there that would want it. There were three men wanted it and there wasn't much between any of the candidates. If Darren [Chapman] or Sean [Maguire] had have got it, they would be saying the same about them now. Expectations have risen since Pat King's time [from 1996 to 2000] and they want success straight away. What do you do? You just have to gather what you have and get on with it.

'I think a lot of people didn't want John in at the start of the year and because results are not going our way they're on his back straight away. I don't see why they are doing it. It's just been a few mistakes, a bit of inexperience that has cost us the last couple of matches.

'From what I gathered, everyone was happy enough. John said at the start of the year that he wanted to freshen things up and he did that by bringing in younger players and some Lisnaskea lads. It needed to be done, to try and change things up a bit.

'I dunno what's going through lads' heads...'

● ● ●

As the Tuesday night training session after the Leitrim game drew to a close, Barry Owens called all the players into a huddle on the training ground. In his fashion, he asked if everyone was prepared to back the manager. If they didn't, they had to speak up now. There were no dissenting voices. To provide some balance to the coverage, he felt a public show of support was necessary.

The disaffected had requested that the GPA should speak to the county board in an effort to resolve their concerns. The county executive was due to meet the following night and Owens felt he should go along to speak for the players left on the panel.

When he got to the county board office, he met the GAA's operations manager Fergal McGill outside. 'He mentioned the GPA involvement to me. He didn't know if the GPA had been in contact with us [the remaining players] at all and he was shocked at that.

'He mentioned that the GPA had been chatting to the lads that had left, and I asked him why had they not make contact with those that remained. He just said "That's a good point." They were chatting to the lads with grievances but they hadn't a viewpoint from the overall panel, just from four or five.

'I was just pissed off with the whole thing, that's why I went along. All of Fermanagh GAA was being dragged down. I wanted it over and done with and I thought it would help resolve the whole thing if we showed that the management had the backing of the players and met the executive to tell them how we felt.

'I was only in the meeting a matter of minutes and I said that we had a number of points to be made – that the players were one hundred percent behind the management. Then they asked me how many had been at training [the night before]. I said all except the one or two that were injured and that I had been in contact with them and they were all behind us. And then I just mentioned that we were disappointed that the GPA hadn't been in contact with any players still left on the panel.'

Owens is not a member of the GPA. He had been in the past but now felt uncomfortable with certain aspects of it. 'I didn't bother signing up for the year. If you read through what you get with them it's not really worth it. You never see anyone being asked down to Croke Park from here. You might see the odd one from Cavan or wherever, but never anyone from Longford or anywhere like that. It's always the big guns wheeled out.

'In fairness they have done a lot of good things, things like their work in player welfare and finding jobs for players over this last few years with the recession. But some of the things players have to get from a county board come to an awful expense. I mean, we get a set of waterproofs every single year. The house would be coming down with them!'

• • •

In Antrim, Paddy Cunningham looked on at the Fermanagh situation with bemusement. When the accusation of the management not providing strength and conditioning programmes and nutritional information was proven false, Cunningham thought of his own setup.

'The Fermanagh thing was funny. We have never received a strength and conditioning programme or any information about nutrition for all the years I have played. As a county player you should know what to do anyway, but it would be good to have a variation and a plan throughout the year so that you are doing the right type of weights for the right time of year.

'There were problems with the county board when things weren't going well at the start of the year, and we had a clear-the-air meeting. We talked to Liam [Bradley, Antrim coach] and Tony McCollum about it. We had no training kit, no wet gear and no boots, just stuff like that. I am the GPA rep so along with Kevin O'Boyle the captain and Aodhan Gallagher we sorted it out. The county board were fine, they gave us an assurance the gear was ordered.'

• • •

After the Wednesday night meeting, players and management got down to business. They travelled down to Kilkenny for a national league game and won 0-22 to 1-3. The county board released a statement four days later, stating they supported O'Neill's position as Fermanagh manager. They also commended the "leadership shown by the senior team captain and players' representative, Barry Owens" and pledged the board's support to the players who had continued to play for the county team. On top of that they turned down the GAA and GPA's joint recommendation that O'Neill's position should be evaluated at the end of the year by a panel that would include figures within the county. When it was made clear that the county board would not have autonomy of the outcome, it was a sacrifice they were unwilling to make.

The departed players countered by emailing a typed statement to media outlets.

We the undersigned would like to express our deep disappointment that the Fermanagh Co Board has chosen to reject the recommendations made under the GPA/GAA Disputes Resolution Protocols.

It is our continued contention that the current management team falls far short of the high standards of organisation and preparation which are required to compete at inter-county standard.

Rather than this season being a launch pad for a rebuilding process, we believe there has been a decline in standards. As a result the undersigned eleven panel members.... have withdrawn to date due to concerns regarding team management...

... We believe the County Board have attempted to drive a wedge between the current squad and the players involved in the Dispute...

...We believe the alarmingly high level of player turnover within the county is a symptom of deep problems which the board are currently unwilling to address...

...We now call on the clubs in Fermanagh to ensure that a comprehensive review is carried out transparently at the end of the season and to ensure that their views are heard clearly on this matter. We believe this is essential for the future health of Fermanagh football...

The statement caused considerable bemusement within the county. Many felt that the players were stretching things by including eleven names. Seamus Quigley hadn't played league football for the county the previous year. James Connolly had not been gaining any gametime of any note, while Liam Lynch and John Mullarkey had not been included in any county squad previous to the 2011 campaign.

The statement certainly irked Owens. 'It pissed me off. Caroline can tell you I was hard to live with for a couple of days. But you know, there was underage training on the Saturday in our club. I went out and had good craic at that and it took my mind off it. That really showed to me what the GAA is all about, underage ones playing the game. All they want to do is play and learn the skills.

'I didn't think too much of the names on the statement to be honest. A lot of them would have been called and said "Aye, I don't care, use my name if you want." They weren't signing anything, they just used the names.

'Some of the names that was on it... I mean, John gave them a chance to play county football and they might never have got that chance with any other county manager! They would have been as well putting just the four names on the statement. I think when they came out and people saw the names they just laughed at it.'

●　●　●

Barry Owens is the player's representative for 2011. No players came to him with concerns about the manager or other issues. In any case, he's here to stay. Since 2007, he hadn't played any league football for his county and he wasn't prepared to miss out.

'I definitely will not be walking. When you look around the county, how many lads would give their right arm to play on the county team? It's an honour for anyone. I know there's a lot of lads in my club would love to pull on the jersey only they haven't had the chance... [This situation] is disrespectful to lads who are still playing, especially the younger lads coming through. They need leaders to point them in the right direction instead of pulling out over silly things.

'I spent enough time standing watching matches without having to go back and do it for no reason at all!'

Last autumn when John O'Neill was being interviewed by the selection committee determining the next Fermanagh manager, he showed them a symbol he had devised. It was a capital 'F' within a circle.

Owens and the remaining players wear their Fermanagh jerseys with the symbols on their backs, just beneath their collars. 'It signifies Fermanagh within the circle. The players, management, county board and supporters. That's what it was meant to be... It's still there, and we're still working towards it.'

CHAPTER ELEVEN

D'yknow What I Mean, Like?

IT'S the first Saturday of April and Val Andrews is making his way from his Dublin home.

His Cavan side are in desperate need of points with just two games remaining if they're to avoid relegation from Division Three. Tonight, Louth are the visitors to Breffni Park. Val shares the journey with Ger Lyons, the team trainer and long-time collaborator through their years over the Dublin underage development squads. Around the time they pass through Navan, a young policeman is getting into his car in Omagh to drive to Enniskillen and work his shift. The car is booby-trapped and the bomb goes off, killing Ronan Kerr. Sometimes in Ulster football, perspective is an elusive quality. On days like this, it shudders the senses.

The lamentations for a GAA member killed in a phoney and long outdated struggle will have to wait. The short-term objective is to pick up the points against Louth and it's looking dicey.

In recent weeks Cavan's U-21 team have been progressing along nicely. Val's co-manager, the indefatigable Terry Hyland, is over the young charges.

Terry is mindful of burnout among the group. Some had long club seasons, some were playing with their universities, and they need the cotton wool treatment. But tonight, some will be thrown in. Youngsters like Gearoid McKiernan, Niall McDermott and Niall Murray are going to fill the role of men to win this pressure-cooker contest.

During the journey to Cavan, a phone call comes from Padraig Dolan, the team's statistician. Val answers.

'Hello? No, Val here... What's the craic?... What?... Can he do it? Well, have a go. We'll go before the game with video clips of workrate and tackling, so for halftime, three to four samples of that... Yeah, positive gear... Therefore you'd want to be leaving it at thirty minutes, cut it at thirty minutes... Ah yeah, and a few scores, yeah... Yeah, yeah. That would be savage, if you could get three or four examples to last about five minutes. So we can come in and see it then. Positive images. Reinforce what I'm saying... Right? You think it's feasible, yeah?... Yeah, I think yeah... Alright, no bother.'

Tonight Cavan are going to try something different. Throughout the first half, Padraig and the cameraman will record the play. Then they'll go into the dressing room five minutes before halftime to edit the clips displaying the battling qualities management are asking for: workrate, tight marking, concentration, and above all, honesty. The squad then will have a quick discussion over some points that need addressing and then go out and play the second half.

In ways it seems indecent to be talking of retaining Division Three league status as something of a goal for Cavan football. This, afterall, is the most storied of the Ulster counties. Home of The Gunner Brady, the Gallant John Joe, and stories of the 1947 All Ireland final win in New York's Polo Grounds against Kerry.

That history has been a double-edged sword for Cavan. They hold the record for Ulster Championship titles with thirty-nine but their last one was in 1997. Before that, you have to go all the way back to 1969. The famous blue jersey of Cavan has been devalued and scorned. Their players have been mocked in their own county as shapers, lads happy enough to strut about in the county polo top the night of a Championship match but not to put the work in to actually achieve something. It's not a flattering portrait but when those from within start musing on the problems, its worth hearing out.

Jason Reilly, the prolific goal-scoring corner forward of the 1997 team, has worked with underage teams in the county in recent times. He tried to put his finger on the problems of the Cavan team before the appointment of Andrews and Hyland and lay some of the blame on the trend of players being attracted to universities on sports scholarships and relegating the county side in their list of priorities. Somewhere along the line, the azzurri lost its allure.

The only way to get it back is hard work. At the meeting of the county board to ratify the management team on August 26, 2010, Andrews set out his manifesto, saying; 'This really is the HOPE programme. H stands for Hard work, O is for Opportunity, P is for Professionalism and E is for Energy, and that's really what we're going with.'

The graft began a little early for them, so much so they were nabbed for having conducted trial sessions including members of the previous year's panel, therefore breaking the GAA's ban on collective training sessions in the months of November and December. They took their scolding but it showed that Val and Terry meant business.

●　●　●

Val. He's a little bit different. An ebullient Dub with floppy hair who could pass for Hugh Grant's older brother on the set of 'Notting Hill'. A Ballymun Kickhams man that never set the world alight as a player. He doesn't come from the traditions that most inter-county managers have, having never played for Dublin. But most managers aren't university lecturers and they haven't had the adventure Val has.

Firstly, there's the name. He was meant to be called Joseph but because his birthdate was February 13, a romantic midwife suggested Valentine when he was a day old.

The name Joseph would go elsewhere. When he met Carmel during his stint with the Civil Service, they would go on to have four children. One of them they named Joseph. He died in August 2006 at sixteen years of age. Due to complications at birth, he was born with hypoxia. He was quadriplegic, blind, couldn't eat and was fed through his stomach. He required twenty-four hour care and he had severe epilepsy. And yet, as Val recalls, 'he could still smile.'

At the time of Joseph's birth, Val's life had been one never-ending carousel of activity. Nothing seemed impossible and tasks were taken on with a reckless abandon.

A high-achiever throughout his childhood and teens, he must be the only living biochemist who had no idea what he wanted to do when he left secondary school.

'I thought I wanted to be a doctor because it was the hardest thing to get into but I didn't apply for any medical courses outside of Dublin, d'yknow what I mean like. Crazy stuff.

'Anyway, I didn't get it, I think I was one or two points off it, but I could have done it in Cork or Galway, but I wouldn't go, d'yknow what I mean, I didn't really wanna be a doctor, so I ended up doing science. Why did I go to UCD? Because my friends were going and the bus stopped there. That's it. I had no plan.'

It was in UCD that the coaching bug bit him again. His first experience of taking a team was in the street leagues of Ballymun when he was only twelve. He served a cruel apprenticeship.

'It was a disaster. You were getting the under-11Bs, or the 10Bs and they wouldn't have a clue. It was on a Saturday morning at eleven o'clock as well which was not good for me, d'yknow what I mean? I never missed one but I was a student!

'We had no support either – you were given a ball and a bag of jerseys. All I did was copy what happened to me at that age, which was, d'yknow what I mean, fire and brimstone. Fire, brimstone and fear – it's a bit like now!

'I remember standing there watching a game in Johnstown Park and the hailstones came down. I had a duffel coat on, the compulsory student duffel coat. And I was standing there, not feeling that well, with the hailstones flying down, a bag of jerseys in one hand, probably dying of hypothermia, just watching the goals go in. If we could get the ball over halfway, it was a good week. I got a bit disheartened because after one halftime team talk I looked out onto the pitch and instead of having fifteen, there was only eleven. Four of them had fucked off home!'

In the 1980s there weren't many jobs open to college graduates, so he did what he could to get by. He had a brief spell selling Polish suits and jeans out of a market stall in the Phoenix Park on Sundays. He drove a yellow mini. And he partied hard. After big games with Ballymun Kickhams, the sessions were legendary. He recalls one party with everybody in the one room, lit by a single lightbulb. The bulb blew and they had to go round to a neighbour's house to borrow one, so that the festivities could resume. The Celtic Tiger was a mile off.

Dublin in the '80s was recession-hit and emigration-sick. He joined the Civil Service but the work there wasn't exactly inspiring. 'Before I got married, Mondays didn't happen. Mondays was just a day off. They wanted me to play the game. The game was dress up, put on a collar, open a few files, write a few letters. A semblance of work basically. I was scruffy and a very unlikely civil servant. Just immature, like.

'TDs would write letters to me, saying something like kids in Carlow are not getting cocoa in the morning. And I'm there saying "Fuck's sake…" I used to bin them. If they wrote in to me more than four times I would take them serious, but I was basically making an executive decision on them!

'The best thing about the Civil Service was that I met Carmel, and we got married. She was working in the same section. The Civil Service was great, solid money, but I couldn't really understand how you only had to answer about four letters a week. You're in there at twenty-five, twenty-six years of age, loads of energy, and you're forced to sit there.'

All that pent-up energy had to go somewhere and Carmel gave him direction. He took it to the limit and Ballymun Kickhams were the ones to gain the most.

'I got married, did a night degree and became chairman of the club because the club was £30,000 in debt. They ran a draw and they weren't so good about collecting money on it.

'At that stage I had changed my life. I wasn't drinking or messin' anymore. I gave up messin'. The club were in the shit and the fella who gave me the job of managing the underage teams gave me the job of chairman. That's how I get jobs – because no-one else will take them.

'So I took that over, developed the pitch, built the walls, got credit off my uncle. They bought twelve acres up beside the airport but then they had to do something with it. The previous guys were getting this and that and consultancy reports on sand types.

'By the time I left I'd wiped out the thirty grand. I doubled the amount of adult teams. I put a team in every division. I developed the grass pitch. I built the surrounds, and then Joseph was born. So my life was changed, emotionally and everything else. It was 1990, I was doing Ballymun, my job, the night degree, three mortgages, the kids, I had plenty of mayhem.'

The birth of Joseph threw him. The focus he had to keep up the plate-

THE BEGINNING... *Jim McGuinness offers his hand and a few words to Mickey Harte before [T]yrone's season begins at Edendork, January 23. [Below left] Ryan McMenamin escaped [p]rospective punishment for his clash in February with Paddy McGrath and [below right] [sh]aring a joke with referee Joe McQuillan a week later against Sligo in Markievicz Park.*

THE TYRONE MAN RYAN McMENAMIN

BACK WHERE WE BELONG... *Ryan McMenamin and his Tyrone side took the scenic route back to this Round Four Qualifier against Roscommon.*

THE MONAGHAN MAN DICK CLERKIN

CAPTAIN, MY CAPTAIN... *Dick Clerkin follows the family tradition of leading Monaghan into battle, in Round One of the Qualifers against Offaly in O'Connor Park.*

THE ANTRIM MAN PADDY CUNNINGHAM

LINING UP THE TARGET... *Paddy Cunningham fought illness to try and recapture the form that made him one of Ulster's most consistent scorers.*

EELING THE LOVE AGAIN... *Kevin Cassidy took weeks of persuasion to be convinced that he eded Donegal, and Donegal needed him.*

THE DOWN MAN **AIDAN CARR**

TRYIN' TO FIND A WAY BACK HOME... *Aidan Carr had to get used to life as a substitute during the 2011 season with the Down side.*

FOREVER DEVOTED... *Illness, cruciate ligament operations and heart trouble could not keep Barry Owens from coming back for Fermanagh duty.*

THE DERRY MEN MICKEY CONLAN AND DANNY DEVLIN

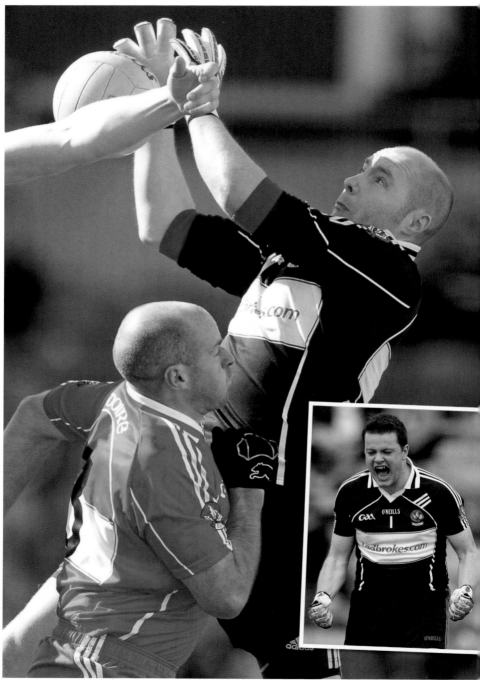

THE CUSTODIANS... *Mickey Conlan and Danny Devlin (inset) came out of nowhere to battle out for the job of Derry netminder.*

THE ARMAGH MAN STEVIE McDONNELL

TRUE FAITH... *Stevie McDonnell won an All-Ireland in 2002, but he was still trying to lead Armagh into another glorious era in 2011.*

THE CAVAN MEN VAL ANDREWS AND TERRY HYLAND

BABY STEPS... *The Cavan U-21 teams' Ulster success under Terry Hyland provided some optimism for the joint management at senior level.*

EN SENSATION... *Seventeen-year-old Patrick McBrearty made his debut for Donegal*
ainst Antrim, wearing hair wax on his hands for grip of the ball.

OWN, BUT UNBOWED... *Barry Owens leads the Fermanagh team off the Celtic Park pitch*
er their Championship defeat.

THIS IS WAR... *Down were not ready for Armagh's enormous appetite for a scrap. Here, Benn* *Coulter and Brendan Donaghy do a bit of sorting out with each other.*

spinning act began to waver. He went to tackle a man in a match and ended up breaking his leg.

'I was going around a very angry, dangerous young man, d'yknow what I mean? There was both anger and disappointment there with Joseph's condition. I tried to take some man's head off in the tackle. Around that time I learned that fear is just the absence of courage. I hadn't been that courageous earlier in my life but at that time I would have killed anybody.'

With reflection, he came to terms with the life he had. He moved into data products and soon learned that the private sector could be the same as his old job with the Civil Service. People talked a bit better and gelled their hair differently but it was more of the same. Looking around for something new to do, he was forced into action when he was laid off.

Tralee was the last place that a wideboy Dub would expect to wind up but it turned out to be the biggest adventure of his life.

● ● ●

In 1993 Val Andrews began a different life as a lecturer in Tralee Institute of Technology. Despite all the traditions of Kerry GAA, the county never had a team in the Sigerson Cup. They never looked likely to either.

A batch of new-wave courses began at this time in the fields of Health and Leisure studies. With the tertiary sector of the economy flourishing, there was ample opportunity for young inter-county players to corner the available markets. Suddenly, Tralee IT was attracting some blue-chip players.

As soon as Andrews entered the college, he got oxter-deep in the football team who at the time were a Division Two outfit. They won promotion out of the sector and gave the Trench Cup a rattle in the first year.

They were happy enough to consolidate their position the next year but then looked at ways of taking it to the next level. They already had some quality players such as Galway's Padraic Joyce and Donegal's Jim McGuinness but the trickle then turned into a flood.

'Health and Leisure is the done thing and I'm starting to get ideas in my head, d'yknow what I mean? So you're going around and you're mooching and approaching players, getting fellas in to do courses. My Civil Service training came in handy for this kind of thing, to know the rules and use them.'

Seamus Moynihan came. So did future Kerry teammates Mike Frank Russell, William Kirby, Tom O'Sullivan, Mike McCarthy and Noel Kennelly. Michael Donnellan parachuted in, Colm Parkinson and Noel Garvan from Laois as well.

Probably their best recruit though wasn't even a player. Pat Flanagan made his entrance to lecture in the college in 1996. A former 100m sprint champion who enjoyed international success, his GAA heritage lay with the famous Mount Sion club in Waterford city and his innovative training techniques would later help Kerry to three consecutive All Ireland finals between 2004 and 2006, winning two.

Upon arriving in Tralee he fell straight in with Andrews, and by the end of the year they were celebrating winning the Sigerson Cup in Coleraine. In 1998 they defended the trophy on their own patch in Tralee. They were all set for the three in a row in 1999 when Andrews' personal life became his priority. The family were due to go back to Dublin because of 'domestic stuff'.

'I thought it was more important that I would do this thing for my family, but the thing that I thought would last months didn't happen. I'd given up the Sigerson and handed it to Vinny O'Shea, Fr Pat O'Donnell and Alan Ringland, but you couldn't come back and say "I'm back, where's me team?"'

The team went on to win the tournament, beating Garda College in the final. Little did Andrews know that it was an incident in the tournament a year previous that would seal the next step of his managerial career.

• • •

Over the winter of 1999, Cavan football was suffering. In 1997 Martin McHugh had taken the team to an Ulster title and a nostalgia-fest of an All Ireland semi-final against old foes Kerry, fifty years after their famous clash in America.

When he decided to call time on his three-year spell in charge, Liam Austin took over, a respected former Down player and All Star. He brought Monaghan legend Hugo Clerkin with him to train the team but the players would keep the new management at arm's length.

The fault lines could be seen months beforehand. A few whispered lines to a county board figure here, a bitching session in a car there. They felt the training Clerkin was conducting wasn't good enough and that there wasn't enough of it. While Liam Austin had appealed to the players to take ownership of their performances and tactics, players felt he wasn't providing enough direction, guidance and input.

The players met and voted that the best course of action was that Austin should take his leave. A measured county board response to this was unlikely, as personality clashes within the board exacerbated the problem. Inertia set in and Austin was incensed when he received no backing from the board.

Austin resigned. He had a parting shot at the players and let it slip that he had bought the entire panel a set of woolly hats for winter training. He also took a verbal swipe at chairman Brendan Keaney for not backing him. The players countered with their own statement, laying the blame at the feet of the management team and absolving the chairman of any blame.

This kind of dispute is now commonplace in the GAA but back then it was new territory. Supporters took sides for and against the players. Inevitable accusations of players being too big for their boots began.

Cavan were without a manager. The league was due to resume in February and they needed somebody in place. They had to act fast but they also had to be seen to make the right decision.

Down in Tralee, Pat Flanagan and Val Andrews were having their usual knock-about chats over their lunch. To this day, they keep a tradition they had started in Tralee of calling each other 'Guru number one' and 'Guru number two'. They were poring over the latest headlines on the Cavan saga when Flanagan leaned into Andrews and said with a half-smile, 'Well, guru number one, would you go for that?'

Andrews saw it as a social experiment.

'Pat Flanagan said to me "You're afraid to apply for it." And I was! I didn't see myself doing county because I'm Val Andrews, I played junior, intermediate and a bit of senior with Ballymun. I'm from Ballymun, like. Even as a college manager I'd ring John O'Mahony or John Maughan – sure I thought they were completely special or something, d'yknow what I mean? But you don't realise that until the end of your first year and I'd say a lot of people don't do it because they'd be afraid to do it.

'We applied on the basis that we wouldn't get it. It was an experience and we wanted to go through the process. We didn't realise that the seventeen other nominations were all flippin' bogus! Once again it's the Val Andrews syndrome of nobody wanting the bleedin' job.

'We seen the nominations and seen the like of Stephen King was meant to be nominated. We thought we would get the nomination, get a bit of publicity, so that if something comes up in Limerick or around there we could go for it. We were having the craic with it, but mind you we were serious when we were in there.'

Even though they had won Sigerson titles, Flanagan and Andrews were aware that such silverware didn't really register with the majority of GAA fans. 'Everybody was saying "Who the hell are these guys? Val Andrews, Kerry?"' To give their candidacy more weight, they needed to get their name out there.

They approached Murt Murphy, a local freelance journalist, to do a piece on them and place it in the *Irish Examiner*. Andrews used to room with Murphy during the Sigerson weekends and found him to be stone mad, brilliant fun and good company.

The interview threatened to get out of control and look like a piss-take. The three men were having too much fun to be able to put much of the content in a national newspaper but one comment slipped the net, possibly due to the mischief of Murphy, when Flanagan described his friend as an 'avant-garde coach'.

The piece appeared in the *Examiner* and went through the wringer as the other papers around the country picked off the quotes and recycled the story for themselves. Job done. Val and Pat had caused a stir.

Somewhere along the line, the phrase 'strict disciplinarian' appeared and grew legs. The Cavan county board, realising they were dealing with a group of strong-willed players, needed someone with a backbone and they liked the sound of Andrews.

The truth wasn't quite as dramatic as that. 'Yer man on RTÉ Radio One interviewed me and says "You're a strict disciplinarian." That came from the Sigerson incident in Galway where Flanagan said if I played Jimmy McGuinness, Mike Frank Russell, William Kirby or Barry O'Shea – if I picked them, he would walk, because the four of them had been acting the goat. So we left the four of them on the line for a quarter-final of the Sigerson. That's where the "strict disciplinarian" thing came in.'

Jim McGuinness would later become one of the most monastic trainers and players in the country. The absence of the Kerry lads could be easily excused – they had just won the All Ireland and were on the party trial – but it wasn't by Flanagan and Andrews. Their regime was like a Navy Seals programme. Collective trainings were arranged for 7am on Mondays, Wednesdays and Fridays, as well as Tuesday and Thursdays evenings. On Saturdays, they could have as many as three sessions focusing on different elements of their game and a challenge match on a Sunday.

With all the attractions that fling themselves at newly-crowned All Ireland champions, the Kerry lads missed a few sessions. They were dropped for the game against UCG. Armed with that evidence, the Cavan board made their move.

'One Friday night the board asked to meet us and we stayed over in the Kilmore Hotel. So we're lying in our beds in The Kilmore the following morning and Flanagan looks over at me and asks "What the fuck have we done?" One, he hadn't really told his mot. Two, we're living in flippin' Tralee, and this is Cavan!

'I think people thought I was going to have a list of fellas who got rid of Austin and I was gonna machine-gun them.'

At their unveiling Pat Flanagan made the promise that Cavan would be the fittest team in the country. It was music to the board's ears, and they filled out the rest of the management team with local men, Seamus Kiernan from Munterconnacht and a certain Terry Hyland from Lacken Celtic.

● ● ●

Positive comments. Upbeat input. Sometimes, Andrews struggles with it and loses his temper. He feels that a lot of the rhetoric of the inter-county game can be boiled down to one question – are you being honest?

In a couple of hours, Cavan face their biggest game of the year to date. They may go on to have a wonderful Championship, and their U-21s have the ability to do wondrous feats, but right here, right now, Cavan badly need to beat Louth.

'At the end of the day, coaching's about expectations. Before you think about winning, there's an expectation you will work, d'yknow what I mean? That you work hard and make tackles. So, if you don't do that, don't come into my dressing room and sit there, because work is all we're asking you to do, and a donkey can do that.

'Running after your man is your decision. Look, we nail our colours to the mast and we strive very hard to be honest. I can stand in front of a group of players and say "I was wrong there, I should have done this, and I didn't." So, that's where my standard is.

'All we're trying to get out of them, and I keep reinforcing this, is to be the best you can be. That's number one. And sometimes we have the wrong fellas on the bus. It will take us time to sort out the group dynamic but that's where we're at.'

What happened in Cavan before Andrews and Hyland took up the post is irrelevant to them. But there are those in Cavan football that say the players' mindset is completely wrong. Last year before they were annihilated by Cork in the qualifiers, some of the players breakfasted on sausages, eggs and rashers. The night before, they had roast beef for dinner. Sports scientists would be appalled that this kind of diet was served to players who were facing seventy minutes of Championship football.

It's not something Andrews is going to worry about though. 'I believe that kicking the ball every evening is more important than worrying about whether to have cornflakes or muesli for breakfast. Boys are looking for improvements in the wrong area, that's the area of sports science, telling you what to eat and that. At the end of the day, your body needs glucose, and that comes from eating pasta or potatoes, it all ends up the same.

'I don't agree with this Yankee school of "Let's hug, kiss and breastfeed." All I want to see is honesty of effort. I keep it simple. A lot of times people are searching for the panacea but sometimes it's bull, these enormous strategies to win.

'The bottom line is, grow a set of balls, mark your man, and win your man-to-man, because that's what it comes down to, no matter what way we distil it. Pulling sweepers or playing in clumps – that's why I lose the head with these lads, they're talking about playing in clumps, or playing in squares. Saying "Oh, the manager didn't tell me, he didn't tell me." Fuck away off lads, d'yknow, because we're all about empowering people. Don't make excuses, Ger marks his man, I mark my man, that's the model. Look at what Dublin have done, just by becoming an honest team. Just an honest team.'

• • •

THE GAME
CAVAN v LOUTH
Saturday, April 2, Throw-in 7.30pm

6.23pm: The Louth team spill out of the team bus along with an expansive entourage of physios, trainers and support staff. Their manager Peter Fitzpatrick is a newly-elected TD in Louth and he stops to acknowledge the congratulations of many as he goes through the back gates of Breffni Park to the dressing rooms.

6.33: The Louth players appear out of the tunnel and begin to inspect the pitch, almost one hour before throw in. The grass is damp but not soaked and the sky is overcast.

6.50: The Cavan squad are in a meeting room in Breffni Park, earnestly studying the clips of previous games where they displayed impressive workrate and hunger. Nobody is speaking, Andrews and Hyland are letting the visuals seep into the players' minds.

6.55: Louth proceed to the pitch out the back of the main stand for their warm-up and go through an impressive array of runs, stretches and sprints.

7.05: Cavan are now emerging for their warm-up. Seanie Johnston, Cavan's captain this season, is notably last out to join the warm-up and strolls casually to take his place. He is not starting tonight due to a cold he had during the week that prevented him from training.

Val is calling the instructions for the warm-up. James Reilly, the Cavan goalkeeper, is being put through his paces by a series of high balls coming in for him to deal with.

Peter Fitzpatrick stands among the drills the Louth team are performing. They all wear different colours of bibs which will come in handy later as they break off into mini-games, separated by the colours. Everything is on the whistle with Louth, everything appears to be sharp.

7.10: Terry Hyland walks across the running track onto the training field, clutching a programme, and goes straight to selector Stephen King to share a joke. The players hoist balls up for each other, getting their handling and kicking right for the contest ahead.

7.15: Everything is a bit more vocal from both camps. Louth are playing mini-games among themselves and their coaches' voices are echoing around the ground. Cavan players are doing a drill of one on one; one player holds the ball and keeps possession, the other is tackling, trying to take the ball off him.

7.18: The entire Cavan team gather at the edge of the running track, and go in together as a group to the dressing rooms. The Louth squad follow them in.

7.26: With the stand at Breffni Park filling up, the Cavan team emerge out of the tunnel to a muted applause and get their team photograph taken. A minute later, Louth follow the same protocall.

7.28: It's announced over the tannoy that David Givney, Cavan's leading midfielder, will be replaced by Niall Murray of the U-21 side. Givney's recurring back injury is of huge concern to Andrews and Hyland.

7.30: Patrick Shalvey of Drumgoon sings the national anthem and on the final note, Val Andrews blesses himself. Gregory Walsh tosses the ball in and the game commences.

2 minutes: A free in for Cavan twenty-five yards out is easily pointed by U-21 attacker Niall McDermott. In the break of play, Andrews runs on and urges on his forwards. Cian Mackey gives him the thumbs up.

6 minutes: Cavan's Damien O'Reilly robs Ray Finnegan of the ball and they have a quick tussle for possession. It's an encouraging sign that Cavan are physically prepared for this battle.

9 minutes: Ray Cullivan hits a shot wide and Andrews and Hyland consult with each other on the sideline. Even at this stage the game is filled with a sick air of dread and tension.

18 minutes: Cavan get out of jail when a ball goes over the top of the defence, and only some smart thinking by James Reilly, who leaves his line to come out and deal smartly with the threat, saves them. Paddy Keenan gets another point shortly after to level the scores, 0-2 apiece.

26 minutes: Niall McDermott converts his second free in two minutes but referee Walsh disallows it for taking it from the wrong spot. Andrews winces. That could be crucial come the end of the game – and the league.

27 minutes: Gearoid McKiernan is putting in the work of a pit pony around the middle, landing a point from distance to open up a two-point lead for Cavan.

31 minutes: The Louth attack are limited in their approach but their high ball in is causing considerable panic. This time the Cavan defence make an utter hash of clearing it and it is scrambled out for a '45 that Brian Donnelly kicks wide. Andrews enters the field to make a switch between Ray Cullivan and Cian Mackey. A spectator roars on for him to "get off the fucking field!" The Cavan manager suspects it was a Louth fan who used to give him more of the same treatment when he was the manager there.

34 minutes: Mark McKeever lands a beauty after some patient build-up play. It leaves Cavan in a good position at halftime, 0-6 to 0-3.

39 minutes: Cavan get a crucial break. The umpires at the goal call in referee Walsh, and after some consulting, Walsh makes his way to Louth corner back Declan Byrne, and issues him his second yellow card, followed by the red. With Louth already playing an extremely negative style of football, this will inhibit them for the rest of the contest but Cavan also need to be careful and not present the referee with a chance to even up the teams.

43 minutes: A mazy run from Niall Murray displays the kind of quality the senior team are missing out on with the absence of the U-21s. He's blatantly taken out of it by a cluster of Louth defenders and Cian Mackey strokes the free over to leave four points between the sides, 0-7 to 0-3.

46 minutes: Cavan ride their luck a little. A free in for Louth from twenty yards is struck by Paraic Smyth but hits the post. Andrews breathes a sigh of relief.

55 minutes: Stephen Jordan has appeared uncomfortable since being introduced at halftime, and is now replaced by Gareth 'Nesty' Smith. Hyland, a former manager of Jordan's at club level, goes over to console him and gives him a pat on the chest.

57 minutes: It took Louth fifteen minutes to get their first score of the first half and now it has taken them twenty-two minutes to get their first of the second half. Eamon McAuley obliges.

59 minutes: Seanie Johnston, Cavan's most dangerous forward, arrives onto the field as a substitute for Ray Cullivan.

60 minutes: Catastrophe for Cavan. Louth's Adrian Reid gets through the net of defenders and takes a strong shot that is excellently parried out by goalkeeper Reilly. Mark Brennan though is following up and blasts the ball into the goal rigging. The boost of a goal could be crucial as the game enters the final ten minutes. Cavan 0-9 Louth 1-4. Character is needed now. Andrews and Hyland go into deep conference in front of the Cavan dugout.

63 minutes: Gearoid McKiernan is in trouble. He's lying prone on the turf while Michael Brennan gets stripped for action. The stretcher arrives to carry McKiernan off, who receives a round of ovation, but this contest, and by extension the season, is in the balance right now.

64 minutes: Louth are now enjoying the majority of possession and look likely to break the Cavan resolve. After another one of their attacks goes just wide, Andrews runs onto the field and then right across it, bellowing encouragement to his players.

66 minutes: The quality of 'Nesty' Smith shows. Known as one of the best foot passers available to the county team, he gives a clever ball to Ronan

Flanagan who squeezes over a vital point to leave a goal between the sides, 0-10 to 1-4.

68 minutes: Louth again send the ball in long and high. Corner back Dane O'Dowd appears to lose the flight of it in the floodlights and it hops loose. Paraic Smyth collects and is straight through on goal but blasts it over the crossbar. There's only two in it again now.

69 minutes: Cavan are barely hanging in. Johnston is feeling the effects of his mid-week cold. He hits one shot wide, and drops another short to the Louth goalkeeper Sean Connor. Then Ronan Flanagan finds him in space and Johnston has the presence of mind to carry the ball into the thirteen-metre line and put it over the bar to leave a goal in it, but it's a dangerous lead with the game opened up and mistakes occurring everywhere.

70 minutes: Terry Hyland is frantically trying to get the attention of the referee so that Keith Fannin can replace Niall Murray. Two high balls floated in by Louth end up with no reward, but Cavan are steadily retreating backwards, defending their lead with increasing desperation.

71 minutes: A sideline ball for Louth is sent into the danger zone. It gets a flick from an attacker and travels right across the face of the goal only to fall wide. Hyland and King scream onto the pitch to their players. The time for thoughtful coaching is gone.

73 minutes: It's over. The referee has blown the whistle three times and Cavan have the win.

• • •

The team gather in the centre of the pitch and go into a huddle, with Andrews at the centre of it. They conduct a ten-minute warm-down and then go into another huddle. Job done, they head for the dressing room with the well wishes of a few straggling home fans ringing in their ears.

Hyland is satisfied with the evening's work. Cavan are another two points closer to safety and survival. He knows where the difference lay in their performance tonight and in previous league games against Limerick and Wexford. While they appeal to the dressing room for men to rise up and become leaders, the leadership came from the youngest men out there: the U-21s who have made it through to the upcoming Ulster final.

'I would say that in the county we would have been criticised up until now for not having played the U-21s. In fairness to Val, we're trying to develop a winning mentality because we've always been the nearly team, we've always had good enough minors.'

The route from being a promising minor to an established, well-rounded senior is a treacherous one. Hyland saw it close up almost a decade ago when his own son, Terry Junior, played on the Cavan team that lost to Derry in the Ulster minor championship. That same Derry team got to the All Ireland final. Of that Cavan minor side, only Mark McKeever came through to be part of the present senior side.

After the post-match meal in Cavan, Terry and Val sit down with their families. Val's wife Carmel and Terry's wife Kathleen are long-time friends who travel to games together along with their children. Carmel will head down the road in front of Val, while he makes the return journey with Ger Lyons.

Sometimes Ger and Val will muse on the evening's events. Sometimes, they just sit in silence, lost in their own thoughts. And other times when Val reckons his conversation is getting what he terms 'a bit ropy', Ger will stick on some music. Guns 'n' Roses is a favourite, and it makes Val howl with laughter.

Tonight needed the forensic approach but even the best laid plans are subject to variables. When they began the league campaign, they would gather the players around for a powerpoint presentation on the game ahead. Thinking back, they feel it was veering on information overload. Players lose their instinct for the game when they have too much to think about.

They changed the format. They went more visual, showing the players video clips, and they did a bit of talking. Tonight though they over-ran their schedule and had to finish the meeting to get out for their warm-up. It made them feel hurried and hassled.

'I was nervous there tonight. You're always more nervous when you have to win and we were terrible out there today; kicking the ball away, dropping the ball. After the ref blew for the first bad handpass, you would think he was going to do that again. I think he blew for four in the first half alone. Some of them were crucial and I don't forgive things like that.

'You see, I try different things with the players but it always ends up the same thing and that is "Man Up." Be honest about the thing. You can have all the fancy stuff you want but do you really want it? That would be my thing.

'That's the first time we went in ahead at halftime ahead since Waterford and things felt right. And at halftime, we tried something different, we tried a bit more technology. So they watched highlights of something positive they did in the first half and had something to focus on, rather than idle chit-chat and nervous energy.

'They had seen all this information, and then I went interactive with them, d'yknow – what have you just seen there? What do you think we need to work on? Showed them tackles and turnovers. That's the first time we have tried it and I don't know of any other county that have tried it. I know Dublin tried it in Croker and it didn't work. Ger does the stats there and he reads them out –

stats for, stats against. Tackles, possessions, how many times you gave the ball away.'

As the crowd exited the ground on the final whistle, there was some questioning the judgement of the management. At halftime they brought on Stephen Jordan only to take him off later again. In most team sports this would be routine but in Gaelic football every switch has to be effective, and if it's not, it's blamed on management.

Andrews will take some of the blame. He's like to think he's as candid and as honest with himself as anyone else and now that the game is over, he'll say straight up that he got it wrong.

'We put on Stephen Jordan and it was a mistake. He was concussed last week and he still looked the same way when he came on. After the first few balls went to him, I said "We're going to have to take him off." Terry said "Nah, leave him on", because there's nothing worse than putting a man on and then having to take him off. Terry knows him well, and loads of players would walk down the tunnel if that happened to them, so I told Terry "Look, you know him and you have a good relationship with him, so go to him." He knew himself anyway, I think he was nearly sort of relieved to come off. We had no trouble with him, he's a fabulous fella.'

Val also knows just like Terry what impact the younger players had. Having them join the senior panel on a permanent basis excites him.

'There's certainly seven or eight of that U-21 team we would be eyeing up. If you say you want honest, hard workers, you have them there.'

They will be along soon enough. The conversation strays away from football for a minute as the headlights guide Val and Ger through Virginia, with people spilling out of pubs and restaurants, enjoying their Saturday night. They will continue through Kells and Navan onwards to home with the outside world oblivious to their journey. They remain quiet and comfortably satisfied with their day's work. Then Ger will fire up Guns 'N' Roses and 'Welcome To The Jungle' will come on. And Val will laugh and say "d'yknow what I mean?"

It's a night like so many, nondescript and dreary, but this was one of the good ones in the madcap world of Val Andrews.

CHAPTER TWELVE

The Waiting Game

WHEN spring turns to summer, a period of rebirth or growth is ushered in. The cycle of nature felt good to Aidan Carr. Fully recovered from the injuries that played havoc with his body and mind through the dizzying 2010 season, he wanted to make his mark. From his county debut, he had been an established member of the side, so being on the margins hurt him badly. The expectation was that he would stroll back onto the side but sport doesn't run in straight lines.

Down opened their league campaign with a trip away to Mayo. James McCartan was able to start with eleven of the team that had played in the All Ireland final the previous year. At one point Down had a handsome lead of seven points but Mayo reeled them in to earn a draw. James Horan had already begun to imbue the westerners with the kind of stubborn resistance that had brought a county championship to Ballintubber a few months earlier.

It had already been a long day for Carr, beginning with a gruelling journey down to Castlebar from Newry. He took his place in the middle of the bus with Benny Coulter and Damian Rafferty. That pair had opened a sports shop in Newry the previous summer and began to live in each others' pockets, sitting beside each other out of habit.

In the immediate vicinity were Ronan Murtagh, Danny Hughes and Ronan Sexton. Ambrose Rogers and Brendan McVeigh planted themselves in the spot beside the bus toilet, willing to hold their noses for the extra leg room.

'Anybody that walks past runs the risk of McVeigh commenting on them,' says Carr. 'Doesn't matter who it is, he'll have a bite. If someone has been in the paper, Brendy will know it and recite it.

'At the back then you have another crew. Dan Gordon will be there, Conor Laverty, Aidan Brannigan. Laverty is the chief messer, he gives Gareth Thornton, our masseur, serious abuse. Gareth was originally from Burren but moved to Ballyholland to play. I'd say he really regrets it because Conor is always at him about it.'

The routine is the same for practically every county on the road to national league fixtures in the depths of February. Someone will press play on a DVD to break the boredom. Kalum King is the man entrusted with the task of picking out the entertainment. Sometimes, the Martial Arts and Ultimate Fighting enthusiast can get it wrong and pick films that reflect his brooding intensity. He got away with a few war movies in 2010 but his tastes had to be toned down. For the spin to Castlebar, they watched the comedy series 'The Inbetweeners' instead.

Carr doesn't know what they watched on the way back though. Three Down subs were used in the game and he wasn't one of them. Rather than brave the five-hour journey back in the coach, he hopped into his father's car and caught a lift back up the road.

The following week Down hosted Galway. The home side spurned a number of goal chances but in injury time Peter Fitzpatrick finally hit the net to give Down a five-point win. Carr got playing the last ten minutes of the game, replacing Mark Poland at centre-forward, but in the Armagh game six days later he wasn't called upon.

When the league resumed in March he replaced Martin Clarke for the final ten minutes as Down were hit by a late scoring blitz from Cork. He got five minutes to impress against Monaghan and tagged on a late point as they cruised to an eight-point win. In the standout league game of their campaign, a narrow defeat to Dublin in front of over 35,000 in Croke Park, he watched as five substitutes entered the action while he remained rooted to his seat.

The unpredictability of his situation is starting to rag him. Places in defence that opened up were closed off with returning heroes who earned their stripes the previous year. The forward line had been posting big tallies too and it has left Carr sitting in no man's land. His versatility had become a burden. When Conor Garvey picked up an injury, Carr was being tried out and utilised as an impact sub coming into the forward line. It's almost as if the thought of Carr as a defender had been forgotten about.

'I'm fit and training all the time but all you can do is wait at the minute. It's just a question of working hard, playing well in training, and waiting for your chance.

'It would probably be a lot different and a lot harder to accept if you weren't making a team that wasn't going well. Boys have nailed down their positions from last year and have done nothing wrong. I've no right to walk back on and demand a place, but it is frustrating.'

The game against Dublin in Croke Park was the third live televised game that Down had featured in over the spring. They're big box office now with four current All Stars. The stardust that Martin Clarke brings to the package is marketable and glamorous and as a team, Down give good television.

'Everything is going great,' concedes Carr. 'The boys were devastated after the manner of the defeat the other night because of that mistake for their goal in the last minute, but we're still in with a chance of making the league final and it was great to be back in Croke Park again. It's the only place you want to play football when you get in there.'

There's also another welcome addition to the Down bench.

As everyone in Ireland knows, John McAreavey was in Mauritius this past

January with his wife Michaela but despite the terrible tragedy that unfolded out there, his subsequent excellent form with Tullylish has ensured he was granted an opportunity with the county to show what he could do. His strength of character amazes his teammates, Carr included.

'His situation is not a topic of conversation in the dressing room, he just joins in with the banter and slagging in the dressing room and I'm sure he's delighted with that. It gives him a bit of a distraction but God knows what goes through his mind when he leaves it. It's a situation you can't even describe.'

Sometimes it's about more than getting your place on a team. For people like John McAreavey, being there among friends and familiar faces is enough.

CHAPTER THIRTEEN

'Always Win
The Wee Battles'

FOOTBALL might often complicate the existence of Ryan McMenamin but when he came over to Ireland from Canada, it was his way of integrating. His only experience of sport before his parents decided they wanted to bring their children up in Tyrone was in the boy scouts in Toronto. There, they would play the national game of ice hockey in indoor halls, chasing a puck around the timber floors.

The Canadian accent helped him out a bit on his first few days at Curly Primary School, between Dromore and Fintona. Everyone wanted to hear him talk and shake his hand. Soon they went back to watching the boy who would eat worms. He needed to diversify to keep the attention of his contemporaries. Mickey Garry and Ned Goodwin were the footballers. He wanted to run with that crew.

By the mid-'90s, he was playing senior football with Dromore St Dympna's. Tyrone minor and U-21 teams never came for him but that was alright; he was studying a Higher National Diploma course in Belfast and drinking his fill. When he finished up college, he had three choices: a degree in Leeds, moving to America, or attending the Tyrone trials he had been invited to along with Colm McCullagh. On a whim he threw in his application for a Civil Service job he thought he had no right to get, as an admin assistant in the veterinary office. Fortune smiled on him. He made the county panel and got the job. So began an illustrious county career that began under Art McRory and Eugene McKenna. Nowadays, Eugene's son is one of the exciting young talents that snap at him for a starting jersey.

During the winter of 2010 he tossed around the thought that his county days may be over. A hamstring injury held him back throughout the season and he never could fully get over it.

'I said to Mickey that I had probably planned to retire, I thought maybe that was it. I wasn't happy with the way I played and I had a nag in the back of my head that my time was up. Mickey said to me "No, it's all in your head." I said I would give it another year after that.'

A chance encounter with Art McRory convinced him he was making the right decision. McMenamin was taking part in a Club Tyrone fundraising event at Drumbo Park where Tyrone GAA people were racing against each other in a novelty handicap run. Lined up against him was his girlfriend Maura, Tyrone camogie player Shauna Jordan, the former tenacious corner-back John Lynch, and Patsy Forbes, a Tyrone star of yesteryear who is European sprint champion in his age group.

'Forbes romped it home, he bate me round the park. Never seen a man take off like it. At the event I met Art. He was standing outside watching the greyhounds racing, he's always been into that has Art, but he wasn't inside with the fundraisers. I told him I was thinking of quitting, that I was fed up with injuries and the like. He told me to stop being a bollocks, stop thinking of my age. So that was that.'

He resisted the calls from local outfit Tummery Athletic and put on hold his annual handful of winter soccer games. Nor did he go up to the field for some recreational kicking about. He just kept up his weights programme and went out every weekend enjoying himself. The hunger came back and demanded that he take his body out for one more tour of duty.

'I had thought of retirement in previous years but your whole mood can turn around in a matter of minutes. There's a great deal of pride tangled up in the whole thing. You want to finish on a high.'

•   •   •

He loves weekends like this one. All the Tyrone panel, backroom team and management are going down to the University of Limerick for a training weekend, ahead of the last two vital league fixtures.

Division Two football is a bit plain for Tyrone tastes. They need promotion. The early stages of the league were played out with the backdrop of fraught emotional trauma. Unsurprisingly, they lost their first two games to Derry and Donegal. They took their anger out on Sligo, Antrim and Laois once they got on their feet. A chance of promotion was still within their grasp but they still needed to beat Kildare and Meath, two of the better sides in the division.

The trip meant taking off for an early Friday finish, but there was enough flexitime in the bank to allow for this. He hopped into the car with his Dromore clubmates Cathal McCarron and Sean O'Neill and they met the bus at the Westenra Hotel in Monaghan before continuing the journey down.

The entertainment has changed through the years. Now McMenamin floats about the back seats and cherry-picks his activities. Michael Harte the physio has his iPad with him and they amuse themselves for a time with a kicking simulation game. Owen Mulligan rules the back seat with an iron fist and sometimes McMenamin takes a seat to watch the Mugsy show unfold. The general rule of thumb is the further back on the bus you go, the more hardcore the messing gets. Davy Harte once likened moving to the back of the bus as 'moving to the dark side'. This weekend the film The Social Network, about the establishment of Facebook, is slotted into the DVD player and helps make the time go by.

Before DVDs and iPads, it was the good old deck of cards. The biggest competitors in the squad were the ones who would hold the card schools. Games took place everywhere. On the bus, in meeting rooms, in hotel bedrooms, wherever there was a flat surface. The morning of the 2003 All Ireland final, McMenamin was engaged in a card game called Dropsies with Peter Canavan, Peter Loughran, Brian McGuigan and Mulligan all in. Kevin Hughes and half a dozen others were there spectating, racheting up the craic and tension as the players waited for the first man to blink. Maura called but McMenamin was eying the £80 in the pot and told her he would have to call her back, he was in the middle of an important hand. Harte never found out about that game, the big game before the biggest game they'd ever play.

By the time they got down to the Castletroy Hotel, it was 9pm. The players were after a long week at work and were set for a weekend of hard work so they just had supper and then flopped into bed.

They were woken from their slumbers the following morning by Tony Donnelly, Harte's trusted lieutenant. He prowls the corridors and stands outside each bedroom door at 7am, remaining there until he gets a response from those inside. Sharing a room with Mulligan, McMenamin had no problem tuning into his frequency of energy and was soon buzzing to get going. Defenders were to train at 10am and attackers at 11am. In between times, players would go along to see team physios Michael Harte and Christina Rafferty, and Cara Horisk, the masseuse.

The forwards focused on their attacking movement in their conditioned games. The defence played small-sided games that conditioned them not to over-commit to going forward but allow runners to spot the opportunity and make breaks. Harte wanted to spend the weekend tweaking a few systems and seeing how they would play out. The flat defence was being worked on. Cork had shown in 2010 how an All Ireland could be won with a traditional formation, so Tyrone were testing their own capabilities.

'Our session was more about balance, shape, and keeping the back six tight,' says McMenamin. 'The four midfielders took part in both sessions, but each of them was over in forty-five minutes. The warm up was the most intense part of it and then we played three games lasting about ten minutes each.

'We couldn't over-commit to getting the ball out of defence, because as soon as you did, the ball was coming straight back in. That meant you had to be switched on to where you were picking up your man.'

Once the pitch work was complete, it was straight onto the next thing.

Stretching would become something every member of the squad was expected to attend to religiously. Ger Hartmann, physiotherapist to the cream of world athletic talent, demonstrated how to get deeper with their stretching by using small ropes. Brian Dooher had been sticking to a stretching regime for the previous six months and remarked to McMenamin in a drill over the weekend that it was the first time in years he was able to run without feeling pain.

While the stretching was going on, Tyrone received a visitor. The Munster rugby coach Tony McGahan had heard Tyrone were in town so he dropped in. He wanted to speak with Harte and quiz him on a few things but instead Harte got him to speak to his group of players.

'It's funny what he touched on, a lot of things that Mickey would emphasise himself. It's strange to see a man from a professional background using the same things that Mickey would touch on. Stuff like stepping out of the box, doing more, taking your opportunities, not confusing routine with commitment. If you want to do anything in life, you have to do something extra.

'He was on about when you are playing to always win the wee battles. He says that Munster always look to win the wee battles, they are famous for winning the last ten minutes of any game they play, but McGahan said that the only reason they do is because they have won the wee battles before that, like getting the first hit in on the man, playing with a high intensity.

'It was interesting, because here was a man like him, wanting to speak to Mickey. It shows that we are used to Mickey and maybe we can take him for granted. When you see the head coach of Munster coming to pick his brains, it shows you the kind of manager he is.'

Harte wasn't into the big speeches that weekend. He wanted to steer clear of all that but he did remind the players what they were there for.

'Any speaking that had to be done was done before training, and the only other time for talking was at the start, to tell us what the weekend was about. As he points out, we are here building for the rest of the year, it has to start now. He was only looking at the one game, and that was Kildare. He told us that the work we would be putting in over the weekend would show against them. There were no team meetings, nothing. We were there to concentrate totally on the training.

'Mickey's still out at every session, watching every drill, cursing if the ball is not played the right way and won't be shy to inform you. I'd say he's very annoyed at the way we went out to Dublin last year, kicking so many wides. He's asking boys to step up and take more responsibility for themselves when they're away from training, not to expect that you train and go home and that's it. We all have our own jobs to look after within the team.

'That's the message from Mickey to the panel. It's not just for lads who are breaking onto the team, or those who are already there; he expects everyone to show the same personal commitment. It's his philosophy of "If one man is able to do it, every man is able to do it."'

After stretching, it was onto core stability exercises, and from that into the pool to relax for a while. At dinner Enda McGinley's mobile phone went missing. Some strange messages were sent to Harte's phone from McGinley, enquiring why he wasn't starting and arguing he should be given more time on the pitch. Harte copped straight away and blamed Mulligan and McMenamin. They protested their innocence with plenty of vigour but nobody believed them.

They got to bed and slept like soldiers. The following morning began with Mass at 9am before a light session of small games. It went on a bit longer and developed into forty minutes of sprinting and tackling drills that made the lungs burn. Team trainer Fergal McCann promised them they would be wrapped up at 11.15am as long as they kept up the effort. Both parties kept their side of the bargain.

Tyrone were on the bus and away back up the road by noon. McMenamin was home by 5pm and free to spend his evening as he chose, feeling good about himself after throwing himself into the training.

'I enjoyed that one. We had something different with the core and stretching work. There was a nice, relaxed atmosphere, no restrictions put on us, it was good fun and there was a good buzz going back up on the bus, especially when you know that every man there, even the injured guys doing their rehab work, put in a big effort.'

All the training and the effort came with an ultimate aim. Tyrone were now sharpened for Kildare.

'We talked about the importance of beating them. They're definitely a top-six team and are big and physical and [Kieran] McGeeney is going to have them well up for us. To beat us in Omagh would give them an enormous lift. Both of us are in the hunt for promotion but whoever wins this one is going to knock the other out of the race.'

The following Sunday, the game was switched to O'Neill Park, Dungannon, since Healy Park is just a long kick away from the murder scene the previous day of PSNI Officer Ronan Kerr. Tyrone bullied Kildare around the field and won convincingly, 0-13 to 0-5.

McMenamin had to come off the field after spilling blood, before being replaced by Sean O'Neill. His competitive instincts led to the injury, going all out for the ball, but it was a sign that he's not finished, but still going strong. A lot like Tyrone themselves.

CHAPTER FOURTEEN

'Ní Neart Go Cur Le Chéile'

AS the watery sun began to drop and the supporters scatted, all that was left for Antrim coach Liam 'Baker' Bradley to do was to entertain the waiting reporters with a few lines. Antrim had just been beaten – well beaten – by Donegal six weeks before the sides met again in the Ulster Championship but that was still too far away for anybody to be getting too excited.

Bradley dispensed with the usual plamás. He was already tetchy about the loss and made a throwaway comment about Donegal having to bring Antrim all the way down to Ballyshannon. The game could have been held in Ballybofey of course, shaving an hour off Antrim's journey time, but that would mean Antrim getting to re-familiarise themselves with the pitch that they made history on in 2009.

While there might have been a sting in his comments, the pragmatic side of Bradley's personality would have had an appreciation for the mind games. In training the previous week, Paddy Cunningham went to contest a high ball against Aaron Douglas and fell awkwardly, doing nerve damage to his shoulder. In Bradley's eyes, it wasn't the worst thing that could happen. It meant that when they played Donegal, they wouldn't be showing their full hand.

So that Sunday, instead of suffering the bus journey, Paddy Cunningham got up at a sensible time and went to Mass before taking himself along to the pool for a stretch and a light workout. Donegal could wait. His body needed the rest but his mind was craving it even more.

• • •

The previous day Cunningham played in a charity match in memory of Donal Maguire, a young man from west Belfast who had committed suicide three years earlier. Two different cousins of Maguire had got in touch and asked Cunningham if he would play and he had no hesitation in committing. Even though his shoulder was aching, he lined out. Any ball that came near him was casually fisted away. It was enough to just fill the jersey for the day and be there for the good cause.

West Belfast is sick with suicide. The social problems of poverty, the abuse of dangerous drugs and alcohol have put a black mark on the soul of Belfast and it is destroying itself from within. Suicide rates have almost tripled since the

Troubles, a sobering thought in itself, and it remains, per capita, one of the highest afflicted regions in Europe.

The Cunninghams were shielded. They had a strong family unit and they had Lamh Dhearg. Cunningham's maternal grandfather was Frank McCague who played for the club and for Antrim. On the other side, he is Paddy Cunningham the Third, with the previous two generations having played hurling and football for the county.

His father, Paddy Senior, had a car-parts business in Derry and Strabane and lived in Derry yet the clubman in him never left Belfast, driving home every weekend to play for Lamh Dhearg, or Hannahstown as they're known locally.

Paddy the younger was fourteen when his father relocated his business to the Falls Road but it didn't take long to fit in. He'd played a bit of football with Ardmore and a tiny bit of hurling with the fledging Na Magha club in Derry. When he started school in St Mary's on Belfast's Glen Road, the PE teacher there, Eddie McToal, was taken by his ability with the feet and the hurl. Within a week, he had the westie twang down, talking like an authentic McCooey while his mother, sister Sinead and brother Ciaran preserved their Derry tones.

He loved school so much that he couldn't wait to go back and teach. Now Eddie McToal is his head of department in the PE faculty of St Mary's. He teaches and coaches in the school, and he watches out for the vulnerable. He tries to show them that's there's another way. There's always another way.

●　　●　　●

The Monday after Antrim qualified for the 2009 Ulster final – the county's first time reaching the provincial decider in thirty-nine years – Cunningham walked into Corpus Christi School, Belfast, where he had begun his first year as a teacher. Everyone – teachers, office staff, the whole shebang – were wearing Antrim tops. 'I don't know where they got the tops from,' says a moved Cunningham. 'They must have robbed a couple of rigs.'

Belfast was buzzing again and it was a thing of wonder. Cunningham brought a few of the players down to the school to meet the kids. Before, one in every ten children might have a GAA jersey of a local clubs or an Antrim top. Suddenly Saffron jerseys were everywhere. Hurling and football became the games of choice during lunchtimes. Antrim were finally moving in the right direction.

Everything about that year was magical. Before the Championship began, Liam Bradley asked Cunningham, his captain for the year, to come up with a team motto. He thought about it for a while and came back with 'Ni neart go cur le cheile.' It translated from Irish to English as 'There is no strength without unity.' They put it on armbands and wore them when beating Donegal and Cavan, before

Cunningham led the team out of the Clones tunnel to face Tyrone in the Ulster final.

Bradley did many good things with Antrim that year and probably his greatest strength was that he had absolutely no ties to anyone there. One of the first things he did was foster the siege mentality. He told them that other teams did not rate them, so it was time to prove them wrong. They started the season with a few wins and positivity seeped in. Players loved the variety of Niall Conway's training sessions. The old dominance of St Gall's and Cargin players was broken with Peter Graham from Creggan sharing the goalkeeping with Sean McGreevy. The coltish Niall McKeever of Portglenone was drafted in and played midfield with authority. Kevin Brady was reinvigorated. James Loughrey came from St Brigid's and tore through everything in his way.

One night Bradley took a phonecall from some of his U-21 players after a championship defeat. The tone was mocking and abusive. Action had to be taken, and CJ McGourty was thrown off the panel for the rest of the year.

That wouldn't have happened in previous years under other managers. Anyone watching Antrim's miserable exit to Cavan in the 2008 Ulster Championship would have thought that McGourty and Cunningham were too similar to play in the same lineup. Now, McGourty was gone and he wasn't being asked back. Bradley's stock among the remaining players grew after that tough call. They learned to trust him implicitly. Cunningham was handed the captaincy after the McKenna Cup campaign and became the main man, hitting an incredible eleven points in the 2009 Ulster final, five of them from play.

Over the past couple of seasons though, that unity has withered.

Having won successive promotions from the bottom rung, Antrim were looking forward in 2011 to a season in which they'd face heavyweights like Tyrone, Meath and Kildare. 'From when I started playing for Antrim it was going to be the most exciting year. Rather than travelling down to Kilkenny, the standard was going to be high and great preparation for Championship.'

Cunningham lived in the gym over the winter, just as he had the winter before that. They had a decent McKenna Cup but then Kildare came to Casement Park for the first game of the league. Once Hugh McGrillen got the introductions out of the way, it wasn't long before Cunningham stood over a free. In the 2010 Championship qualifier game down in Newbridge, he had a late free to seal it for Antrim. It was from serious distance but he thought he might scrape it over. Instead, he was put off when Johnny Doyle walked right across his path as he was stepping up. Doyle tried the same stunt again this time and as soon as the ball left Cunningham's foot he knew it was over, so he barrelled straight into Doyle for retribution and picked up a yellow card.

He finished that game level with Doyle as the top scorer on eight points, but the gulf was clear for everyone to see. Division Two was full of teams that played to a defensive system and neutralised the most dangerous attackers. 'If Kildare looked at Antrim, they would have looked at who did our scoring over the last few years and realised if they marked me tightly, they'd have won half the battle. I was getting close attention.'

Kildare's Ronan Sweeney was lined out as a full forward, but his job was to stand in front of Cunningham, blocking off the space for his runs. The teams in this league were cute but Antrim weren't helping themselves.

'Whenever Niall Conway came in with Baker in the first year, it was a massive gulf in class compared to what we were doing before, it was brilliant.

'But our pre-season this year was same from when Baker and Niall and Paddy McNeill took over first. Circuits out on the pitch, again. It became boring and monotonous. I haven't had a weights programme ever from when I started with Antrim which is unbelievable. Only I'm a PE teacher and I have a mindset and I know what I have to do, but as for the rest of the boys...

'I said to Baker about not having a weights programme but he reckoned he was happy enough with what they were doing out on the pitch. He said "I don't want big strong men that aren't able to move" but what they were doing was more of an endurance test rather than developing anything. Doing weights thirty seconds on, thirty seconds off. There's a place for that but not in pre-season when you should be trying to bulk up. You aren't aiming to peak in February.'

The little things weren't being looked after. It was April before the team received any training gear for wet conditions.

'The county board felt we had too many on the panel for the amount of gear. We have Tony McCollum looking after us as our county liaison officer. Tony is top class, he and his wife Frances go to every match, it doesn't matter where it is. And Tony was hitting his head against a brick wall.'

When they conducted warm-ups before league games, they were a raggle-taggle outfit all wearing different training tops and various club and jerseys. Players begged Tony for shorts and socks on match-day and had to buy their own gloves when such equipment should have been a formality.

Cunningham and a few other experienced players approached team captain Kevin O'Boyle with their concerns. They set up a meeting with the county board and got a fair hearing and their gear straight away but it should never even have come to that.

For the first time since Bradley arrived, they went on a losing streak throughout the league. Bradley had always been bullish and demanded that his players believe in themselves, but everyone was being pulled into a morass, with injuries and defections depleting the squad.

'You were used to winning, so losing was affecting morale. We tried to be realistic and say we weren't going out to win Division Two, just to stay in it, but things were down in the dumps. Players weren't enjoying the matches, weren't enjoying the training, including myself. I haven't enjoyed this season whatsoever. I haven't liked the setup, the atmosphere. I told Baker this and I wasn't the only one.

'There's been no craic. All through the league the management were ridiculously negative about everything and there's nothing worse when you're getting beat. You need something to turn it around too. We were going nowhere. We actually felt we were going backwards, back to the bad old days.'

●　　●　　●

On top of all that, Cunningham had something else to cope with. He has Crohn's Disease, an inflammatory disease of the intestines, whereby the body's immune system attacks the gastrointestinal tract. The symptoms are vicious, causing abdominal pain, vomiting and diarrhea. It is notoriously difficult to treat and causes lethargy and weight loss.

During the league it robbed him of his strength and his energy. When critics scoffed and said he had no power or was incapable of breaking a tackle, they had no idea that this was a man running on a flat battery. He felt sleepy all the time and anything he ate he wasn't getting the nutritional benefit.

When he was fourteen, he had glandular fever and had surgery. His condition was detected at that point. It led to doctors removing six inches of his small bowel.

'I never really talk about it. I've had it since I was a kid and I don't let it get me down. There's other people that have it and they don't play sport or do anything. I just said to myself that I would never let it get me down. So I fight it and away I go.'

That attitude still prevails. The league has been a write-off but Cunningham still feels there's time to get their house in order for Championship. In a one-off match, anything can happen. Championship makes optimists of them all.

CHAPTER FIFTEEN

'That's How I Roll'

MICKEY C at thirty-three is not the goalkeeper he was – he's better, wiser, more in tune with the cadences of a team on the attack. He can spot danger a mile off and get everything in place to deal with it.

While outfield players over the age of thirty have to deal with the annual speculation over whether they'll give – or get – another year, attitudes towards goalkeepers are gradually changing.

In soccer, Jens Lehmann has just re-signed for Arsenal on a short-term deal at the age of forty-one. Edwin van der Sar has insisted this year will be his last as a player for Manchester United but his form is as good as ever; at the age of thirty-eight, he was voted the best goalkeeper in all Europe in 2009.

With the advances of sports science and heightened awareness of stretching, core stability and flexibility, goalkeepers can go on for much longer in Gaelic Games too. Brendan Cummins is regarded as one of the best shot-stoppers in hurling history and was thirty-five when helping Tipperary to the 2010 All Ireland.

When Liam Bradley took over as manager of Antrim, he brought a distinct Derry flavour to his backroom. His assistant manager was Niall Conway who soon recruited his clubmate Conlan to help out coaching the goalkeepers. While he was there, Conlan learned plenty about Sean McGreevy. Nobody's quite sure how old McGreevy is and he hardly shouts it out, but Conlan knew he was around forty when he came on as a late sub in the 2009 Ulster final. Along with John Finucane and Peter Graham, the goalkeeping fraternity fed off each other, but the greatest lesson that Conlan took away was that it's never too late.

The pursuit of excellence has become the norm among the subculture that's GAA goalkeeping. Books have been written about their singular focus and the appetite for courses and drills in their specialist position is always rising. During the winter of 2007, former Cavan goalkeeper Paul O'Dowd hosted a goalkeeping clinic at St Gall's club in Belfast. One of the first people waiting for his arrival at the Milltown venue was Conlan. At the finish O'Dowd appealed to those present to give him feedback on the course and Conlan replied, 'I thought it would be, how would you say, more high-falutin', sir!'

He also made it his business to attend a similar session at Jordanstown University given by the ex-Republic of Ireland soccer goalkeeper Packie Bonner. Learning his trade was a life-long venture to Mickey C. The more he learned, the better he got, but his name stayed out of the frame where Derry was concerned.

'When I was playing before, personally I don't even think I was ready for it.

I was getting an opportunity where, yes I appreciated it, but I only thought I was a keeper. Whereas now, I know I'm ready for it. That's the main reason I'm back. I thought I didn't do myself any justice when I was there. Even at that, people might have thought "Aye, he was a decent enough keeper, he was good enough" but I don't think I was anywhere near it.'

There was the odd wobble in form. In 2009 Ballinderry were beaten in the Derry championship quarter-final against Glenullin. Conleith Gilligan was taken off and it looked like it might have been the end of the road for him and Conlan. They knew they had to take action so they embarked on a commando-style training regime.

Most mornings they could be found over the winter down at the Ballinderry ground at 6.30am, working out in the gym. The gym is a mobile hut with not much in the way of heating but they generated their own warmth. Huge snowfalls and harsh frosts of -12C didn't deter them. They stuck to a programme laid out by Martin McElkennon and then took what they learned to Jordanstown where they gained qualifications in strength and conditioning.

The risk is that every goal he concedes will turn him into scapegoat-fodder. He knows that if he loses a ball in the sun and it drops past him, that Brennan will be criticised. He knows that his age will be brought up, that the whole experiment is a high-wire act.

● ● ●

When he first came into the team, he was given little sympathy. The regular goalkeeper in 2000 was Dungiven's Eoin McCloskey but he aggravated a hip injury against Meath in the National League final, a week before their first round Ulster Championship match against Cavan. Conlan got his chance but his first game for his county wouldn't be at a pitch opening in a country backwater, nor in the casually-contested McKenna Cup. It would come under the glare of the nation.

'That morning the nerves were hanging out of me. But Eamonn Coleman knew Cavan football inside out and instead of revving men up or being cross, it was all constructive. We had a game-plan we had to stick to and it wasn't a ranting and raving affair.'

Fintan Cahill burgled a goal midway through the first half to keep Cavan briefly in touch but that was as good as it got for the home team as Derry turned in a powerful display to win 2-13 to 1-5. Conlan was up and running but even more pertinent was that he was Coleman's goalie.

'Coleman would have been ruthless. If you weren't playing well, you wouldn't be on. Some of his wee clichés and sayings were unreal, he was just such a passionate wee man about football. I think the reason he done so well was because his enthusiasm rubbed off on other people. He just lived for it.'

He didn't pamper his players either. One night Conlan and Paddy Bradley skipped Derry training. Instead, they went out for an important session with Jordanstown in the lead-up to the Sigerson Cup. The next night they went back and Coleman let them have it.

'Eamonn put me and Paddy in the middle of the circle. He says "Do you mind tellin' these boys where youse were at?"

'We said we were away with Jordanstown, we'd a Sigerson to prepare for. And Eamonn just said "Boys, Anthony Tohill was playing Sigerson football all his life and I bet ye he doesn't know where his Sigerson medals is! These two boys are running round looking after one! This is what matters! Yis have to come here!"'

The other players forming the circle abused the students, saying they were good for nothing, fancy boys that thought they were something. Some of the jokers of the team went away overboard, just to see if they would react. They had to stand there and take it. They thought it would be just for a minute, but it dragged on and on.

'Some boys said to us after "Holy Ghost, how did ye stand that there, like?"

'Another time we all met in the Elk and Willie Anderson was in there, the Irish rugby man. We were all sitting round at the tables and chairs and Eamonn says "Right boys, this is the exercise tonight. We're going to go round each player and youse are going to tell each man what their strengths and weaknesses are."

'I was sitting there and it came round to me. I started thinking "Jays, what's these boys going to tell me? Are they going to tell me I'm clean useless here or what?"

'Next thing, Eamonn says to me "Why can't you play here like you play for Ballinderry? When you come here, you play like a number two goalkeeper!"

'I would never have taken that personal, I just knew how passionate he was about the sport. I knew that any criticism I was going to take from this man, I was going to go away and work on it.'

Conlan's time would come again. But this time, he's a goalkeeper with experience.

'In my eyes, it's not just about saving shots. You can do a lot in a game. The more vocal you are, the better the relationship you have with other boys. If you want them boys to work for ya and to do what you're calling and seeing, well sure you mightn't have a shot to save. That's the way I look at it now.

'I wouldn't have been able to shout at Kieran McKeever, Sean Marty, Henry Downey and them boys. You wouldn't have been doing what you're doing now. Henry Downey was centre-half back then. Like, how would I have roared at Henry? You can imagine: "Henry, hold your position, sir!" Aye right!

'I feel I have more games under my belt now and realise that when you go out to play football, there's a chance that you could be injured next week. You might not play another game again. So I'm making sure I'm ready for every game.

'When I was just playing club football I found myself a bit more relaxed even though you'd be doing the hard training and want to see the results for it as well. But now that I've been called back into the county I've had to have a lot of discipline, watching everything I put into my mouth. I'm nervous, yes, because I care. I'm trying to leave my mark, to make sure everybody's alright, make sure I'm in the right frame of mind.'

● ● ●

Heading into the last couple of games, Derry were close to where they needed to be. If they could beat Meath and Antrim, they would be halfway to a league final place and promotion, but they still needed results going for them elsewhere with Tyrone, Kildare, Donegal and Laois all still in the chase.

After rotating his goalkeepers throughout the league, John Brennan assured Conlan he would be getting the last two league games. 'It's like he would say to any man; he just took me to one side and said "Look, Danny's been playing very well and now it's your chance to play well and stake a claim to the number one jersey."

'When you're not playing all the time and then your chance comes along, you do be a bit edgy. Maybe holding back on things you'd normally do, not taking risks, being a bit flat-footed.'

The first half of the Meath game left him shell-shocked. Derry were being carved up through the centre by Shane O'Rourke and then Joe Sheridan helped himself to two goals in quick succession.

'Once the first goal went past me, I thought "Oh my God! What's happening here?" And then for the second goal, I was left totally exposed because everybody had chased the ball and left Joe Sheridan standing on his own on the edge of the square.

'At halftime I had a word with myself. "Frig this here, I'm just gonna go for it. This could be my second-last league game ever and I have to give this my best shot." I went out in the second half and I thought I lifted my game a good bit. I was doing a lot more talking than what I was doing in the first half, which I thought would be impossible. I moved the ball when I got it and came out at free kicks and offered myself to the freetaker. Just trying to contribute more. It keeps my mind on it that bit more. As the man says, that's how I roll.'

Derry changed tack in the second half. Martin Donaghy and Sean Leo McGoldrick carried the ball more and they made some defensive readjustments.

They clawed the gap back and went ahead. There was still time for Cian Ward to grab an opportunistic goal and make things sweaty, but a late scoring spurt made for a bit of comfort at the final whistle.

Even though Brennan had assured Conlan he would be playing the last two games, he endured a terrible week of nerves, fearful that he might pay a price for the three goals conceded against Meath. It wasn't until Brennan called out the team, with Conlan in goals, that he relaxed. He went out and did everything right. He kept a clean sheet and at the other end, Paddy Bradley kicked five points to relegate his father's Antrim side.

Derry didn't make it to the league final. Laois beat Donegal in the final game, leaving a league final between those two teams. But that didn't matter to Conlan. He had kept a clean sheet and was back in pole position, Derry's Number One.

CHAPTER SIXTEEN

The Traps Are Set

THE last day of the league was a strange one for Stevie McDonnell and Armagh, just as it had been a strange league in all. They stayed up and retained their Division One status but the satisfaction in that alone was tempered by anti-climax.

They'd been beaten on that last day in Cork after a late surge from the home team, and after the long bus journey back, McDonnell had it with cabin fever. He got a taxi into Newry and met up with Ciaran McKeever in Bellini's Bar for a few pints. The Down lads had spent too long cooped up themselves after their visit to Killarney, so Benny Coulter and John and Marty Clarke joined them to make up a quintet. They spent a few minutes swapping war stories of the day. Down had been two points down in the last minute of their game when Coulter blasted the ball goalwards only for Marc Ó Sé to block it with his foot. Referee Rory Hickey waved away all the appeals. C'est la vie.

McDonnell and Coulter regularly meet up at lunchtimes for pots of tea and idle chat. They go back a long way. They bonded over International Rules series through the years and are held up as two of the most consistent performers for Ireland in the hybrid game.

This particular night was seven weeks out from their head-to-head clash in the Ulster Championship but there was nobody wanting to go down that line. Instead, they spent some time watching Rory McIlroy's game fall apart at the Augusta Masters.

'It's important that you're friendly with guys,' says McDonnell. 'You can't stop talking to them because of a match. But we all realise that we're going out to cross the line and beat each other because that's the way football is.'

● ● ●

Armagh's league opened under the glare of the television cameras for the unveiling of the new Athletics Grounds and a visit from the Dubs. They put up a good show but were closed out late on by their guests. They overturned Monaghan with the benefit of a late Brian Mallon goal in a game they had no right to win. They wanted to put a run together but fell to Down in the next game. They beat Mayo away, then fell to Kerry.

Their form was schizophrenic. They had Galway at home in the second-last game, a team who were without a point all year. A win would see Armagh safe but Galway turned it into a shootout, putting 1-20 on the board to Armagh's 0-18.

Down in Cork, Armagh scrapped and scraped. In the early stages of the second half, McDonnell took an excellent pass in from Micheál O'Rourke and worked a fistpass for Aaron Kernan to flash to the net and draw level. Shortly after, Cork's Eoin Cadogan was breaking out of defence when McDonnell grappled with him in a tackle. Cadogan swung his arm back and Maurice Condon awarded the Corkman a red card.

Armagh strived to push on for victory but they couldn't find the extra gear as Cork sped away for victory. It was a long drive home.

• • •

Surviving in the top flight wasn't something that Armagh teams used to aspire to. Back in 2005, McDonnell ran up a majestic ten points during the defeat of Wexford in the league final. It was the first time Armagh had won the competition but in his acceptance speech Kieran McGeeney appealed for supporters to give them space to prepare for the Championship before dropping the microphone with a thud.

Great teams become distant memories. McDonnell is now an old warrior clinging onto those times, trying to bridge the gap to the next great team. Throughout the league there was frustration and he couldn't wait for the Crossmaglen Rangers players to win the All Ireland club and get back to county football. In February he sat down and considered their return.

'They'll certainly celebrate an All Ireland if they get it, but Jamie Clarke doesn't drink, Aaron Kernan will take it easy, they're very committed to the [Armagh] cause. They're mad keen to get back playing for Armagh rather than being on the outside looking in. As a team, it will be great to have those boys back, hopefully with an All Ireland in their pockets.'

Crossmaglen's success has its benefits too. The 2002 Armagh team had a generous smattering of their attitude to complement immense characters like McGeeney and Paul McGrane.

'I think as a county that we should be taking a huge amount of confidence over what Crossmaglen do on a consistent basis. They go out with no fear of any team. The old Armagh team of the last decade used to do that, stamp our authority on each match. It's something that we have to instil into our mentality and our game-plan.

'The physicality hasn't gone out of Armagh but we had very strong-minded players back then, players that never really panicked under pressure. Now we're lacking in that experience to cope with situations. In 2003 we were four points down against Dublin and in my thirteen years playing with Armagh, that second-half performance was definitely the best that we ever produced as a team in terms of physicality, knowing that we were in complete control of the match. Even when we were four down, I really believed we were going to win. It's having that belief in your teammates and your style of play and that's what we need to find within this squad. When the Cross boys come back, we'll rediscover it.'

• • •

Other little things are gnawing at McDonnell. This was the first league season where he didn't hit a goal. It's become a bit of an issue. When he clattered a rebound past Ronan Gallagher in the 2008 Ulster final replay, he became the all-time highest goalscorer from Ulster in championship football with his eighteenth goal. His close friend Benny Coulter was four behind him at that point but Benny's goal against Kildare in the 2010 All Ireland semi-final edged him in front of McDonnell.

'I set myself the target of five [goals in this league],' says McDonnell. 'I think goalscoring is a very instinctive thing. I got myself into a couple of opportunities against Galway and I hit the post with one. The other one went over the bar. Even against Cork, I had one blocked by Michael Shields in the first five minutes. They weren't clear-cut chances but I got myself in those positions.

'I'm still happy that I'm finding myself in those positions, I've scored goals long enough that I know how to do it. I know that if the chance presents itself in the Championship I'll put it away. Before every game, you set yourself a target. You might not always reach it but you just get over that and move on.'

Goalscoring is a private demon that he feels he can slay but there is an irritation at the level of scrutiny Paddy O'Rourke is receiving as Armagh manager.

'We're all aware of the criticism and Paddy is aware of it as well. Ultimately, when an outside man comes into the job he's going to have knives out for him regardless. People have to realise that Paddy O'Rourke came in last year and we had been struggling in Division Two for a couple of years. We were promoted and won the final. We had a decent run in the Championship with five games.

'This year we've maintained our position in Division One. While we were lucky in the end, we still did it without the Cross boys, so maybe they have to cut him some slack.

'I would be of the opinion that Paddy sets us up before the match, sends us out to do a job and then it's up to the players when we cross that line to perform. A lot of times over the course of matches that we lost, it was our fault, and all the blame shouldn't be falling back on the manager.'

O'Rourke made a clever move at the start of the year when he brought in Des Jennings. The respected sports psychologist worked closely with the panel in

2002 and 2003 during a time when Armagh were at their height. In Oisín McConville's autobiography The Gambler, he wrote of how he felt some standards were allowed to slip when Jennings left the camp.

In years since, Ross Carr would take Jennings in with the Down squad and when Dan Gordon lifted the 2008 McKenna Cup, he would praise the work of Jennings from the podium in Casement Park.

Jennings' return to Armagh was greeted with glee by McDonnell, aware that Jennings would also have serious insight into the Down players they'd face in the Ulster Championship opener.

'We would always have had a lot of time for Des and what he did, getting the message across to players and making them feel good about themselves. I personally don't think Armagh ever replaced what Des offered so I was delighted when Paddy asked him back in.'

The previous man hadn't inspired such fondness. Dr John Kremer is regarded as the godfather of sport psychology in Ulster and had been working with GAA teams ever since the early 1990s when Dessie Ryan brought him into work with the Queen's University Sigerson team that featured the McNulty brothers. With Justin McNulty coaching Armagh in 2010 he was brought in to the Orchard county setup but for all his expertise and experience, the chemistry just wasn't right this time.

'In fairness, for the first night or two that John came in he was good, but then he started doing things that went against the players, criticising them. He was lucky one or two times that he didn't get the head ripped off him. In my opinion, I wouldn't have him anywhere near us at all.

'Des is all about making the players feel good about themselves, trying to get them to perform to their highest possible level. It's worked for a lot of the players in the league and he will have them performing in the Championship.'

To beat Down in seven weeks' time, Jennings' expertise will be required to boost the mood of the younger players following an indifferent league campaign.

'We know we have the talent to beat Down. It's down to making the younger boys in particular believe. It's mind training and when you look at the games we played against Down over the past couple of years, they might have beat us in the league by a point but in the second half we had opportunities to beat them. Last year we beat them in the league final, because we were very focused after our league beating in the Marshes.

'The fact they beat us in the league this year won't do us any harm at all. It might work in our favour. If we can get all of our players believing we can get the result, we will.

'The first thing they're going to do is to try and stop me and Jamie. They'll feel that myself and Jamie are the only scoring threats. What I would do is get the other forwards thinking that they'll do the scoring and we have plenty of boys who can.

'The half-forward line needs to be pushing up. I'm not a fan of being defensive. I believe the way football is now it doesn't work. It might have worked a few years ago but at the highest level now you need to go at teams. In the Down match I think we'll take a risk and go at them.

'We know all about the Down forwards but we would be very confident, man for man, that our defence can hold their forward line. We have to push up more. It's not something they will be expecting from us. I'd like to think we'll be able to do it.'

Down's greatest strength is their confidence. Armagh though are thinking that in this instance it could border into arrogance and that could be their downfall.

The traps have been laid. Armagh are going for the ambush.

CHAPTER SEVENTEEN

Love And Hurt

GETTING the stitches in was the most painful part; the rest he put down to just one of those things.

Martin McElroy had the ball in Monaghan training and Dick Clerkin moved in to tackle. McElroy is smaller than him so Clerkin had to lean over the top to get the angle right. Then McElroy went to push off and caught him. Next thing, there was blood in the mouth and the familiar metallic tang that is always recognisable yet always a shock. Clerkin's tooth sliced through his lower gum and snagged itself on the other side. If he was able to smile at the time, it would have been one of satisfaction.

The intensity is back.

• • •

Life after Banty was always going to be difficult. Then, as well as getting to know a new management and new methods, they had to deal with a number of injuries and the retirement of some key players. Yet, for most of the league, they had been hugely competitive. They surprised everyone including themselves in the first game by beating Galway and then dominated Armagh before coughing up a goal and a few points to somehow end up on the losing side. Two ballsy displays against Cork and Dublin gave them belief they were progressing. The thought was whipped away with harsh lessons from Down and Kerry.

For the previous six years Seamus McEnaney had built a solid team and commanded serious loyalty from his players. They repaid it but inevitably, the panel grew stale with lack of competition for places.

Eamonn McEneaney was forced to perform a lot of surgery. When Kerry rolled into Inniskeen, he looked around the dressing room at the wounded and lame. From the team that started the 2010 Ulster final, only Clerkin, Colin Walshe, Darren Hughes and Conor McManus were able to start. Young talent is getting its head, as much out of necessity as anything.

Some games, you get away with it. But Kerry never underestimate teams. Monaghan had attempted to mug them a few times before and gave them a few uncomfortable Championship afternoons. So when Kerry spotted a side of greenhorns in white and blue, they put on the knuckle-dusters for the day.

They were eleven points up at halftime. Monaghan took over half an hour to get their first point. By the end they had clawed it back to a six-point gap.

To Clerkin, there was no point going over the top about it all.

'Ten of our team were U-21 against Kerry. You put that against a team that has more All Irelands and All Stars than we've games under our belt, it's an apples-and-oranges comparison. To be even competing at that level is a credit to us. Over the last six or seven years, we have never been on the end of a hiding. We always compete, we always stay there. From eleven points down at halftime, we worked our way back into the game. How many teams would have been able to do that? That alone can give you great heart.

'It would be a lot worse a situation if you were playing at your best, and still ending up being beat by that margin, to not be within an ass's roar.'

The Tuesday training session after, Monaghan broke with routine. It had been Eamonn McEneaney's habit to sit down with the players for five or ten minutes in the dressing room and talk about the weekend's game. It's always measured, where they cover what happened, what was lacking, and it's rounded off with a small bit of interaction between players and management. This time, McEneaney took them all out onto the pitch and asked them to show him what kind of fight they had in them.

'We maybe realised that the time for talking was over. The intensity was an issue. It had been a trademark of ours for years and it was there in the early part of the league, but then we patted ourselves on the back for the decent performances. The intensity hadn't been good enough in recent games.'

A lot of players were carrying the residue of poor performance in their engines, so they were glad to get straight down to business. They went through their new-style warmup, almost entirely of ball drills and shooting exercises. It's another subtle shift in emphasis that has impressed Clerkin. Then some small-sided games began and things got feisty.

'We got the bit between our teeth which is great to see. I probably deserved a slap tonight. Marty McElroy, he's not that big, but he's strong, he had the ball, I went to slap into him, and the heel of his hand shot out and caught me on the bottom lip. My tooth went out through it.

'It's one of these things that will happen from time to time in training. James Turley got a bit of an elbow there too tonight. It does you no harm. When we're training hard there are plenty of knocks and bumps all the time. The odd bust-up in training doesn't hurt either.

'I think it's a signal that we're heading back to that level we attained in 2007. We have a lot of guys coming back to training, the likes of Tommy Freeman and Eoin Lennon, but we have to bring it into matches. We spoke about it earlier in the year, that we didn't want any complacency. Everybody's place should be in jeopardy.'

For years it felt like the county team was a closed shop, so Clerkin is taking the positives out of this campaign. So much so, that he feels even relegation would not be a trauma for this crop of players.

'When you go back to the start of the year and look at the panel we had initially, how many of those guys would leap out at you? I'd far rather be slightly off the pace with a young panel, than off the pace with an older panel, which they were calling us last year. I think our average age last weekend was about twenty-three, and if you take me out of it, it would be a lot lower again.

'The boys that might have been coming back from serious injury were perhaps being held back a little bit during the league, but they'll be back for the Championship and desperately hungry for football. In Championship the intensity is higher, you have the buzz, the excitement, the media coverage related to the game.

'The Ulster Championship, no matter what they might say, has always a bit more bite to it than any other provincial Championship. It's still a special thing to be in. There is a certain desperation there. And once you win a game in the Championship, whatever you did over the winter and spring doesn't matter a damn.'

●　　●　　●

That's it tweeps, am officially a #mandown. Popped the big ? over in paris and thankfully I got the answer I had hoped for!! #AlisonClerkin
@dickclerkin8, Twitter, 17th April

There has been another sign that he has truly becoming one of the more elder statesmen of the team. After the Kerry match he spotted a gap between the end of the league campaign and a club game so he booked a few days in Paris for Alison and himself. He was on a mission.

They got to Paris on a Wednesday and set about making a list of all the tourist attractions they wanted to see. A self-confessed gastronome, he was looking forward to see how the French chefs would wow him. They booked into a hotel between the Eiffel Tower and the Champs Élysées, and headed out. Notre Dame, the Tower itself, a boat trip on the River Seine; they covered a lot of bases.

The following day, Clerkin felt under pressure. It would be one of the most important days of his life. He would propose to Alison.

The thing was where to ask her. On the Eiffel Tower? Too cheesy. They wandered into the Louvre with Clerkin seeking inspiration for the perfect moment but he felt the experience no more rewarding than a visit to a suburban shopping centre. A painting here, a Reubenesque statue there; he realised that while he could take a picture of nearly every building in Paris, fine art wasn't doing it for him. He paid his dues to the Mona Lisa, but he was faking it.

Wandering aimlessly in the Ancient Egypt section, the pair thought they would make a break for it, but their maps were hopeless, and they kept ending up in the same place wondering how in God's name they could get out.

Eventually, they located the exit. It was a beautiful day and a setting as they took a seat on a bench with a baguette.

'It felt as good a time as any. I popped the question. It wasn't totally private but it was intimate to a point.

'The first response that you're always looking for was "Are you serious?" "Of course I'm serious."'

Alison accepted and broke into a big smile. While Dick might have felt there had been the odd hint coming at home, she was still in mild shock. They thought they might go back to Notre Dame after the Louvre, but instead they boarded the tour bus and sailed round the city as the light died on the evening. Two young people in love, enjoying the glow.

There was no ring but he had it figured out. The following day they travelled to the diamond wholesale capital of Europe. 'We went to Antwerp and got sized up. Alison took her time because she wouldn't have known what she wanted, but it only took us an hour. It was beautiful, different, something you just wouldn't get at home. That wasn't the reason we went; it was more to get something original. When it was that close, why not?'

The following day, they were on a tight schedule. They were flying into Dublin for 3pm and Clerkin had a club game for Currin against Sean McDermott's at 7pm. The plan was to get home and visit her parents with the good news in Monaghan town and proceed from there to his parents in Scotshouse before making the game.

After collecting their baggage, they made it back to the car. The lights had been left on and the battery was completely flat. Looking around, there wasn't a soul about to jump-start it either.

'I started panicking. Alison went to get a roll because we had nothing to eat. By the time she got back, I had pushed the car up the middle of the park and down, twice, trying to jump start it on a flat surface. The car is a big two-litre diesel Honda and I was trying to get it up to a decent speed but there wasn't a beat out of it. The sweat was pouring off me! I was ready to die.'

A rescue service came to their aid a couple of hours later. He turned the nose of the car towards the game. He arrived late, but took the field and kicked a point in a good win for the club. The following day, they spread the good news.

Dick Clerkin can smile now.

Love is in the air.

And so is Championship.

CHAPTER EIGHTEEN
True Blue Terry

TERRY Hyland had to learn fast when he was thrust into the job of Cavan selector. It was Val Andrews' first county job too, so the two knew that they had to trust each other immediately.

He wasn't a high-profile former county player, he wasn't even a man who was given a spin in a McKenna Cup.

Terry Hyland is everyman. He may be a businessman who has succeeded by having a keen brain and a sharp eye, but he's not someone who courts, demands or needs attention. He's just another Cavan man with a passion to see them get back to where they once where. Long before his time, but that doesn't matter.

Cavan is in a strange place. Half of the county love football. Not in a pleasant pastime or diversion sense, but in a scary sense. They are preoccupied and irritated with football. Sometimes they hate football, what it does to them, how it teases and mocks. But Cavan is football. It's just that not enough of them seem to care anymore.

Hyland is Cavan. To the very marrow of him, he is a manifestation of the passion that can envelop the county.

Lacken is his club and he first kicked a ball for them in 1970 as a boy. He had plenty of ability and he was strong as an ox so they threw him into midfield. He made it with the seniors in 1978 and he played there in midfield for seventeen seasons. Pretty much every bone in his body got broken in those years but it didn't stop him coming back from more. His ankles snapped. Legs were broken. The cruciate ligament in his right leg went. Ribs were cracked and broken. Two discs were once removed from his neck and they had to open him up on another occasion to insert pins to brace his shoulders. When Cavan go to away games now, he has to drive. The bus journeys play havoc with his aching joints.

And when the seniors cast him to the scrapheap? He just dropped down a level and played with the juniors. No biggie.

A friend asked him if he would take the Cavan Masters team – football for men over forty – and he was glad to accept. He was the trainer and when he turned forty himself he slotted straight into the team and got to wear the blue jersey. They captured two All Ireland titles in the late '90s but his motivation soon switched.

'I think the reason I stayed involved for so long was I could see an opportunity to play club football with my own sons. Create a small bit of history, you know. I remember playing midfield with Mark, my second son, in a junior match and it went very well. I was forty-five at that stage but sometimes the mind keeps telling you you're probably younger than you are.'

He found he got great pleasure from coaching. There was nothing fancy to his philosophy, he just played it as he saw it. In 1993 he brought Lacken to the county intermediate final. He stepped down after another year and went to Knockbride and took them to an intermediate final in 1997. Back to Lacken for another spell then, in which they reached the senior county semi-final in 2000.

When the county spell ended he took a break for himself, but soon got itchy feet. He landed the intermediate championship as Lacken manager in 2004. A few years later he took Lavey to the same title, and they beat all in front of them until the Ulster club final.

All the while, he kept up his involvement with the Cavan junior team, and the county U-21 footballers. And when Val hitched his wagons for a spell in charge of Louth, he hopped on board.

'I'm not a high-profile kind of guy. I never cherry-pick. If a club asked me and they were a decent bunch of fellas I would go with them. I don't go looking for championships. I always believe in the honest type of footballer. Sometimes you see men who go around and get ticks on their CVs, and maybe my CV doesn't tick up the same as everybody else, but I'm a great believer in that if you display honesty, you'll get honesty.'

That quality carried Cavan a long way in 2001. By then Andrews and Hyland could put their own stamp on the side. They brought a few new faces in that surprised many but worked out exceptionally well. 'Terry was instrumental in that,' recalls Andrews. 'I recall saying to him "Here, we have to change." He had a saying about lads who were an honest gasún, and we took that as a concept. Terry would say "Look, there's this lad, he's an honest gasún," and I would say "Get him in."'

Hyland's expertise on the line grew. 'Terry's a businessman,' continues Andrews, 'He takes decisions, he thinks on his feet. He came up with a suggestion of moving Edward Jackson to midfield [in the 2001 Ulster semi-final against Monaghan]. Lo and behold it worked. Nobody to this day knows that but everyone was saying "Jayz, Val's great on the line!"'

It brought them far. All the way to an Ulster final in fact, when they were in front of Tyrone at halftime. They were pipped in the end and it remains the one that got away in Cavan football.

• • •

One that didn't get away was this year's Ulster U-21 title. Hyland was in his second year looking after the team and there had been a reasonable amount of optimism that they could progress. He surrounded himself with good people:

Joe McCarthy, Ronan Carolan and Anthony Forde, people who had been there with the last successful U-21 side and the 1997 seniors.

They beat Fermanagh in the first round, the reigning champions Donegal in the semi-final, and then there was that glorious night in Enniskillen when they captured the provincial crown, beating Tyrone in the final. Cavan men and women spilled onto the pitch at the final whistle, delirious to have some success. Hyland stayed away from the grand gestures and whooping it up. Jose Mourinho, he's not. A zealous photographer pointed a three-foot lens in his face and told him to start cheering. He just smiled back. It wasn't about him.

'I was bowled over with the amount of well-wishes I got. I suppose it's the age of the mobile phone and I got a serious amount of text messages. But I'm only a conduit for the management team and the players. I see the management as a co-operative. I stand up in front but I'm only a front for the work of everyone behind me.'

The same group of players had shown up well against Tyrone as minors in the Ulster Championship a few years back, so there had been a decision to keep them together and focused at their own level. It meant that the senior team could not expect the likes of Gearoid McKiernan, Niall Murray, Barry Reilly and Niall McDermott to train with them, although they would play the odd senior game. But keeping them apart meant another few nights out of the house for Hyland. Some nights, he trained the U-21s before heading straight on to senior training.

'Terry had the U-21s, his emotional energy went into that,' says Andrews. 'That's where he does everything, so he stays nice and calm in his role in the seniors. I don't know how he does what he does because he's out every day!

'Honestly, he is amazing, like. I would look at him and like, I mean, in one fortnight, he had done thirteen days with teams, something mad, like!'

Three days after they won Ulster, they were expected to play Wexford in the All Ireland semi-final. The ridiculous scheduling was highlighted in the media and the GAA's fixture-makers caught some well-deserved flak on the issue. Yet Cavan managed to dig in and win, only to be beaten in the final by a superior Galway side.

Hyland skipped off to his little bolthole in Spain and escaped the slings and arrows. Even though his side had brought honour to the county with their first Ulster U-21 title in fifteen years, he knew all about the old maxim of the closeness of a pat on the back and a kick on the ass.

'We always seem to have promising minors and the thing we do with promising minors in Cavan is hoof them straight onto the senior panel. They aren't fit for it, they aren't mentally fit for it, and by the time they're twenty-three they're either physically or mentally burned out.'

'In Cavan, we're not bad footballers, we just don't believe we're good enough, and sometimes it's just that belief factor you have to get across. Be straight and honest in your dealings with them, don't tell them any lies. Okay, they may not agree with you, but they can't come back and say "Well he twisted this, he said something different."'

Honesty and integrity. With him it's never for Hyland's sake but Cavan's.

CHAPTER NINETEEN

The Big Date

DONEGAL v ANTRIM
Preliminary Round, Pairc MacCumhail, Ballybofey, May 15

DONEGAL were to open the Championship with another home draw. It was the fourth consecutive year they had that advantage but the expectation had become oppressive.

Ballybofey had been a cruel venue for them as they fell to Derry, Antrim and Down in each year. Every time, they ended their first day weighing up their chances in the purgatory of the qualifiers system. That couldn't be allowed to continue.

If preparations were too casual before, that couldn't be a complaint now. When Kevin Cassidy came back to join the Jim McGuinness project, he promised to himself that he would give it everything. That extended to bringing his trainers on a family holiday to Lanzarote in February. Every morning before Sarah and the twins were up, he would be on the roads from 7am, running in the punishing heat from Puerto del Carmen to the Old Town and back. With his hotel surrounded by hills, it was the ideal place to punish himself with steep climbs. He stuck to his manager's prescribed regime and conducted his own personal warm-weather training camp.

The Friday after Donegal beat Laois in the Division Two league final in Croke Park, the group headed to Breaffy House Hotel in Castlebar, a retreat for county teams with full-sized pitches, weights rooms, ice baths; everything they could ask for. On arrival they went straight into the pool for a recovery session. After that there was a meal and then it was straight to bed.

They trained for two and a half hours on the Saturday morning from 9am. Once it was finished, they were ordered back into their beds for a couple of hours. After the siesta it was time for rub downs and the ice baths. A bit of light relief came later with ten-pin bowling in the town but it was soon back to work and a psychology session conducted by McGuinness, a sport psychologist himself. He covered various scenarios in games, asked them how they would cope with it, how they could retain their shape, and how they'd stay mentally strong when the pressures of a Championship match was upon them.

On Sunday morning they were out on the pitches for a two-hour session that involved serious stamina work. Then it was lunch before the bus brought them straight home. The following week training tapered off, something that surprised the players.

'We thought that we might have been killed in training this week,' mused Cassidy a week out from the Antrim game. 'My own personal opinion is that Jim has the season planned out. He's not disrespecting Antrim or anything like that but he doesn't want to peak too early.

'You'll see a good performance against Antrim, but we have no speedwork whatsoever done. That's his plan definitely, because he talks about the Kerrys of this world, how they don't have to peak until July and August of the year.'

Cassidy's motivation is Antrim, but for his manager, it is the date – May 15.

'Jim never mentions Antrim. He just says the same thing over and over. May 15, May 15. There is no Antrim, it's irrelevant to him. That's not a bad thing. During the league his message wasn't "Laois do this, Laois do that", it's "Donegal do this, Donegal do that." That's how he prepares. What's the point about worrying about other teams? We have to worry about ourselves.

'When the U-21s lost in the All Ireland final against Dublin, Jim said he walked away from that game the happiest he felt all year. The team gave absolutely everything and a bit of luck beat them on the day. You can't complain about that. That's all he's looking for. He has a saying, that there's nothing to compare to walking off the field having given everything you can. That's the direction we're going in.

'It's a cause and it's a dream. Sometimes you can train and just go through it. Other times I come off the training field and I feel better than after a match that we've won. Because you put in that extra effort, it's being put in as something that is for a greater cause.

'People always ask what's Jim doing that is different to John Joe. It's just simple things that he organises. He gets us on the one boat, not for an Ulster title or an All Ireland title, but to be the best you can be, to look after your own performance. Fair enough if Antrim beat you by six or seven points, shake hands and walk away. But there's nothing worse than coming off and thinking "If I hadn't gone out that Saturday night" or "I wish I had have done those extra runs" or "I wish I had have trained harder."'

• • •

For the last weekend of April, Antrim were camped in The Radisson Blue Hotel in Rosses Point, Sligo.

They needed a big lift. While Donegal won Division Two, Antrim finished dead last in the same division. Morale was low, their confidence shot to pieces. To lighten the mood, team selector Niall Conway spilt the panel into teams for a table quiz once they arrived on a Friday night. Paddy Cunningham was in a team with his clubmate Conor Murray, Brian Neeson and Sean O'Neill, and they answered most of the questions on sport, books, politics and history to claim the prize.

When they arose on Saturday morning, there would be no heavy lifting. Instead, they were presented with the choice of a fishing rod or a golf club. Paddy teamed up with Liam Bradley in a fourball against Kevin McGourty and Murray. Despite the various stunts the opposition tried to pull and the muddled score cards, they had fun.

Later that evening, they had a meeting to decide how they would deal with Donegal. They no longer had the element of surprise which they had in 2009. Now they needed to box clever with their formation and offer a few decades of the rosary that their injured comrades would recover in time to play. They touched on trying different formations and trying to confuse Donegal with their lineout.

The analysis wasn't far-reaching enough to satisfy Cunningham.

'There's no point in saying that we won't look at them and concentrate on our own strengths. We have to sit down and look at their strengths, and not just the week before and then start working on them.

'Obviously they have [Michael] Murphy and [Colm] McFadden and we need two men set aside to mark them. We can't stand off at midfield and let them pump quality ball in them two men. Our workrate needs to be upped, right across the field.

'It's very important we exploit some of their weaknesses. Two years ago we exploited their full-back line. Mick McCann gave Neil McGee the run around and I pulled Karl Lacey out to give the two lads in the full-forward line a bit of space and it worked very well. I think we need to sit down now to see what we can do and how we can do it.'

They had one more meeting that day with renowned performance coach, Caroline Currid. She had worked with Tyrone when they won Sam Maguire in 2008, and had spent the last two years with Tipperary, culminating in their Liam McCarthy Cup in 2010. Now, she was with the Dublin team and she was urging caution to the Antrim players.

'She said herself that one session wasn't going to work miracles or make dramatic changes. One session with a woman like that, with her expertise, it wasn't going to make any difference. You needed her in from day one, to be there the whole time. She did say that if any of us needed to speak to her or have a yarn or whatever, to ring her. But that was two weeks before Championship.'

● ● ●

On the Sunday morning of their camp in Sligo, the squad rose as one to get

Mass. They headed straight to the pool for a session afterwards, then travelled for a challenge match against Mayo in Kiltimagh.

They were buried, 3-10 to 0-11. It confirmed everything Cunningham had suspected.

'That was a complete disaster. The match was due to start at 1pm but we didn't get to the pitch until 1.15pm. We got off the bus, got changed and straight out for a two minute warm-up. Mayo had been warming up for half an hour and hit the ground running. Things had been good after the golf, the quiz and a talk from Caroline and there was a bit more hope coming into the thing.

'Then we go and get beat by that much. I didn't feel we needed that match. Fair enough we were in Sligo, but I thought we would have been better off playing a lesser team. We got nothing out of the game and I'd say if you asked Mayo, they would say they got nothing out of it either.

'There was the usual negative message after it. No fight, no passion, all these clichéd phrases. We were second to the ball, running into tackles, all these things that are happening and that you know are happening, but no solution to them.

'It got to the point that you didn't want to listen. Before you would go into the dressing room, you knew what was going to happen.'

●   ●   ●

On the Friday before the opening game of Championship 2011, Kevin Cassidy was sitting at home watching The Late Late Show when his mobile rang. It was Jim McGuinness with some important information.

Up to then Cassidy thought he would probably be marking Kevin McGourty. Even when there were reports that McGourty was unfit, Cassidy thought it could either be a spoof story or else he would be on somebody like Sean Burke. Rory Gallagher had even given him a few DVDs of St Gall's in action, so Cassidy could familiarise himself with little tics that give away McGourty's intentions.

Now Jim was able to tell him that he would be on Lamh Dhearg's Brendan Herron. Ulster football is a small world and word can get out very easily. Advantage Donegal.

The Villa Rose Hotel in Ballybofey was their meeting place on Sunday at noon. After a lunch of chicken and pasta, they got down to business. The management team highlighted the danger of conceding frees that Cunningham would convert. They were also shown his tendency to steal a few yards.

Positionally, they suspected that Antrim forward Mark Sweeney would drop in to pick up Mark McHugh, freeing up Anto Healy as an extra defender. Aodhan Gallagher would also drop from midfield into a deep position to pick up

Rory Kavanagh's runs with the ball. Conor Murray would switch from half-forward to midfield.

A fortnight out from the game, 'Baker' Bradley played a mind game, remarking that Donegal had been playing a defensive style of football since their league game in Ballyshannon, going so far as to label it as 'puke football'. Bradley was gearing his team to do much the same.

'I think he's a man under pressure to be honest,' says Cassidy. 'That's one thing you don't do, is come out and say something like that about a team, especially a week before the game. It's music to our ears.

'A reporter called me up about it and asked if I would want to comment on it but I told him I would prefer to wait until Sunday. The way it came across to me is that they're under pressure. They're stretched with the two McGourtys out and this year I think we'll be a lot more aware of how they're going to play, especially with Rory there, because he knows them inside out.'

Before Donegal left the Villa Rose, McGuinness showed his players some pictures of the scenes after the defeats to Derry, Antrim and Down in the three previous years, with Donegal players sat with their heads in their hands, others sunken to their knees.

'Lads,' he told them, 'it's time to get off our knees and win a Championship match.'

● ● ●

Only a day earlier from Cassidy getting that Late Late phonecall from Jim McGuinness, Paddy Cunningham underwent a colonoscopy in hospital. His Crohn's Disease had flared up again, causing him serious pain.

It was one of the worst possible lead-ins to a Championship game, having to undergo an operation of that nature the Thursday before his biggest game of the year, and being unable to eat from the Tuesday, but Cunningham felt such an inconvenience was impossible as he had already cancelled a previous appointment; President Mary McAleese was coming to visit his school and he was expected to do the meet-and-greet duties. If he dodged this one, he would have been discharged and forced to go back to his GP.

He had to be sedated for the operation and was drank fluids to clear out his system. So little wonder that come gameday, Cunningham felt he had little energy and was running on empty.

He had informed the Antrim management of the procedure, but he kept certain elements of it from them, such as the fasting and the fluids he was forced to drink. Later, Cunningham would reflect that he was only fit for twenty minutes at best but he was desperate to turn the season around with a big performance.

Antrim had an early start that Sunday. All the city-based players had grouped at Casement Park, and the team bus collected their south-west contingent at the Elk Inn in Toomebridge. From there they took the Derry road to a petrol station on the Glenshane Pass where Liam Bradley and Niall Conway stepped onto the coach. Their stop-off came at the Everglades Hotel in Derry city. Unsurprisingly, their meal was pasta and chicken.

When the bus rolled into McCumhaill Park at 2pm, the players stretched their legs by getting a look at the minor match for ten minutes, before they had to tog out. But it was a much less assured dressing room than the one down the hallway, at least in Paddy Cunningham's mind.

'All week I've tried to stay as positive as I can. But I was still thinking in the back of my mind, had we enough work done? We were worried about the injuries we were carrying.'

● ● ●

Matchday was sodden and miserable. It would require a mixture of guts and intelligence to win. On such Sundays, winning's the only thing that matters. Aesthetics don't come into it.

At 3.21pm the tradition pre-match parade began. Three minutes later the announcement came over the tannoy that the precocious Patrick McBrearty, who had played in the minor curtain-raiser, would be on the bench for the senior Donegal team.

Right on 3.30pm referee Maurice Deegan hoisted the ball in the air, and Championship 2011 began.

Before the first minute was complete, Antrim's Championship debutant Rickey Johnston fouled Donegal captain Michael Murphy and Colm McFadden duly curled over the free for the first score of the day and the summer.

On six minutes came Cassidy's first involvement. He pushed upfield and got himself into a scoring position but hooked his shot wide of the near post.

The pattern for the game had been set even in those initial stages. Both sides had opted for caution and Antrim seemed surprised that Donegal had read their intentions.

On fourteen minutes though a crossfield ball was directed at Cunningham and Anthony Thompson clipped his heels. Free-in for Antrim.

Cunningham has a particularly curious, unorthodox routine. He'll begin his run-up only to slow down and stamp his feet in a little jig, before taking another couple of steps and then kicking the ball through his laces and over the crossbar. It works though. He's in the top bracket of dead-ball kickers in the country.

Like the golfer that tinkers with his stroke even after the perfect round, he always feels there's room for improvement. When he trains with Antrim, he spends half an hour to forty-five minutes working on his technique. On a night off, he will take himself to the Lamh Dearg pitch with a bag of balls. He always goes alone. If somebody else is there, he runs the risk of chatting, or kicking about, and not working on his craft with the focus required.

His style is just something that evolved, unselfconsciously. 'I never really planned it, and then after it worked for me, I just continued on from then. I've been doing it for three or four years but I think now I want to change it. I need a new routine. It's not that I've lost confidence in it or anything, but I think I need to freshen it up a bit.'

Along with scores from play, it helped him to a scoring tally of 3-57 in 2009, the year they reached an Ulster final, in eleven league and Championship games. The following year, he was the highest scoring forward in Ulster, playing the same amount of games, only this time helping himself to 3-73. During the difficult league campaign this year, he kept his side of the bargain with thirty-eight points in six games, thirty-two of them from frees.

'I think my average has dropped slightly. My target is not to miss any frees at all, ever. You're going to miss at some stage, but I think I'm missing too many. You might not notice it in newspaper reports or whatever but I need to change it a wee bit.'

While Thompson stayed down receiving treatment, Cunningham's mind began to wander. It was a simple chance, twenty-one yards out and central. The crowd had it chalked down as a point.

As he began his run-up, the catcalls came. Players were shouting at him. Kevin Cassidy asked the ref to watch where he was taking the free from. He put it wide. Unbelievable.

'The first free was terrible. Obviously McGuinness and Rory Gallagher had their tactics worked out and they knew that we get a lot of scores from frees. With the first one, there was such a long delay that I think I had too much time to think. It was a terrible miss.'

Donegal were controlling the game with Cassidy influential. He broke forward with regularity and as he did, gradually broke the will of his marker Herron.

Donegal's disciplined defence was starving Cunningham of possession. It would take until the twenty-third minute for him to get his second touch of the game. It was another free, only this time the angle was tighter and the distance greater.

Cassidy was on his case again, even pointing to the ref where he felt the free should have been taken from.

Cunningham went through the routine and thumped it over. As he back-pedalled into his position, he had a word for Cassidy.

'Will that do ye, Kevin?'

'Cassidy and a few others were at me flat out about missing the first one,' recalls Cunningham. 'Chirping and chirping and chirping, the whole backline were. They were obviously told to do that and even at halftime on the way in, a couple of their subs were at me.

'On the first one, I was so annoyed with myself. I don't think I've missed one as handy in my life. But I was never going to miss the second one because Cassidy was just doing my head in.'

Cunningham was right. It was a stunt Donegal were willing to pull.

'We were told before the game to get onto him and the ref right away,' admits Cassidy. 'Anything at all to put him off.'

The fortunes of the two players mirrored that of their team. While Cassidy was exerting himself and enjoying the game, Cunningham's exasperation grew. Just before halftime he missed another free, albeit from a tight angle. As the teams made their way in, Donegal were three points to the good.

In Antrim's dressing room, the mood was foul. Donegal's was serene.

Heading out for the second half, Cunningham was deep in conversation with fellow attackers Kevin Niblock and Tomas McCann. They also were baffled with the system they had been asked to play.

Donegal gained a platform at midfield and started piling on the scores. Liam Bradley became agitated on the line.

Cassidy picked up on their disharmony. 'There seemed to be a lot of arguments among each other. Baker was screaming instructions onto the field and they weren't really following them. He was screaming at Tomas McCann to go centre-forward so Lacey would have to pick him up, but he wanted to go inside. There was a lot of that, over and back. They didn't seem to be that together.'

He has been there before. 'When negativity starts to seep into a camp, it's a cancer to a team. We had that problem last year. You have to stay so positive, because you train so hard, and if you start being negative, you're fucked.'

On fifty minutes Cunningham took a pass from Conor Murray. He rode a tackle from Martin McElhinney but Paddy McGrath was onto him like a flash. Cunningham linked into McGrath's tackling hand and went down to try and win the free.

He lay on the ground but referee Maurice Deegan wasn't buying it. Free out.

Seven minutes later, his day was over. Liam Bradley sent Mark Dougan on for him. As Dougan ran on, Cunningham looked at the substitute's board, scarcely believing what he could see.

'I can't remember the last time I was taken off. Never, ever, I don't think.'

He made his way off the field, and took his place on the bench. Nobody on the sideline went over to him.

Dougan looked lively, hitting a point on sixty-four minutes. Three minutes later though he came in from the right side with Karl Lacey hanging out of him. Both players fell to the ground before Dougan swung an elbow at Lacey's head. Red card.

In injury time Mark McHugh cut through for a Donegal goal. There was only enough time to take the kick out. Game over. Donegal 1-10 Antrim 0-7.

• • •

After the whistle, Cunningham sought out Lacey. The two of them had been close as teammates for Jordanstown and they shook hands. Before the match he had verbally sparred with Neil McGee too, something he calls 'ganching', but now he could only congratulate McGee. In truth, McGee and Donegal were always going to be the winners.

'Preparation wasn't as good as it could have been. Probably last week training was good but it was too little, too late. We only talked about how we were going to mark Murphy and McFadden last week. We were very, very defensive and we didn't have a notion of how we were going to go upfront, especially against Donegal who put so many behind the ball.

'You were never going to beat a blanket defence with more or less two men inside and one half-forward. I think it was damage limitation. We were more concerned about them than ourselves and we didn't play to our strengths at all.

'If you look at the statistics throughout the year we had a problem with scoring. If you have one or two players doing ninety percent of your scoring then it's evident that you need to work on things upfront. But we weren't working at that at all in training. All we worked on was defence.'

He got dressed and the group went through the usual post-mortem routine. Instead of going back in the bus though, he met his girlfriend Claire who had found the drive down tricky. They made for Derry and stopped off in the Icon restaurant for dinner.

By the time Cunningham got back home to Belfast, his parents were watching The Sunday Game. He sat with them and listened to the talking heads savage the game as a spectacle. Cunningham went through the masochism of watching the defeat but he couldn't give tuppence for the critics' views.

Neither could Cassidy. He recorded the live game and sat down to watch it when he got home. He could see the point in some of the opinions but it wasn't going to be a source of grieving to him.

'At halftime I thought the pundits were terrible negative on us. We had spoken about that, and Jim has spoken a lot about it, and we don't really care. For years we have gone out and played good honest football and people have said

"Ah, they're [Donegal] decent, honest footballers." That's no good to you. You want to win a few games.'

The game had its own fascinations. Cunningham felt there had been information leaked somewhere from the Antrim camp.

'If you listened to their players afterwards in the interviews, they said how unbelievable McGuinness and Gallagher were in knowing exactly where our players were going to play, how they were going to play. They knew everything about us.

'I would say that comes from boys talking out of turn. It's a small enough world out there and loose talk like that spreads.'

Antrim's players were released to their clubs for a fortnight, before resuming training for a qualifier against an opponent they won't know for a full month upon their return. Cunningham is relishing the break. The team has gone stale and there's disillusionment there. He just wants to go back to having fun.

Donegal though know that their summer is only beginning. In the quiet of the dressing room when they sat on the benches, drained after their exertions, McGuinness told them that they could go to their clubs for the week but to keep themselves right for hard training on their return.

They can deal with that though. At least now they're off their knees.

CHAPTER TWENTY

An Air Of Inevitability

DERRY v FERMANAGH
First Round, Celtic Park, May 22

THE pain didn't come at the point of contact. He could feel something alright when he put his boot to the turf but nothing greater than a little prick, like sitting on a thumb tack. Yet Mickey Conlan knew.

He had to try another one. How else would he know? So he waited until the next kickout. The kicking tee was in his hand and he dribbled the ball out to the fourteen-yard line. The ball was placed on the pedestal and he took his steps back.

There was still a choice to be made. He could put his hand up and get a physio over. He could even try a short kickout and disguise the injury, get through it by playing a game of bluff. But he had to know it wasn't this same, irritating injury that always seemed to plague him halfway through the season for the last few years.

So he kicked the thing and put all his weight behind it. And then he let out a roar, the pain mingling with the frustration, the panic and the realisation that after everything, after putting his family, his work and his friendships on the backburner to wear the Derry colours and march behind the band on Championship day, it could all be taken away from him.

This wasn't the way the comeback was supposed to go.

• • •

Up to then life had been treating him very well from the time he'd jacked in the delivery job at the bakery to play county football. He was working three days a week for his brother-in-law Fintan Martin. It involved managing the office of Fintan's metal partitioning and suspended ceilings business, doing runs to the bank and driving workers to their various locations; a breeze really. It also left Thursday and Friday free to take some fitness classes and build up a client base for his new personal training business. Whenever he'd think about the gamble he'd taken, he'd smile and say to himself that he never wanted to see that bread van again.

With the benefit of proper rest, his reflexes and mind were sharper than ever. A clean sheet against Antrim was an encouraging end to the season, the kind of thing a goalkeeper needs before preparing for Championship. In the in-house games, he was lining up for the stronger selection. He was in pole position to play against Fermanagh in the Ulster Championship. Life was good.

Then a fortnight before Championship, they went for a weekend retreat, down to Dunboyne Castle Hotel.

After checking in on the Friday evening they went for a fitness test in the hotel gym. Conlan had worked on his stamina relentlessly throughout the winter and spring, pushing him up into mid-table among the squad, enough to be holding his own, certainly for a goalkeeper. The test was a rigorous assessment: incline treadmill running, the stationary bike, rowing machine, step-up tests, strength tests, sit-up tests, bench presses. It was an evening full of strain and grunts, but he was happy to do it and the results were good.

The following day, the team boarded the bus to Aughrim to face Wicklow in a challenge match. The journey was ninety minutes long and along the way Conlan began to stiffen up. By the time they pulled into the car park, he was glad to get out and stretch the legs. The team togged out, got their instructions from John Brennan, and the game commenced.

He was playing well and feeling even better. Then he kicked that ball out to the wing. And then he kicked out another ball, and that was it.

'I thought "Jesus Christ, not again!" The only thing I could think about was that I wouldn't be able to start against Fermanagh, after training hard all year.

'I get emotional about it. Especially when I'm on my own. You want to play at the highest level and then a wee thing like that can deprive you of it.'

When they got back to the hotel he called Paula and broke the news to her. She shared his disappointment but talked about how he was going to get it sorted, that he had to remain positive.

That evening as Conlan was applying the ice on the injury, a certain melancholy came over him. Meath legend Colm O'Rourke arrived in to give a talk to the squad. He told them he always felt Derry were blessed with skilful footballers but were serial underachievers. If you wanted success, he said, you had to commit everything to the pursuit of perfection. No half measures. Each man had to be ruthless with each other. If they felt a teammate wasn't putting in the required effort, he had to be told. Anything else was a waste of time.

O'Rourke was speaking from experience. He had soldiered with mediocre Meath teams for the first half of his career before success arrived. And for him it was candour as much as talent that delivered it.

With that advice ringing in his ears, Conlan took himself off to bed early with an icepack for company.

The following Tuesday evening one of the Derry physios, Anne Boylan, assessed Conlan's injury and diagnosed that he had a grade one tear.

He took a week off training altogether. The only thing to cure a muscle tear is rest, but in his mind, he couldn't rest, at least not for any longer.

On the Sunday morning, one week out from the Fermanagh match, Conlan was put through his paces by another physio, Conor Henry. It was all twists and turns but he got through it and thought 'Brilliant, I'm gonna make it.'

It would be on the Tuesday night that they'd would make a call on it.

'We went and done another tough training session in Celtic Park. At that stage Conor had me out and Dr Michael Logan was there too. After the session I had to finish up with some kicking and they were assessing me. After I hit about sixteen kickouts, the doctor said that I wasn't kicking it one hundred percent. I wasn't kicking it one hundred percent, but I was using my natural kick which I felt would have got me through the game.

'In my own head I was holding back a little. I was saying to myself that I would hold out until the Friday night and be passed to play at the last minute.'

That Friday night John Brennan called him aside. He wouldn't even be togging out.

'John was good because he laid his cards on the table. He said he had been speaking to the doctor and he'd felt that I'd been holding back. Whenever I'd got injured, John had called Barry Gillis back into the panel as cover, and now Barry was going to be his number two with Danny Devlin starting. He didn't want me going in and then putting my hand up after five or ten minutes, needing to be taken off. He said he hoped that I was okay about it but he just didn't want to take the risk.'

From being the likely number one for the start of the Championship, Conlan was now just one of three keepers fighting it out for the position. The most dramatic inter-county comeback of 2011 was on ice. Like his leg.

• • •

One man sure of his place at Celtic Park was Barry Owens.

The one and only time he had faced Derry in the Championship before was on a muggy and windy Saturday afternoon in Healy Park for the 2008 Ulster semi-final. He hadn't been long back with the Fermanagh panel after his heart operation, and after spending the first few weeks running on grass getting used to the air in his lungs again, he joined in with the games, wearing a luminous bib to warn teammates not to tackle him. A few lads got great craic out of it, saying they were going to bust him the next time he went for a ball, but he made progress rapidly. In no time the bib was gone.

He'd returned to a team and setup he barely recognised. Fermanagh had the ultra-organised Malachy O'Rourke in charge with Leo 'Dropsy' McBride as his drill sergeant. O'Rourke's former county teammate Paul Coyle was selector and Peter Leonard doubled up as another selector with a talent for sorting out logistics.

It was a player-friendly environment. They now had the benefit of multiple physios at training. They had a sports psychologist. When they arrived at training, their kit would be freshly laundered and laid out for them on their peg. All they had to bring were their football boots and the right attitude.

Two weeks before the semi-final, O'Rourke approached Owens with an unusual request. 'He just said "Look, we might try you at full forward. We don't expect you to do much running or whatever. Just hang in there, get the ball and lay it off."'

Derry had opened up a gap in the first half but four consecutive points led Fermanagh back into the light. They were still trailing though when Owens was sent onto the field in the fifty-third minute and to everyone's amazement, took up at full forward. Waiting to mark him was Kevin McCloy, the All Star full back from the previous year. Owens had won the award for that position in 2004 and 2006.

A minute later, a ball dropped short around the square and Owens ghosted in behind McCloy to fist to the net. Fermanagh were in front and three minutes later their force of nature for a captain, Marty McGrath, burst through to score a fine point. Fermanagh kept working manically and at the final whistle the pitch was invaded with delirious fans. For only the fourth time in the county's history, Fermanagh would play in the Ulster final.

All that though was three seasons back. When Owens looked around this particular Fermanagh dressing room, he couldn't see any of the men that did battle against Derry on that famous night. He was captaining a side of rookies and not necessarily the best young talent in the county either.

Recent challenge matches had given him some encouragement though. They drew with Leitrim. On a wet Wednesday night in Clones, they were seven points down to Monaghan at halftime and stormed their way to a draw by the finish. To Owens it showed what could be gained by going at the throat of your opponents.

Others weren't inclined to see it that way. His opposing captain in Clones was Dick Clerkin.

'It was worse than a bad in-house training game. We didn't play well and there were a lot of lads disinterested. Fermanagh in fairness kept going and got a draw out of it. It's no disrespect to Fermanagh, I would have fairly close links and good friends up there, but after that night I really feared for them going up to Derry.'

Clerkin spoke with John O'Neill after the game and could feel his exasperation. 'Jesus,' O'Neill remarked, 'that's another two half-backs we're down.'

Yet as much sympathy Clerkin had for the Fermanagh manager, he had even more for their captain.

'I feel awful sorry for Barry Owens. He's a super player and a role model, as honest as the day is long, and you can see he's still giving it his best. I know of other boys who put their name to that letter [from the disaffected players] who I wouldn't give tuppence for. Ten of them wouldn't be worth one Barry Owens. It's sad to see what's happening there.'

● ● ●

To stay with Derry, Fermanagh needed to turn the game into a dogfight. When Owens considered the personnel, he wasn't so sure that could be done.

'I don't think our lads can play that defensive style because they're all young and inexperienced. If things don't go well for them, the heads could drop, so we're as well going for it at the start.

'What would worry me is strength-wise, especially after losing Tommy, James, Shane McDermott not being there, big Seamy Quigley. That's a lot of big lads gone.

'He's [John O'Neill] on about bringing back the wing-half forwards when Derry have the ball to stop them and get a wall up in front of our defence of midfield, half-backs and half-forwards. We've been trying out these tactics since the last league match. I suppose he has watched a right few videos of Derry, how they play it, what they do, and how we can counteract it.

'If we're to beat Derry, it will be down to the like of Sean Quigley, Cecil [Daniel Kille], Ryan Jones. They'll be the three main men. If they all have a good day, we'll not be that far away. Cecil's not that young, but the rest of them are, and that's a lot of pressure on them.'

● ● ●

In every utterance he made, John Brennan played it cautious. Whenever the subject of their game against Fermanagh came up within the camp, his message was consistent. 'I'm fearing this match. We know nothing about Fermanagh. It's Championship football, they've nothing to lose, they're going to throw everything at us.' He extended the attitude to press interviews.

It struck the right note for Conlan. 'He was brutally honest in that he knew nothing about their players and that he thought they would pour every ounce of their body into the match. He never let his guard down at all in respect to Fermanagh. I was very impressed by that.'

For Conlan though it didn't feel like the weekend of a Championship match.

He didn't get that usual anxiety. His diet would normally be meticulous but it was an inch he was willing to concede now that he would spend the day on the bench.

'I had an Indian takeaway on Saturday evening. Normally I'd be checking my gloves to see if they were alright, seeing if my boots were alright. I would have all them ready to go on a Saturday evening.

'If I hadn't have picked up that injury, I'd have been out the back of the house, kicking the ball off the wall the way I do the day before big games. I imagine different things happening in a game. If I had a wee dummy to do I would practise it like mad so that when it comes to the game it's just something that comes natural to me. Changing feet, different wee things. Practising high balls and thinking whenever I get it what foot I should explode off. Sometimes out there I'd let a roar out of me. "MY BALL!" You could hear it down Scotstown Lane!'

But no one heard it that Saturday night.

He woke up on matchday and put on his Derry tracksuit. If he was going to get something out of the day, it would be a bit of physio treatment while the team were out doing their warmup, so he put on a pair of shorts underneath his bottoms.

Conleith Gilligan gave him a lift. Kevin McGuckin was already in the car. The three of them had started out all those years ago with the Ballinderry U-12s.

They met the team bus at the Oakleaf restaurant on the Glenshane Pass and had lunch before going to the Steelstown pitch for their warmup. Conlan stayed out of the dressing room while they got kitted out. As they filed out onto the field, he went inside to get his rub.

Once that was taken care of, he went outside to help the team goalkeeping coach Johnny Kelly put Danny Devlin and Barry Gillis through their routines. He had already spoken to Danny and given some advice in the week leading up to the game, telling him to treat it like any other game, to put everything out of his head and play his own game. They finished up, packed everything onto the bus and snaked their way through the narrow streets of Derry city to Celtic Park.

Some of the players went out to watch some of the minor match and sample the atmosphere. Conlan stayed with other panel members who hadn't made the matchday squad. As the rest of the team went into the dressing room, Conlan thought he'd leave it for ten minutes. When he went to enter, the door was already locked.

●　●　●

At 3.17pm, Barry Owens shook the hand of his Derry counterpart Mark Lynch and referee Joe McQuillan. It was Owens' thirty-eighth Championship appearance but his first time captaining Fermanagh for the first round of the Ulster Championship.

It felt anything but a Championship atmosphere, with an attendance of just 5,646. When both sides met in 2008, over 14,000 were present.

There were many reasons for the low figure. The recession in Ireland had decimated the disposable income of many families. An inflexible attitude to ticketing prices by the Ulster Council had also soured attitudes. Above all else, people knew this was a nothing game. Whereas before Fermanagh had been formidable first-round opposition, boasting the best first-day record in the entire province for the previous decade, this was only a shadow Fermanagh side playing, up against a Derry team that finally seemed to be all pulling in the one direction.

The crash could be seen even before the impact. When Derry came out to conduct their warm-up, cones were laid out in impressive patterns. Players fizzed about on the balls of their feet and looked hungry to get stuck in. Fermanagh's warmup was conducted at half-pace, casual and rudimentary. Players jogged in straight lines, turned, and joined the back of a slow-moving queue. They looked like they were winging it. Those players who walked away earlier in the year had felt the management were winging it all along.

At the throw-in, Cailean O'Boyle moved in to mark Owens. Terry O'Flanagan put Fermanagh ahead with a free. Within fifteen minutes though, the game was over as a contest.

A quick free released Eoin Bradley and he burned Michael Jones for pace. He headed directly to goal from an angle on the right side of the post, waiting for James McGrath to commit himself before threading it past. Owens was frantically sprinting back and dived at the shot, only to feel the ball whistle past his fingers on the way to the net. He was instantly switched onto Bradley.

Playing with a strong wind at their backs, Derry pressed on. With ten players taller than six foot compared to Fermanagh's two, they outmuscled and bullied their callow opponents. Mark Lynch, Sean Leo McGoldrick, Conleith Gilligan and Enda Muldoon were all hoisting their shots into the air, letting the breeze carry the ball over the bar.

Fermanagh's lack of a sweeper and their refusal to pack the defence was astonishing. By the end of the first quarter Derry were nine points up. By halftime they were 1-12 to 0-2 ahead, having hit eleven wides.

The second half would begin with another series of points for Derry before they mentally switched off without the stimulus of a challenge. Fermanagh had hit the crossbar twice in the first half and may have had a penalty call rejected, but there was a canyon between the standards of the sides. Derry coach John Brennan would later reflect on the nature of the game and say that it wasn't even up to the challenge of a training session.

'When you look back on it, you would think we definitely should have had a sweeper,' Barry Owens would reflect. 'But they were hitting it over from fifty, sixty yards; I dunno if a sweeper would have stopped that. It was very disheartening. Just after the goal they got four, five, six points in a row. When that happens, your confidence just goes completely.

'If it was a close match, I'd be pissed off for a few hours afterwards. But when you're beat as convincingly as we were, it's water off a duck's back at this stage.'

From his position on the bench, Mickey Conlan had a chance to judge the performance and he liked what he saw.

'All the players were on the same wavelength and it showed in the first-half performance. Once Eoin scored the goal, Derry began moving the ball well and playing well. Everything seemed slick.'

Owens and some of the Fermanagh players journeyed down the road to Enniskillen and stopped at Brewster Park for a few pints before heading up the town. In the past, The Corner Bar has been the scene of great celebration but on this night Owens, Chris Breen, Hughie Brady and Paul McCusker were hardly feted as heroes. He was hardly expecting it any other way.

The Derry side made their way from Celtic Park to Henry Downey's bar in Derry city for a meal. After that for Conlan it was off home to Paula and the kids.

An unsatisfying game and an unsatisfactory day was at last drawing to a close.

CHAPTER TWENTY-ONE

Ambush

ARMAGH v DOWN

First Round, Athletic Grounds, May 28

THE game between Antrim and Donegal had been pulled apart and over-analysed. The Derry walkover was not even worthy of further comment. Even before the Celtic Park match, the usual arguments were aired by commentators weary from the lack of razzmatazz in the opening weeks.

Immediately after the first game, Martin McHugh offered his solution. 'Take the Armagh-Down Ulster game to headquarters with, say Laois v Offaly and have a big double-bill Championship Sunday in Dublin to get things going.'

That was the clever thing to do, but in the conservative world of Ulster GAA, it was only wishful thinking. The game would be played in The Athletic Grounds.

Armagh were delighted with the draw, and the unfamiliar role of underdog suited them. They would be hosting their first Ulster Championship game in sixteen years and they had the All Ireland finalists coming to town. Tactical football would have a part in it, but it would mainly be about who wanted it more.

The BBC Championship coverage for this game milked the history of the fixture. They opened the programme with some footage of past encounters and some contributions from past protagonists. Barney Carr, Down's coach when they brought Sam Maguire north in the 1960s, captured the essence of the rivalry. 'We always had that sense that every time we met them, it was a local derby.'

The footage cut to scenes of hard tackling; of busted noses and snarled threats; games played in grounds that had grassy banks and crowds not afraid to sneak a few bottles of beer in with them.

One clip was of a famous incident from the 1999 Ulster final between the two teams, when Down's wing-forward Ross Carr raised his hands and shoved Armagh manager Brian Canavan in the face over a disputed line ball. Ross then appeared onscreen. 'The real rivalry is south Down and south Armagh. The melting pot is in Newry.'

Oisín McConville was the next talking head. 'It's harum-scarum when it comes to Armagh-Down fixtures. When I first started playing with Armagh, people used to say to me that it doesn't matter if you win another game as long as you beat Down.'

As the coverage ramped up as throw-in time approached, clips of supporters arriving at the Athletic Grounds were screened. One gentleman in his Armagh colours said he was a Manchester United fan but he was taping their Champions

League final against Barcelona, because 'I have to see my nephew scoring 1-6 here tonight.' The BBC correspondent asked him who was his nephew and he replied, 'Stevie McDonnell.'

Sitting in co-commentary for the BBC, Tyrone legend Peter Canavan set the tone for what was to unfold when he said, 'This is where the Championship really starts.'

● ● ●

Twenty years ago, Aidan Carr's father Ross was at a crossroads with his football. The previous summer had been a write-off. He played in a drawn Ulster Championship game against Armagh, was dropped for the replay and left off the county squad for the 1991 national league.

He went back to basics with his club, Clonduff. Frank Dawson had finished up with the Down hurlers and took over as coach. Carr reacted favourably to the new regime. He rediscovered a bit of form and more importantly, the appetite for the game.

Following up some scouting reports, the Down management team of Pete McGrath and John Murphy checked him out in a county league game. After liking what they saw, they invited him to rejoin the Down panel. Their first-round Championship game against Armagh was a month away.

There was no need to twist his arm. Down was unfinished business and he wanted to give it a serious lash. 'Even at that early stage, listening to Pete and John, they had a definite design on the summer, on the Championship game, but they definitely exaggerated the passion that was among the players. The first night I went to training, twelve people trained. There was also about seven or eight there with injuries, but there wasn't twenty-five or there wasn't thirty. When we got to the All Ireland final, we needed two changing rooms to hold the players that were on the panel.'

McGrath had played a confidence trick on Carr but he was back for good. They beat Armagh at Newry, in a game impossible to draw any other positives from. But it was only the start for the team and they would finish the year as All Ireland champions and bridge a gap back to 1968.

Alongside the McCartans, the Carr family tree is considered royalty in Down football. Ross's uncle Barney was the manager of the county team when they made the breakthrough in the '60s. His brother Aidan was on the county panel that won the All Ireland junior title of 1946.

He played with other brothers Hugh and Gerry on the Warrenpoint team, but when he met and married Rosemary Bradley, he moved out to 'the country' and settled in the sheep farming community of Hilltown. The Bradley family kept a newsagents shop on the Main Street until the 1950s and the building is now the house where Aidan's son Ross and Theresa Carr are bringing up their family.

'Where we grew up,' says Ross, 'we were brought up with everything that is GAA. Daddy and all his brothers playing for Down, my uncle Barney managing the '60s team. Then mummy's brothers, the Bradleys, all played for Clonduff here. It was just a GAA house.'

When he broke onto the Clonduff senior team, he had to change. The Down players were his heroes, none more so than Colm McAlarney, but now they were pushing him around the field.

'You went from being in awe of them to actually playing on the same pitch as them. It was phenomenal. At the same time at home you were never under any pressure to be the best you could be or to outdo somebody else. It was just... you weren't going to be doing anything else. It's like it was in your DNA.'

Ross passed the same DNA on to his son, whom he christened Aidan. Towards the end of his time on the field, Ross got to play on a team alongside his son. It's something he cherishes but he wishes it had been crowned with a county title.

'It cracked me up that I couldn't win a championship with him. By 2002 I knew we wouldn't. We'd won a championship in 2000 with the backbone of the team being all minors but they had won everything along the way up so by the time they won a senior championship they felt they had nothing else to prove. The age gap was too great for me to have an influence. I couldn't relate to them.

'There was one particular game against a local club team down here in which we had been winning by four or five points at halftime and we ended up getting well beat. We were doing the warmdown and my head at this stage was buzzing, I didn't have a good game into the bargain. And three or four of the young boys were talking about meeting each other up the street in five minutes, or going to play pool or whatever it was. It just got to me and I let a volley of abuse at them.

'Then I went to training on Sunday morning and knew after that day I wouldn't be back. What I didn't want to happen was fall out with Aidan's friends. It's alright if you're shouting and roaring at footballers, but if you're effin' and blinding at your kid's friends, telling them "If you're gonna carry on like that get the fuck up the road..." That was the reasoning for it.'

● ● ●

Ross Carr would become Down manager but it was a fraught path. Pete McGrath had paid for keeping faith in Ross's generation for too long. Paddy O'Rourke was Ross's captain in 1991 and he had his turn as manager but as ever in Ulster football, it ended badly.

'Paddy was one of the reasons that we won All Irelands in the '90s. He was a phenomenal leader. I was watching a documentary recently and they were talking about Franz Beckenbauer being the manager's lieutenant on the field for West Germany. That's what Paddy was for us.

'When Paddy's time as county manager was over, the county chairman and secretary and treasurer at the time asked me if I would be interested in taking over. DJ Kane and I had to make sure that Paddy was okay with us taking on the job. We probably took it because we felt at that particular time that players weren't respecting the Down jersey the way it should be respected. We wanted to straighten it out a wee bit. Now, that was a wee bit naïve too, because you go in with a preconception of what you will do, and that it will all be great and grand and four All Irelands later...'

He was aware that at some stage he would be handing his son his starting Championship inter-county debut. Accusations of nepotism always dog county managers that play their relatives.

'Mickey and Mark Harte got it and Mark suffered from it. Apart from one or two games, Mark was scoring consistently. We played an Errigal Ciarán team in Newry in 2000 in the first round of the Ulster club championship and it was Mark Harte who scored the goal that beat us.

'Mark suffered because of people using it as an excuse to get at somebody. We have all got to understand that the average pundit hasn't got a clue about what goes on or what's required to play county football. A lot of them go to games, they never attend training sessions, they don't see performances in club matches, so you have to take it with a pinch of salt.'

The promise that Aidan's group had shown when Ross was their minor manager was sufficient temptation. He knew the job would take time but he was willing to stay in for the long haul.

In Ulster football though, nobody gets to stay in for the long-haul without trophies. Carr might have masterminded the demise of Tyrone in the 2008 Ulster Championship the same year Mickey Harte's team went on to win the All Ireland but a year later he was out of favour.

'In hindsight, we did some things wrong, some huge mistakes. To this day, my biggest regret, and I will take it to the grave, is that Aidan should have started against Wicklow in the qualifying game [in 2009]. He got suspended after the Fermanagh game up in Brewster Park. He missed the first qualifying game but came on against Laois for Paul Murphy and had a great game.

'We were out a fortnight later and I should have backed my instincts. Maybe it was because we were suffering so much for picking Aidan, but Aidan was the best half-back we had at that time, bar none. His performances in training and everything, he should have got playing. And had he have been playing, we would have won. That, to me, is my biggest regret – not from a father's point of view, but from a manager's point of view. I let a player down because of an emotional decision, which I hadn't done before, and that will haunt me for a while. Hopefully, Aidan won't hold it against me for as long as I will hold it against myself.'

After the Wicklow defeat, Ross and DJ were living on borrowed time as a management duo.

'We didn't leave the job, we were pushed, and that's where it became bitter. We'd felt that we had been asked to do a job and then not given the time to do it. In fairness, the people who asked us to do the job were equally shafted three months into our appointment.

'A new county board came in with their own designs on how things should be done, and from the very outset it wasn't a case of if we were going to be pushed, it was when.

'Once I got over the disappointment and the anger of how it was handled, I would be very philosophical about the whole thing. You know as soon as you take it that the chances of it ending successfully are very slight.

'Every other county in Ireland are trying to win a provincial or the All Ireland title but how many have a realistic chance? In 2006 when we took over, how many teams had a realistic chance of winning an All Ireland? Three or four?

'It was the manner in the way it ended that hurt us and angered us a lot, given the service we had given. That's not to blow smoke up our own asses or anything but we know what we did for Down, as part of a unit. We knew the sacrifices as a management team that we as families gave.

'Certain things happen that you catch yourself on. If you keep being that bitter, the only people that suffer are the people that feel the bitterness. The people who you think done you wrong, they don't think about it, so you just catch yourself on and get on with it.'

In 2010, under new manager James McCartan, Down pulled off the unexpected and went on a helter-skelter run through the qualifier series all the way to the All Ireland final. Ross sat in the stands and watched Down play but there was a sickening feeling that his son Aidan was unable to force himself onto the team with injury holding him back.

'Last year, when Down were going well, of course I wanted Down to win, I wanted Down to win the All Ireland, but it was very frustrating. I tried to remain impartial from being the father of a player to what a manager would be looking for. But I was under no illusion that in our campaigns, Aidan was in the top five half-backs in Ireland. I don't think I was being clouded in that judgement because he was picked to go and play for Ulster. Sean Boylan picked him to go to the Irish International Rules trials and put him on standby to go to Australia.

'I remember during last year, meeting other managers at functions, notable ones such as Jack O'Connor and John Evans and them asking me what the story was with Aidan, why he wasn't figuring? Anthony Tohill asked the same. That gave us a bit of comfort, that how highly I rated Aidan wasn't just a doting dad syndrome, it was a fair judgement.

'I think it was very difficult for Aidan to enjoy the campaign, knowing what the family went through the previous year, and to his eternal credit, he was very disciplined and very committed to the Down cause. But it was bittersweet for the family.'

• • •

This season, Ross got back into management, helping out with the Clonduff senior camogie team. He played a bit of hurling himself in his youth, though he's not claiming to have been much good.

'I'm not sure you could call it hurling. It was a bastardised version, a mixture of everything, but it was great fun back in the early '80s. We won a junior version or something like that. I think I played in three hurling finals and used the stick once. I kicked it every time I got it. There's actually a photograph of me playing and you would think I was cutting thistles!'

The new role means he gets to spend a lot of time with his daughters, Fionnuala and Sarah-Louise.

In the football world, he remains frustrated. Watching Aidan this year has him feeling that his son has been taken for granted, that his talents are going to waste.

'I'd be annoyed from a father's point of view that he's not getting a run. I think he has been abused in terms of not been given a chance. I'm not saying this from a father's point of view but from a pure football point of view, I cannot for the life of me understand how he is not getting a game. Obviously last year while it was difficult, Aidan's fitness wouldn't have let him come in and play at the level Down were playing at.

'This year is totally different. Aidan knows what was being asked of him in games, to rectify what areas of improvement he needed to work on, and I saw him in the McKenna Cup games, and he was Down's best player in those games.

'The management said they were going to give everybody a chance to get themselves involved this year. They knew after last year that they needed to look at new positions and new players, to find extra options. But it's been bullshit, because they haven't. They've given him just five or ten minute cameo roles.

'I understand that managers see players in a different light. Like the old saying, doctors differ, patients die. But you can't have gone from being one of the best half-backs in Ireland two or three years ago to being not even in the top twenty-four in your own county. It's just not right, given the performances of people who've been given numerous opportunities.

'Personally, and myself and Theresa have talked about it, I would sacrifice both my All Ireland medals to see Aidan winning an All Ireland medal. I know the joy it brings.'

●　●　●

The year started brightly enough for Aidan. He got two full games in the Dr McKenna Cup, and while he was disappointed with how he went against Antrim, he felt better about his performance a few days later against Armagh. His first target for the year was to keep injury-free but that has been the easy part. He hasn't missed a single training session and has looked after himself, getting his hamstrings rubbed out regularly.

In the league, he was an unused sub against Mayo on the opening day. Against Galway he appeared as a sub with twelve minutes to go. His play was rushed and looking back he feels his performance probably justified the management's decision not to play him.

Armagh were up next but he never got on. He got eight minutes to impress against Cork, and the last three minutes against Monaghan. Despite chipping in with a point, he found himself an unused substitute again against Dublin.

The day of the Dublin game, Carr missed out on a club match. He felt it would have been more beneficial to him to have a game under his belt. His patience wore thin. He was named on the matchday squad to play Kerry in Killarney on the closing day of the league, but he approached the manager James McCartan and asked if he could be excused.

'I had said to James during the week of the Kerry game that if I wasn't going to be involved, I would rather stay at home and train with the club. Karma working out the way it did, Kalum [King] got taken off in the first half and I could have been with a shout. And the club had nothing on, so I ended up just training by myself. That has probably gone against me as well.

'It was a hard conversation to have with James. One of my best friends, Finbarr McConville, got married that day and I was groomsman. I made a call, I had a great day at the wedding, but I had no drink or anything while all the rest of the boys were having the craic. They were drinking shots and all that. I didn't do it because I didn't want to be seen, with Down having a match and me drinking.

'It left me thinking, if I had have went to Kerry, it might have been me that they brought on for Kalum and I would have had more than a full half. I can see why the management would look at it a different way, not going to a national league game.

'That's not how I feel at all, but there can be an impression that I did. I had reached the point where I was going to Kerry on a Saturday afternoon, travelling five or six hours. And on a Sunday, going by the previous weeks, I was going to get five or six minutes. At that stage I just wasn't happy to do that.'

As the league went on, it had become apparent that Carr's face just doesn't fit. Throughout the year, the Down management of James McCartan, Brian McIver, Jerome Johnston and Paddy Tally met with each player individually for an exchange of views. Carr had his after the first game of the season.

'After that chat it made me very happy because I worked on a lot of stuff that James had asked me to. My off-the-ball work, tackling off the ball, chasing, pushing off, and cutting out what they call the 'impossible pass' all the time; the outside of the boot or the crossfield pass. It's probably always my first option whenever I could pop the ball ten yards in front of me and then go ahead.

'They're looking for a certain style. Hard-working players, definitely. Possibly I'm not at that level. I don't think I'm lazy. It's probably a subconscious thing; my first reaction is to stop a player going past me, so I'll not push up that tight on him and sell myself short that he loses me in the turn. They like pressure, pressure, pressure, they're very like how Pep Guardiola has Barcelona. They want the forwards to put pressure on to win the ball back. I would never have really done that before, so it's just probably changing or adapting to do that as well.'

He has worked on the elements they wanted to see improvements on, and during recent weeks he was pushing strongly for inclusion with his performances in challenge matches.

In one week alone, Down played Cavan, Offaly and Louth. He started against Cavan as a wing-forward but it was his substitute appearance against Offaly that really encouraged him. He only got fifteen minutes as a third midfielder but managed to kick a goal and two points.

It pushed him into the team for the Louth game, where he started at centre-forward at the Abbey Christian Brothers' pitch. Again though, like the Galway league match, it took him time to relax into it.

'It was an absolutely horrible start. Everything I tried went wrong. It got so bad, I was considering walking off. The first ball I got I went to hit a short pass and it was cut out. Next ball was a sideline, I went to hit it back to the keeper and put it out for a fifty. The next two kicks I got I gave it away.

'I knew that it was a turning point, because some fellas who'd be regulars on the team and had been injured were coming back to full fitness. James had said to me before the match that he needed another big one out of me. I kinda put myself under too much pressure at the start. James and Brian said to me after that they were actually feeling sorry for me after the start I had.'

Despite that terrible opening period, Aidan settled himself and finished strongly, hitting five points. A fortnight later though Down played Limerick and he only got ten minutes. Injured players such as Declan Rooney, Kalum King, Danny Hughes and Martin Clarke all came back in and he was squeezed out.

'It kind of knocks your confidence a bit, to see that they're putting out a strong team and you're not on it. And then, to only get ten minutes, it's very frustrating.'

It's tempting to say that playing for Down is his birthright, and while he knows it doesn't work like that, it hurts that he finds himself where he is. For now the squad morale draws him back night after night.

'I really want to play for Down. Growing up, I was always going to training with Daddy and they were successful at that time. I grew up knowing a lot of people that were heroes all over Ireland and they knew me by my first name. I loved it. I remember whenever the training was over I could hit shots against Neil Collins or Mickey McVeigh.

'I would have spent a lot of time with Damian Watson, who was the waterboy back then, and is still with us now, so I would bring water to players, collect balls... From no age, I wanted to be a Down footballer. To opt out of that, would be very, very hard. While I'm there, there's always a chance. It could be because you're really forcing it, or it could be that it falls on your lap.'

His father admits he can't see the sense in the situation. 'We're pretty philosophical as a family. We understand that good and bad and things can happen, but Aidan's an incredible person, outside of football. He's become an incredible man, an incredible son and brother. The people in here think the world of him. So when he goes outside into his life, we know the qualities he can bring, whether it be work, or sport or whatever. I know, that he's an asset to Down. Everybody I talk to knows that he is an asset to Down.

'So why is he not playing? He's one of the best footballers in Down. In his position, I don't think there are three better half-backs. I know he feels he can play centre-half forward. Mark Poland has done a remarkable job there but Aidan gives Down something there that Mark doesn't give them in being a physical presence. Down are lacking mobility in the middle of the field which will sooner or later come against them and which Aidan can give them. So from a football point of view I cannot understand his exclusion. But I can't come up with the answers. Only the managers can come up with the answers.

'It's difficult for us as a family to sit and watch what, to us, feels an incredible injustice. It's totally unexplainable to me and all we hope for is that his perseverance and application will get rewarded.

'It's a huge decision for Aidan to make here. Does he go along as a journeyman, or does he say "No, that's enough for me"? The hardest thing to do is to keep going to training and having to prove to yourself that you're good enough. It's obvious the management don't rate him.

"What should they do? They should cut him loose, tell him "You're not in our plans.""

The most pressing concern at this stage is whether Aidan will be named on the matchday panel for the Armagh game. At this point he's not even sure of that.

'I hope I'm in the panel. If you're not going to make the first fifteen, you hope that you're one of the players that they will turn to, should they need you. It's a surreal feeling because whenever you think of Championship you get caught up in the emotion and the excitement. Down versus Armagh in the Athletic Grounds; you're hoping it's a good evening, that the weather is good, conditions are perfect. And then you get a reality check and realise that there's quite a possibility that you'll spend most your time sitting watching it.

'I find it very hard to sit and watch. Going into games knowing you're in there from the start, flying fit and have a real chance to dictate what happens in a game, you just go out and thrive in it. But sitting and watching it, you can become over-critical of what happens on the pitch and you get lost in the emotion of it; you see things that you don't see when you're on the pitch.

'When you're on the pitch you don't get carried away because you have a job to do and you just go and do it. On the sideline, you have time to think that five minutes ago we were on top and now we've hit three wides or the referee's not giving us anything. You worry about all that and get sidetracked a bit.'

He had enough experience of going out as a sub the year before and he doesn't want the embarrassment any longer.

'When it comes to match day there's a divide. The team go out, then they parade around the pitch, subs go behind the goals to kick the balls out... It's then that you really notice it. It's shit.'

• • •

Across the border, Armagh lay in camouflage. The consensus was that Armagh were going badly. Analysis in print and from commentators all spoke of rows in the camp and player discontent with the management.

Yet, in recent weeks, the panel had become a close unit. A link to the past had been re-established. Oisín McConville was brought into the setup to act as forwards coach, and Paul McGrane was back to work with the midfielders. It was becoming just like old times for Stevie McDonnell.

If any team had a disruptive run-in to the game, it was Down. The press box at the Athletic Grounds hummed with chat about Martin Clarke leaving in three days' time to sign a rolling option for Collingwood to retain his registration. It was the worst-kept secret in Ulster that Clarke was intending to return to Australia. In the weeks leading up to the game, Clarke's focus was derailed on a couple of occasions, with lapses of discipline going unpunished by management. Fringe players of the Down panel became increasingly exasperated by the kid-gloves treatment of their brightest star.

The omens were promising for Armagh. It was a wet evening and the rain would not abate. Down had a habit of playing poorly in the rain in recent years. They ran out in their tracksuit tops; Armagh emerged with just their jerseys on. It was clear that they meant business.

After five minutes the game had yet to take on a pattern. Down had successfully converted two frees before Armagh's Malachy Mackin kicked a lineball across to Charlie Vernon who sent it in the direction of Stevie McDonnell.

Unknown to everyone outside the Armagh camp, McDonnell hadn't trained for three weeks with a pubic bone injury. Hard ground at this time of year can harm him, and when it starts to hurt, the only thing to cure it is rest. He could have continued to train but the danger is that the condition can develop into osteitis pubis.

His familiar opponent Dan Gordon was onto the ball first and took it at chest height. Gordon went to handpass it to Kevin McKernan but Micheál O'Rourke got the slightest touch to it. Tony Kernan collected the ball and released it to Kieran Toner, who laid off to the onrushing Ciaran McKeever. His shot was blocked by Martin Clarke but the ball continued into Tony Kernan. Kernan had his back to the goal but gave a beautiful reverse pass to Jamie Clarke, the silky Armagh forward with the mop of Bob Dylan curls and an eye for goal. Clarke stroked it to the net and the Athletic Grounds erupted.

Already alarm bells were ringing for Down. Picking up Clarke was James McCartan's brother Daniel. While he may be blessed with a big heart, this match-up would be a risk. On nine minutes, O'Rourke found Clarke with a searching ball and Clarke skipped past a challenge before pointing.

Two minutes later then McCartan fouled Clarke, allowing Stevie McDonnell to step up and stroke the free over. When Aaron Kernan stretched the Armagh lead to six points on nineteen minutes, Down were drowning.

Martin Clarke picked up a loose ball in midfield with Ciaran McKeever tight to him. Clarke flighted the ball down the left touchline to Benny Coulter. He checked inside full-back Brendan Donaghy and laid the ball off to the sprite-like Mark Poland. He turned outside and inside in an instant, beating Kevin Dyas and wrong-footing Donaghy, before dropping the ball onto his left foot and slotted it to the net for what would be considered one of the goals of the Championship. With its awareness, balance and agility, it almost rivalled anything Lionel Messi would produce in the Champions League final taking place at the same time in Wembley.

Aidan Carr was there in the flesh watching Messi. When the Down team was announced after training after the Thursday night session, he wasn't even included in the subs. He couldn't bear to be so close to the action and yet so removed. So he booked his flight that evening. A ticket was sourced for him and he went to London for his Saturday night.

Sitting in the crowd of 87,695, Carr could almost drool as the Little Flea and his Barca teammates out-passed Man United and strolled to their win. Or what he watched of it. Half the time, he was sitting looking on his phone at the live score updates on the BBC Northern Ireland website. It was good to be at Wembley; but he was only distracting himself from the pain of not having a say in Armagh. What made it worse was the way that Armagh scores dominated the updates.

Down may have halted the rot but Armagh were irresistible. Malachy Mackin hit a point and James McCartan had to make a change. He withdrew full-forward John Clarke and put in Conor Maginn. As the half drew to a close, Down forced their way back into the reckoning with some strong running from sub Maginn. The halftime score was Armagh 1-8 Down 1-6.

At halftime the 13,107 crowd buzzed with anticipation. In the revamped stadium, spectators were packed incredibly tight against the sideline, making the pitch a hothouse of pressure and tension. Peter Canavan wasn't wrong, the Championship was finally truly here.

Down dominated the opening ten minutes of the second half, an excellent Martin Clarke free nosing them in front for the first time. Armagh hadn't scored in twenty minutes and all the momentum seemed to be with Down.

Then Aaron Kernan led the Armagh revival by stroking over a free. Shortly after, McDonnell and Jamie Clarke combined for a point and Armagh were in the lead again.

From the kickout Down engineered a goal chance for Benny Coulter but just as Coulter was about to unleash a piledriver, his marker Brendan Donaghy got back and gave him a little nudge in the back. Coulter lost his balance and hit the ball with his shin. Goalkeeper Hearty collected it comfortably. A minute later, James McCartan surprisingly took Coulter off.

Armagh now had the momentum and tagged on points from Tony Kernan, Mackin and Billy Joe Padden. The television cameras focused on the Down management team of McCartan, Paddy Tally and Jerome Johnston in heated debate along the sideline with some five minutes left. Aaron Kernan added another score to leave five points in it with just a couple of minutes to go.

With nothing to lose, Down rolled the dice again. Dan McCartan found himself in an attacking position and fisted the ball across the face of the goal towards a charging herd of Mourne forwards. Brendan Donaghy fisted it away but only as far as Kevin McKernan. His shot was bound for the bottom corner but Paul Duffy spread his body in front of it. The ball hit off his thighs and amazingly trickled wide. Hearty swallowed Duffy up in a bearhug. On the line, James McCartan sank to his knees and put his hands on his head in disbelief.

The resultant '45 was floated in by Martin Clarke but Charlie Vernon caught it. The referee blew his whistle. Down, All Ireland finalists of 2010, had been ambushed and were out of the Championship after just one game.

Paddy O'Rourke, a Down man to his marrow, remained a picture of serenity at the final whistle.

While the television crews whisked O'Rourke off for interviews, Stevie McDonnell gathered all the Armagh players into a huddle. He spoke clearly and forcefully, telling the players to forget about Down, that chapter was over. From now on, their focus had to be on Derry.

Their unified display had shocked and surprised many who were waiting to see Armagh fall apart. Just where had it come from?

'There has been a lot of talk about discontent and shite like this, within the camp, and people looking for the manager out and all this, but it couldn't be further from the truth,' says McDonnell. 'It showed out there. At this time of year there are rumours going around about every team. Down are no different but there are a lot of them going around about Down at the minute. That game showed they weren't united.'

In years past, Armagh would have been addressed by Kieran McGeeney. His message was always simple but delivered with frightening intensity. McDonnell had gauged the mood over the last few weeks and didn't see rallying calls as necessary.

'I knew, with the attitude of boys in training in the last few weeks, we were going to do it. Sometimes you don't have to say too much to players because you just know by their attitude and their body language.

'Fair enough, people weren't giving us any chance. They were maybe judging that on what they seen during the league. But there's a big step up from the league to Championship football. We were without the Crossmaglen contingent for the majority of the league, and you look what Aaron Kernan, Tony Kernan, Paul Hearty and Jamie done to that team; they make a huge difference. We are certainly well up for it and I knew there was no way going into that game we were going to lose that match. Our focus was on Down, nobody else, and that was it.

'We wanted that game more. Down did a bit of speaking about winning an Ulster title. They weren't winning an Ulster title off our back. That was a guarantee.'

Once the talking was over, they headed into the dressing rooms with the cheers of the crowd ringing in their ears. It had been a long time since they had felt that love from their own. Armagh were back.

McDonnell couldn't leave the ground straight away. Man of the Match Billy Joe Padden had been selected for random drug testing. They had travelled to the game together so instead of dashing off with the rest of the group, the captain waited for their Mayo import for two hours while he tried unsuccessfully to urinate. From such a high to a humiliating exercise was Padden's lot.

• • •

First thing on Sunday morning, Stevie McDonnell went to the swimming pool for a recovery session. Ciaran McKeever was already in it doing his stretching exercises, draining the lactic acid from his legs.

McDonnell is captain of the team and McKeever is vice-captain. As far as they were concerned, it was straight down to business.

'We have to be responsible now. We're county footballers and we've done a lot of work to get ourselves in the position we are in now, a great position, because even still, nobody's expecting anything from us.

'We have no time to waste, just three weeks to prepare ourselves as individuals and as a team. That time will fly and if we're not fully focused, we'll be caught on the hop.

• • •

The Saturday night had ended for McDonnell driving back with Padden to Newry, two Liverpool fans delighted that Man United had got their comeuppance. Aidan Carr sat in Wembley a dejected United fan watching the trophy presentation, before idling back to an apartment owned by his company.

As McDonnell and McKeever stretched their muscles and looked forward to the summer stretching out in front of them, Carr sat in the departures lounge in Gatwick Airport waiting for a flight home, wondering where exactly his career for Down had gone. He would be back at the next training, having to prove a point to himself, all over again.

CHAPTER TWENTY-TWO

'I'll Try Not To Let You Down...'

TYRONE v MONAGHAN
First Round, Omagh, June 5

ON Friday evening, May 20, Dick Clerkin was going through his usual warmup routine on the pitch at Parnell Park. Most challenge matches at this time of the year normally fall into two categories: a club pitch opening that usually involves a lot of waiting around while the local clergy bless the field, or the experimental type played behind closed doors.

This was against Dublin though, so it was always going to be different. There was a crowd there. There were photographers dotted along the sidelines. It mattered.

In that quiet and understated manner of his, Eamonn McEneaney approached Clerkin and took him to one side. 'Dick, I'm going to give you the nod for the captaincy this year.' It took a moment for it to sink in and then Clerkin responded. 'Listen, thanks very much. I'll try not to let you down.' Job done, McEneaney marched off to speak with others.

After a long week at work it was some tonic. He didn't get emotional straightaway but one of the first people he thought about was his father. Hugo Clerkin had held the county captaincy himself and Dick knew just how proud he would be.

During the league, the manager played a wait-and-see game, rotating the captaincy between senior players like Paul Finlay, Conor McManus, Darren Hughes and Dessie Mone. Clerkin had it for the Cork and Kerry games and while he was hopeful of retaining it for Championship, he was given no indication that he would.

In Gaelic football there isn't the same fuss surrounding the captaincy as there is in other sports. Most accept the job and try to lead by example. Some can immortalise themselves in the role. Any retrospective look at Kieran McGeeney's career is impossible without picturing him as the man who led Armagh into so many battles. When Peter Canavan lifted Sam Maguire in 2003, every neutral in the country was delighted that he had the privilege as captain.

Most of the time the captaincy is more about leading by deed than utterance. Anybody can be captain of a team, but those who come to be regarded as good at the role are the ones who have constantly backed themselves to do the right thing in the heat of battle.

Damian Freeman had been a sterling Monaghan captain for the previous three years. Vinny Corey held the role for the three years before that. Sometimes Clerkin felt a tinge of frustration that perhaps the honour was not shared out more often.

The Monaghan side went back into the dressing rooms for the final talk when the manager addressed them, breaking the news. The team broke into a spontaneous round of applause. Some got up to shake his hand. There was a caveat to the captaincy though.

'He said that he was giving it to me because he had been concerned about things. Our tackle count wasn't as good as it needed to be. He said "I'm going to be naming you captain but I'm putting the gun to your head for leadership in this regard. I want you to set the standard in terms of workrate, tackling and that's where you're going to show your leadership, because we're missing that."

'In fairness I maybe hadn't worked as hard in some of the games. It's something that I had to bring back into my game. Eamonn probably realised that, as well as rewarding me with the captaincy for time served.'

McEneaney told all his players that he expected at least six tackles over the next hour from each of them. When they reported back to the dressing room at halftime, the statistics had it that Clerkin had already made thirteen tackles. You could nearly hear from the stands his heart beat with pride.

• • •

The week before they opened their Championship campaign, Tyrone embarked on their traditional weekend retreat. There was a lot of work to do before they would play Monaghan.

They met at the Westenra Hotel, Monaghan, by 5.30 on the Friday evening. On the team coach Cathal McCarron was banned from picking the videos after the fiasco of the previous weekend away and his choice of Jackass. The task was passed to Joe McMahon.

That McMahon was there was a minor miracle. Six weeks earlier he had been playing for Omagh St Enda's in a league game when an opponent struck him off the ball, breaking his jaw and knocking out a number of his teeth. By the time of this trip though, McMahon was already back training with the county squad. His fast recovery drew admiration from Ryan McMenamin. 'He looks in good shape. Maybe the two weeks sipping soup through a straw helped the big guy! He just needs now to work on his match fitness and that will come.'

They were heading for the Castleknock Hotel, hardly unfamiliar territory for the squad. Friday night was pretty relaxed but the work started with a training session on the Saturday morning. Anyone who was not able to take part in full training went to the gym for a supervised session.

Later they had a strategy meeting and discussed Monaghan, what they were likely to do and how they could short-circuit it. Afterwards Mickey Harte left the players to their own devices which meant an evening of Champion's League final football or the Armagh game with Down. When the Tyrone team came to organise a sweepstake, they eschewed the action in Wembley for the Ulster Championship.

'We normally would go away the weekend before our first Championship game. It gets the heads right. We got a good weekend's work done. We got on top of the niggly injuries. A lot of the boys were getting rubs. I think the physios probably worked the hardest of all of us.'

A lot has been made of the collective age of this Tyrone team. Philip Jordan had flirted with the thought of retirement, even skipping a couple of sessions, but he was tempted back. Given the dedication of the players, it was no surprise that they had stuck to the stretching programme that Ger Hartmann had devised for them over the Limerick weekend during the league. As a man with plenty of miles on the clock, McMenamin can feel the benefits.

'I would have stuck to the routines, getting it done about three or four times a week, and on the days of a game, once or twice that morning. You use a bit of rope to stretch your legs. There's no wild science behind it, but it's helped Brian Dooher a lot, given him more flexibility. It's probably a good help psychologically as well.

'It's one of those things that you always think as a younger man "Aye, it would be a good thing to do" but you never actually do. You always think you'll never need it. If you could go back again you would do things differently, like learning to take frees off the ground!'

The rest of the week they stuck with their trusted methods. They met on Tuesday and Thursday for training and gathered at Kelly's Inn for a video analysis session on Saturday morning, focusing on the new players and new emphasis of play Eamonn McEneaney had introduced to Monaghan.

McMenamin left knowing that he was playing centre-back. While he is assured in this position at club level, it hasn't been a place he has played much for Tyrone.

'Whenever you play on the Tyrone team, you have to be prepared to play anywhere. Mickey expects that if you're picked corner back you will play corner back, and if you're picked centre half you will play centre half. It's probably been the strength of Tyrone down through the years that players can play in different positions.'

That night McMenamin slept soundly, knowing all angles were covered.

• • •

On Saturday evening, Monaghan had their team meeting in Dermot McArdle's bowling alley in Castleblaney. The side named by Mickey Harte had a couple of surprises, so they needed to get their heads around a few things.

Clerkin had thought he might be on Kevin Hughes which would have suited him. He had unfinished business left over from the 2010 Ulster final when he had let himself be bullied out of it. But Hughes was on the bench, so Clerkin would be tracking Sean Cavanagh.

Their pre-Championship preparations had been different. After the league they had played five challenge games. On the way home from playing Sligo, they stopped off for a sneaky feed in Supermacs. Clerkin got a whipped ice cream after and never felt bad about it for one second.

They beat Meath comfortably and Clerkin was surprised that a team of Seamus McEnaney and Martin McElkennon would be so tame. As well as that, there were games against Dublin and Cork. That wouldn't have happened before, playing challenge games against teams of that calibre, but this team needed tests like that.

'Let's be realistic here, we have basically half our Championship team and panel from last year and replaced them with U-21s and guys that people said were also-rans, that they had their chance and weren't good enough under Banty's time. That's a huge changeover.

'I have to say I would be very happy with how the younger lads have come on and how the experienced lads are as hungry as ever. I still see myself with three or four years left with Monaghan, rather than having one game down the tracks and if you lose your whole world ends, which can be made out to be the case. Our boys are going to go up there and play with no baggage.

'One thing Eamonn has tried to bring into our play is to play it as we see it, to think on our feet. It doesn't have to be played at one hundred miles an hour, it doesn't have to be direct ball into Tommy [Freeman] all the time. Maybe it's a bit simplistic to say that's how we used to play, but it wasn't far off that. The Ulster final last year and Fermanagh in '08 were days we were clueless.

'Playing Dublin and Cork, they're two of the best teams in the country, and they were at their best, putting good teams out. It was very heartening. With all due respect to Tyrone, they aren't at that level now. I don't care what anybody says, if they were being honest, and Mickey Harte has said it himself, Tyrone are not in the top bracket anymore.'

• • •

Come 3.10pm on Sunday, Dick Clerkin fulfilled a dream. He came marching out of the Healy Park tunnel with his troops behind him. The rain was tipping down. A group of photographers huddled in a mass in front of a bench for the obligatory team snap, taking shelter underneath golfing umbrellas. They hardly sat for a matter of seconds before they went of to the far sideline to begin a handpassing drill, concentrating in picking a path through heavy traffic.

Four minutes later, Tyrone dusted off the howitzers for another season as they charged out, bristling with purpose. Over the last few seasons, watching Tyrone's pre-match warmup is a thing of beauty. Half the players pull bibs over their heads and they all spread out to the various cones to run a drill. With perfect synchronisation and everybody in possession of a ball, they are given the signal to start.

Tyrone are in red, Monaghan are in blue. There are no gimmicks and no twisting of the tail stunts that have characterised meetings between these two in the Ulster finals of 2007 and 2010. In '07, Seamus McEnaney reneged on a ruling by the Ulster Council that Monaghan should wear blue jerseys, taking the field in their traditional white. In his mind, he justified it by a gentleman's agreement with Mickey Harte earlier in the year, when he made a throwaway comment that Tyrone would change for the Ulster final.

In the 2010 Ulster final, Monaghan were believed to have taken Tyrone's dressing room. In their defence, they would say that they were just going to the room that they usually occupied. There was a slight innocence to the mistake, but it gave Tyrone an aggravation that they could carry onto the field with them.

This was a vastly-changed Monaghan side. While the defence had a new look, the attack was vastly reshaped. In New York, the Leitrim GAA team over there would boast a full forward line of Tommy Freeman, Rory Woods and Kieran Tavey, all Monaghan men.

Tommy Freeman had become a victim of the recession. A carpenter by trade, he had recently married and had just built a house. With work drying up, he was forced to go Stateside. He played in a couple of league games and then overnight, he was gone. There was no tearful announcement in any dressing room, he just slipped away quietly. It was left to McEneaney to break the news to the team.

Clerkin had sympathy for his friend. 'Maybe he just felt bad about it and didn't want to chat to boys face to face. I got the feeling off Tommy this year that he needed a break. He's been on the go a long time, injuries were troubling him. He got hammered over that Derry game in '09 with the tamest headbutt in the world and the suspension.

'There was a tough end with his club last year. He missed that penalty with the last kick of the game in the county final to win it which was heartbreaking for him. He and Damian [Freeman, brother] carried the team in that game but

I was chatting to him around Christmas and he had said he was awful disappointed about it.

'Sometimes people just need a break and Tommy is still young. If he needs that to get the hunger back, so be it. Plus, he hadn't any work and had just built a house and got married. How can you enjoy your football when these things are hanging over you?'

•   •   •

While Ryan McMenamin sleeps soundly the night before any match, the second he opens his eyes he is up and buzzing. His diet is meticulous in the week of a match and reservoirs of water pass his lips.

As ever, Kelly's Inn was the meeting place, at 12.40pm. The usual carload of Cathal McCarron in the driving seat along with Sean O'Neill brought a welcome sense of familiarity. Once more, the Tyrone management brought them through a quick video session and tactical talk. After that, it was off to Healy Park.

The Tyrone dressing room is always a bubbly scene. They don't have to wait for men to make their voices heard with so many characters about. 'I'm in a good corner with Mugsy [Owen Mulligan], Hub [Kevin Hughes] and Johnny Curran. It can be very enlightening! Mugsy was telling me a few stories and when he goes into storytelling mode about his own adventures, it's good fun. Maybe it's not the sort of thing you should be talking about forty-five minutes before you're going out to play a Championship match, but it's good craic!

'Mickey doesn't say much before the game. In Kelly's Inn he spoke to us, but only for about ten minutes or so. Tony Donnelly spoke there too and Mickey would put his own spin on it. When we're doing the warmup, Fergal McCann would be very chatty, and as it increases in intensity a lot of the players start talking, everyone takes their own lead from it. Before we go out, Mickey always has the final say, and once that's over, we hit the field.

'I don't even remember Mickey's message. It's always more or less key points and what we've been practising during the week. Then he wishes us luck and that's that.'

•   •   •

Match referee Cormac Reilly was about to throw the ball in for the start of the game when he observed a lot of pulling and dragging between the midfield quartet. He set the ball down and had a word with Clerkin and Sean Cavanagh. Clerkin felt he needed to stand up and lead the way as captain. His side had one player over the age of thirty and their average age was twenty-two. Tyrone were fielding seven players over thirty. Their average age was twenty-eight.

Within a minute of play finally commencing, Clerkin played a long ball in to Paul Finlay who was tugged, resulting in a free which Conor McManus tapped over. For the remainder of that opening quarter Monaghan would hold their own, either staying a nose ahead or at least level until a decisive sequence of play on eighteen minutes.

Monaghan's Kieran Duffy took an extra solo at the wrong time, allowing Aidan Cassidy to swallow him up and scoop the ball to Peter Harte. He smoothly transferred the ball to Stephen O'Neill who carried it and released it at just the right time to Brian McGuigan, loitering with intent. McGuigan threw out a body swerve with his hips and dropped it onto his left foot to crack the ball past goalkeeper Mark Keogh. Suddenly Tyrone were two points ahead.

Monaghan began to get frustrated. Off the ball, Stephen Gollogly and Philip Jordan were snapping at each other when Gollogly threw out a leg, half-tripping, half-kicking. As Reilly consulted with linesman Paudie Hughes who spotted the incident, Monaghan got Gollogly off the pitch and James Turley on. It was an unorthodox move, but they got away with it, as Reilly booked only Jordan.

Soon after, Brian Dooher kicked a sideline ball down the line when Sean Cavanagh pushed Clerkin to the ground. As play continued with McMenamin creeping upfield for a shot that fell short, Cavanagh and Clerkin wrestled on the ground. Reilly stopped the play and showed yellow cards to both of them.

A few minutes later Clerkin and Cavanagh had another run in – literally. Eoin Lennon seemed to have caught a kickout of Keogh's only to drop it, allowing Cavanagh to come from behind and gather the ball. He passed the ball straight away to McGuigan and set off looking for the return. Standing in front of him was Clerkin. Neither man was conceding ground. They crashed into each other and went to ground.

The crowd roared in the stands. On the television coverage, co-commentator Martin McHugh remarked, 'Dick Clerkin could be in bother here, Dick Clerkin hit Cavanagh late.'

The replays showed that Cavanagh started his run and Clerkin was caught like a rabbit in the headlights. He could have moved to avoid him but he hadn't much time. This was Cavanagh's fifty-fifth Championship match and he was playing a clever game. He stayed on the deck as Reilly called the play back. Clerkin knew he was in trouble.

'I was on the stand side and the crowd were roaring. The Tyrone line were roaring at the linesman too. You could see them going mad the first time when he got the yellow card, as if it were an injustice. The linesman was slightly influenced by what was going on behind him as well, but for a man with my experience, I should have known.'

McMenamin spotted the incident himself. 'Dick knew what he was doing. When Sean went to do the one-two, Dick knew that he wasn't going past for the return. He did stop him from getting to the ball, and in the rules, that's a yellow-card offence. I think he probably had his card marked from tangling before.'

Cormac Reilly conferred with linesman Con Reynolds. He went straight over to Clerkin, gave him his second yellow card, and the red. Clerkin was gone. The promise he had made to McEneaney that he wouldn't let him down was broken but he felt he had received rough justice.

'I was marking him tight but he was grabbing me as much as I was grabbing him. He jumped into me. Without a doubt. He didn't try to go round me and when he ran into me he went to ground straight away. He knows how to deal with guys that want to mark him tight and how to get them a yellow card. I'll put it like this: for a man his size and his athleticism, he goes down easy. I'm strong enough but I'm not that bloody strong! He has a stone weight on me and I shouldn't be able to put a man like that down with minimal effort. It was frustrating, but I was annoyed at myself that I allowed myself to be codded like that.

'I would have to put my hands up and take some of the blame.'

A cheer went up from the crowd. They had their red card, Monaghan were down to fourteen men, and the crude portrayal of Clerkin gained currency.

'For a few years there, I got a profile, a caricature almost, of being this ogre, this Neanderthal from Monaghan. I had to take it tongue in cheek for a while but after a couple of years I began to realise that this had stuck, with the jokes you would get when you were out. Boys saying to me "You're not that big!" And I was left wondering what they were on about.

'The picture that was being painted was one of a big thug that did nothing but go around knocking people around. But that had been allowed to develop and I had no way of counteracting it – not that you would try it.'

The main stand in Healy Park is elevated and the crowd can sometimes seem on top of the pitch, especially in a pressure cooker atmosphere. Some heroes had a go at Clerkin, abusing him from the safety of their seats and behind the cordon of stewards. He could hear the odd remark, but he was caught in the initial shock of what had just happened. He had to get off the field, hold his head high, and not react. In the recent past, some players have reacted childishly to a referee's decision, but all Clerkin could see was the bench and where he was going to take his seat. As a captain, he had to keep his dignity and the walk was a test of it.

'I could take the stance that the referee was wrong but I was playing close to the line. I was marking tight, maybe in some people's minds, too tight. If I wanted to hide behind what some people said I could. At the end of the day, I gave the referee his opportunity to send me off.

'I went straight in and sat in the dugout. I was distraught, sitting there. My first time sent off in the Championship. I got a second yellow card after the game in '07 against Kerry, but it was over by that time.

'I was disappointed with the referee. A tick, or a speaking to, I don't think anyone would have argued with that. He never spoke one word after he gave the first card, and then the same for the second. It was just bang, bang – you're off.'

●　　●　　●

Monaghan were aggrieved and lost their discipline for a spell. It takes a cool head to play Tyrone but with so much youth in the line up Monaghan were failing the test. After a rash challenge from Conor Galligan on Davy Harte, a bit of sorting out commenced. Once it was tidied up, Reilly booked Darren Hughes. Cavanagh tapped over the free, followed closely by a Stephen O'Neill special, showing off his balance and his ability with either foot.

At halftime, there was organisational work to be carried out. Just at the sending off, Tyrone assistant manager Tony Donnelly entered the field and spoke to McMenamin. They structured the formation so that he was the free man, lying between the half and full back lines.

In the first play of the second half, the merits of his switch were displayed. Monaghan played a high ball in and McMenamin cleaned it up, ran the ball out and played his pass. His influence would grow.

After exchanging points, Monaghan had an attack but Conor Gormley dispossessed Christopher McGuinness. He got the ball to Martin Swift, onto Jordan, and then to Brian McGuigan. Dessie Mone came straight at McGuigan, who showcased his upper-body strength by blasting through him. McGuigan played it into the rampant Mark Donnelly, who lost Galligan on the turn. Galligan recovered to foul Donnelly in the box. Penalty for Tyrone.

The move, from Gormley's tackle to the foul, has taken twenty-one seconds and is a study in fluidity.

If they goal from the penalty, Tyrone will be eight points up.

Martin Penrose blasts wide.

Eight minutes later just as Tyrone appear in complete control, Monaghan get a break. Mark Downey puts a ball in that Dermot Carlin drops. It falls to Conor McManus and as he pulls back his shooting foot, McMenamin pushes him in the back, onto the ground. Monaghan penalty and a booking for McMenamin.

Darren Hughes drills the ball to Pascal McConnell's left as he commits to going to his right. Suddenly, there's only two in it.

Tyrone needed to be careful here. A slip on the wet surface would be all that was needed for Reilly to even up the teams.

Monaghan though couldn't make inroads into that two-point margin that Tyrone clung to with all their experience and might. While they kept Monaghan in touch with a few silly frees, Owen Mulligan came on and added another edge to the Tyrone attack. The game winded down with an untidy finish. Mone received a red card after catching Jordan around the neck.

Some verbals followed, with McMenamin in the thick of the exchanges. Brian Dooher came over, grabbed his teammate and pointed downfield. Obediently, McMenamin trotted back into defence.

Shortly after, with tensions simmering and tempers frayed, Reilly blows the long whistle to signify the end. Monaghan's Ulster dream is gone for yet another year. Tyrone are in another semi-final.

● ● ●

There is no great celebration. Tyrone go straight into their stretching and warmdown routine. Clerkin comes onto the field wearing a tracksuit top and joins the team huddle.

Tyrone huddle up and Mickey Harte goes into the centre. He jabs his index finger towards the turf, delivering the message emphatically. What had just unfolded would not suffice if they wanted to win the Ulster title. McMenamin realises it.

'We have a pile of work to do. That proves it. We won't get anywhere near Cavan or Donegal with that, but we got through the first round. I'm sure Down, Monaghan or Antrim would love to be the same as us, playing bad and winning. You take the positives out of it and look at it collectively as well – we could be a lot better.

'It's becoming an expectation that the kind of football you play in August has to be played in January and February, let alone June. If you don't play 100 percent, there are always going to be people on your back.'

Monaghan traditionally put up a battle that's feisty, even nasty. They were prepared to take Tyrone down a hard road and Tyrone were ready for it.

'We weren't surprised by them at all,' says McMenamin. 'We expected them to come out and play like a team that came in under the radar. There was talk that they had nothing to lose, but there was also talk that they thought the best time to play Tyrone was in the first round.

'We knew that they would come out with eight of the boys hurting from the Ulster final last year. That was going to be a big factor, and with a new manager in as well... You were expecting a lot of fire from them.'

Clerkin felt that there could have been a bit more end product for all the fight in the Monaghan team. 'Tyrone will do well not to believe what they are saying about them being in control. Our boys were annoyed at the way we let them win. You could take a moral victory out of that game and pat each other on the back but Tyrone were there to be beaten. That might look a good Tyrone side on paper but I don't care what anybody says...'

● ● ●

Life goes on. That evening, Clerkin attended a school reunion of Alison's in the Hillgrove Hotel. Dessie Mone had attended the school too so the two of them paired off and had a few drinks. After a few, they began to take more notice of what was happening outside their world rather than inside it. There was a lot of history and politics being discussed and that got Clerkin animated and thinking about other things again. While he may enter a tunnel-vision for the Championship, it's good to realise that it's not the focus of everybody's day.

'I wasn't looking forward to it but I started to enjoy it. It takes the attention off things, makes you realise it's not all that people in Monaghan care about on the day. I could have taken the hump, but part of being captain is taking responsibility, keeping the head up.'

The Tyrone team made their way back to Kelly's Inn for their post-match meal. Once that was over, McMenamin escaped the goldfish bowl by heading straight to Rossnowlagh. He had the following day off work and planned to get some surfing in.

He got down at about 8.30pm. He is friendly with the locals and hung around the hotel lounge, enjoying a few drinks and chatting with them, watching The Sunday Game on television.

Conditions weren't great on the Monday. The waves weren't coming in at Rossnowlagh, so he headed over to Tullan Strand. There wasn't much happening there either.

It was a wasted journey but it was nice to get off the treadmill for an evening. Dromore have a club fixture in the next week, and after that, Tyrone will get their head down and see what they have to do to beat the winners of Cavan and Donegal.

It's going to be a long summer. He's sure of that.

CHAPTER TWENTY-THREE

'The Motto Is Family'

CAVAN v DONEGAL

First Round, Breffni Park, June 12

EIGHT o'clock on a Friday evening and two nights before they finally partake in the 2011 Ulster Championship, the footballers of Cavan emerge onto one of the famous theatres in all the province – Breffni Park.

There was a time when a visit to this place meant defeat and a lesson from the masters of Ulster football. In 1904, Cavan first reached top of the pile in Ulster with three Championship titles. Antrim shot out ahead of them, gathering eight titles by 1913, but Antrim's tally had been surpassed again a further nine years later.

To this day Cavan remain top of the Ulster roll of honour, with five All Irelands and thirty-nine Ulster wins in total, but things are so much different now. The structure of Breffni Park is now a stark reflection of how Cavan have yet to enter into the twenty-first century of the footballing world. It is a romantic venue but the corners are clogged with dust. The toilets are dark and uninviting, covered with rogue cobwebs. The stand could use a coat of paint and bird droppings spatter the seats. It exudes a faded glamour that seems out of place in the modern age. An evening studying the confines of Breffni Park is the equivalent of a Kiss Me Quick hat and a saucy beachside postcard scene of Blackpool in its heyday.

Cavan's last Ulster final was ten years ago and you have to go back fourteen years since Martin McHugh brought them to the promised land of the winners' podium on Ulster final day. After McHugh delivered the title he needed to take a step back from management to devote more time to his business and family.

In two days' time, one of the children that McHugh stepped down to spend time with will be playing for Donegal, looking to blow past Cavan into the Ulster semi-final. Mark McHugh is an embodiment of Jim McGuinness's coaching philosophy. Ultra-fit and impervious to fatigue, he planted the winning goal against Antrim and immediately got up to sprint into position for the kickout.

McGuinness may have enjoyed Sigerson Cup success in the late '90s as captain of the galaxy of stars that Andrews was able to gather in his time at Tralee IT, but it was his spell at University of Ulster Jordanstown, winning the college competition with them again as captain in 2001, that shaped him.

In Ulster, much of the modern day football philosophy comes from a pivotal moment. When Anthony Tohill broke his leg while training as a rookie for Melbourne Demons in the Australian Football League, he returned home to study in Queen's University and play for Derry. He brought back a modernised attitude towards training and physical preparation. His new friends in the college engineering faculty – Kieran McGeeney, Cathal O'Rourke and Paul Brewster – lapped it up. Outside of training on the pitch, they set up camp in the Queen's gym, relentlessly urging each other to lift more, lift heavier, become bigger, faster, stronger.

They formed the nucleus of the Sigerson-winning team of 1993 and their template gained further credence. At the time Armagh were basic cannon-fodder yet McGeeney would still tell people on nights out that he expected nothing less than an All Ireland in his career. They'd laugh at him but he wasn't even smiling. He was winning his All Ireland.

Cavan are disconnected from that mindset, that culture which permeated the gym in Queen's and then beyond. Their star players looked more towards the Dublin colleges for their education and made the college team their priority. Those left behind in the county without the scholarship schemes and the college perks grew resentful.

Football in the county has become inverted. Players have become frightened of taking responsibility. Management teams have been whistled in and charged out, all departing by issuing damning verdicts on the lack of drive among the county footballers. County panels have huge turnovers from year to year. There's little continuity. There's no 'nursery' school like Derry have enjoyed with St Pat's Maghera or Fermanagh have in St Michael's, Enniskillen. Cavan have become a basket case caught on a carousel of underachievement.

Yet before any Championship match, there's always hope. And on this Friday, the players have one final run out before their first game of the summer.

Just moments earlier there was a serene hush over the ground. The bountiful rainfall had turned the grass the colour of an Augustan fairway and swallows dipped their flight to skim a few inches off the dew.

John Wren is a Corkman living in Cavan since 1969 yet is still considered a blow-in. He takes immense pride in his job as head groundsman, coming to understand the science of turf and grass through patience and care. The playing surface will get another trim and then a brushing the following morning. He would like to experiment and cut the circle and square formations he admires on other sporting fields, but they won't fork out for the machinery.

Occasionally, the players will mention that they don't think the bounce is big enough on the pitch, and he patiently explains that it is sand-based and when it rains, the wet sand dulls the impact. He believes the Cavan senior panel receive far too much criticism and stands up for them all the time. Instead, he reserves his ire for the early tackle Tadgh Kennelly put in on his countyman Nicholas Murphy in the opening seconds of the 2009 All Ireland final.

Just as he walks off, Val Andrews comes down the tunnel, swapping banter with the county public relations officer Declan Woods, the county chairman Tom O'Reilly, and team selector Stephen King, the man who lifted the Anglo-Celt Cup in 1997. The players emerge too.

Within five minutes, they're into a loosening up drill. Team trainer Ger Lyons calls the instructions. Co-manager Terry Hyland comes out and takes up his position alongside King and Woods. The players are handpassing the ball. Lyons calls out the instructions. 'One-two! Move the ball! One-two! Move the ball!' They move to another area of the field and Lyons makes the area smaller. The calls get quicker as the heartrate increases. Lyons then takes them through a series of dynamic stretches: lunges, high kicks, pivots.

A chasing pack handpassing game is then commenced, led by Andrews. It seems impossible to decipher as neither team is wearing bibs. Confusion comes over the exercise. Players seem distracted and some are nattering to each other. The drill breaks down twice and eventually a player stops the ball to appeal to the players on his side to raise their hands and identify themselves. Andrews will later concede that he made a personal mistake with this drill. He felt it was too complex, too close to the game.

Some of the county minor team emerge from the tunnel. They take their seats in the main stand for a look and a chance to drag out a summer's evening.

James Reilly, the stalwart Cavan goalkeeper popularly known as 'Miller', has set his kicking tee up twenty metres in from the sideline. He is booming massive kicks straight in the direction of Tomás Corr and Ray Cullivan for them to leap and catch.

Hyland now is down at the town-end goals working with some backs and forwards in a traditional exercise, stopping the play occasionally to draw his players in to deliver instruction. Andrews is at the other end of the field, leading the shooting drills.

At 9.22, the players form a huddle in the middle of the field. Laughter comes from the circle before there is hush. It only lasts a minute before Lyons takes them through their warmdown.

Five minutes later the players head down the tunnel. The next time they will see this pitch, the eyes of Ulster will be on them and Donegal. They are taking on the most highly-organised and motivated side in the country at the moment. In their minds they will be thinking that the heavy lifting is done, but in truth it's not even started.

Tom O'Reilly turns to John Wren, the other last person out on the field, and remarks, 'John, the field is a credit to you.'

The players eat a meal together, and before they leave, are handed a laminated sheet of the match day schedule which reads:

MATCH DAY SCHEDULE

1.50pm	❑ Meet in Breffni Park
	❑ Ogham stamp
	❑ Tog out (warm up tops, shorts, socks)
	❑ Rubs
	❑ Strapping
	❑ Hydration / Nutrition
2.25pm	❑ Team meeting upstairs
	❑ Video Analysis
2.40pm	❑ Team jog to back pitch (paired off)
	❑ Warm up 1 – Back pitch
	❑ Kick, Catch & Score
	❑ Dynamic Warm Up
	❑ Static Stretching minimal
3pm	❑ Return to dressing room (paired off)
	❑ Hydration
	❑ Visualisation
	❑ Breathing
3.06pm	❑ Team put on jerseys
	❑ Team focus

3.09pm	❑ Main Pitch and Team Photo (1-26)
	❑ Warm up 2
	❑ Reaction & Speed Drills x 5 (5 mins)
	❑ 3 v 3 Goal Game (5 mins)
	❑ Kick around (2 mins)
3.22pm	❑ Team Parade
3.27pm	❑ National Anthem
4.08pm	**Half Time**
	- injury assessment
	- cold towels
	- drinks/hydration
	- food
	- video snippets
	- Statistical Analysis
	- Talk
	- Warm up
4.25pm	❑ Second half
5.02pm	❑ Final Whistle
	❑ Victory
	❑ Warm Down
5.45pm	❑ Meal in Kilmore Hotel

Feardhacht is Firinne

On it, the Cavan county crest motto is printed. 'Feardhacht is Firinne.' It translates into English as 'Manliness and Truth.'

• • •

Val Andrews and Terry Hyland are doing a good impression of two people taking it all in their stride but privately they must have worries. With the commitments of the county U-21s in getting to the All Ireland final and exam commitments on top of that, they've only had twelve days to prepare for Donegal. As Val puts it, at times it's felt like 'a bleedin' Railway Cup gig'.

All year the two men have been preaching a diet of weights, weights and more weights. They're trying to bring through what's almost an entirely new team, and one thing you need in Ulster is some grunt and heft. Little by little, Cavan are beginning to learn lessons. There will be some hard examinations along the road and they will fail some of these dreadfully but the rot has to be stopped.

Andrews is a devotee of Daniel Coyle's book, The Talent Code, and the theory of 10,000 hours of deliberate practice leading to perfection. Mozart was not born with the talent of grand pianist; he became good because he played the piano. Lessons of this kind do not sink in easy in Year One of any project. They need time. They don't have time.

Come the week of the game, Andrews and Hyland had a fully-booked calendar. On the Monday night, they trained the county junior team for an hour. The Tuesday was a sharp, hour-long session with the senior side. Twenty-four hours later they were on the sideline against Kilkenny in the Leinster junior championship. 'Now that was pressure!' quips Andrews, but the team won comfortably. The following night, Andrews drove up the road to discuss tactics with Hyland.

They had already picked their team the previous weekend. A few calls were marginal. Gareth 'Nesty' Smith just missed out. Mark McKeever was expected to be named for his ability and experience, but over the past six weeks he has been dogged by an injury that would struggle against Donegal's running game. Other than that, the team effectively picked itself.

'We didn't spend that long,' says Hyland. 'When you go to a race meeting you look down at the card and you pick x amount of horses. You should never change your mind, because those are the horses you picked. Then you start deliberating and you always find a reason "Why did I not pick that fella?" It's like going in to buy a shirt. Usually the first one you see is the one you end up buying anyway.'

The turnover of players is starkly illustrated by Andrews. 'There are basically three fellas that started against Fermanagh [in the 2010 Ulster Championship]. Before we started this Championship, there was thirteen left of last year's squad. Now we have eight or nine debutants. It's the right way to go. The last time we were here in 2001, we had nine debutants. In Louth it was the same. We seem to get these jobs when there is a clearout needed. But this one? We're not leaving until we win something! No matter if he [Terry] wins it, as long as one of us wins something.'

Of course, Hyland has already won the Ulster U-21 Championship this season. But expecting too much from that group is dangerous. After losing the biggest game of their young lives, a good number of them went straight into the pressure of exams, living on their wits for another spell.

In the league game against Louth, the Cavan backroom team were able to record clips of the opening half, and relay it to the team at halftime. They will not be able to do it in this game because the Ulster Council forbid it. They have a trick up their sleeve to get round that particular obstacle, it's in the match day schedule after all, but the regulation is another form of hassle they could do without.

When GAA players and managers are invited to reflect on their careers, one thing they will always get round to talking about is the friendships they have made through the games. Although this is a brutal game and expectations are often savage, it's refreshing to see the mutual friendship between the co-managers. It's a double-act, with Hyland the straight man, the Ernie Wise to Andrews' wise-cracking Eric Morecambe. A partnership in perfect harmony, illustrated by Val's account of a recent day spent in the hospitality of Hyland and his wife Kathleen.

Andrews: 'He's married to a caterer! Myself and Ger [Lyons] went for a meal there one day before the game. Right, no bother, we said. So we went up, Ger's a Dub like myself, and sit down. Grand, like. And then it's "Right, what will you have?"

'First of all, where I'm from, you don't get a choice, but then you're asked if you want beef, chicken, or a bit of fish? I'm looking at Ger – now this is after the soup, of course – and we knew we were in trouble because there was a raaaake of silver either side of the plate...'

Hyland: 'I was afraid the boys might lift it and I wanted it put away...'

Andrews: 'She solved our conundrum of what we were going to eat by giving us a bit of everything! It was like three dinners! I thought it was a big special dinner and everything, but it wasn't! We got that into us, and it was "You'll have a bit of dessert" and we were like "Yeah, grand thanks." And out came five desserts! Ah stop!

'But she's a great cook, Kathleen. You [points at Terry] should open a restaurant! Get out of this football and off we go!'

The weekend of a game is a demanding time for both players and management. Physically – and especially mentally.

'You're lying wide awake at three in the morning,' says Andrews, 'saying the fifty times table and you realise "Feck me, why am I doing this for?" And you're saying, "Full back line...Ah, Jaysus..."'

'But you still do it. For the challenge, for the adrenaline. You do it to test yourself, your emotions. This is bad for you. This is physiologically bad for you. It raises your blood pressure and my blood pressure wouldn't be the best anyway. Maybe Terry's a bit more relaxed, but...'

'Not really,' Terry interjects. 'You can be relaxed looking, but inside is a different story. A bit like when your horse is coming to the winning line, y'know.'

The day before the game, he will have business to attend to. Val is gearing himself up for a forty-mile cycle that will be enough to get him off to sleep that night.

'What we want is a performance,' says Val. 'If the performance is there, we'll be there with ten minutes to go.

'We believe we'll do the old northsider job then. You know, just come in and lift it.'

• • •

The Monday before the Cavan-Donegal showdown, while Val and Terry were training the Cavan junior side, they would have been totally unaware of an incident elsewhere that could have turned horribly nasty.

The Donegal squad had just wrapped up training in Termon when Mark McHugh drove out through the gates of the ground. In the car with him were Jason Noctor, Patrick McBrearty and Michael Hegarty. One moment they were on the road, the next the car was lying on its roof in a river. A split second of carelessness was all it took, and despite their panic when the water began to leak into the car, they all got out without anything more than mild embarrassment.

It was a bad week for cars in the McHugh household. Kevin Cassidy's brother Stephen works as a sale rep for Martin McHugh. He had an accident in the company car and it joined Mark's car on the write-off list.

Later on in the week, Donegal were back out training doing a shooting drill and a wayward shot carried over the ballstop. Mark had parked his new car behind the goals and the ball crashed through the windscreen. Bad luck comes in threes.

That weekend Cassidy did everything right. The win against Antrim has done nothing to sate the ambition of the Donegal players. On the Saturday morning, Cassidy went through his usual routine of bringing a bag of balls up to the Gaoth Dobhair pitch and took one hundred shots.

McGuinness has ramped up training. The commitment required is still fierce but the periodisation training is kicking in. Players are now concentrating on sprint work and sharpening their speed of thought.

On the morning of the match, their thought processes were about to get another stir around. After a light snack in Donegal, they made their way to the Farnham Arms Hotel, a ten-minute drive to Breffni Park. Cassidy was having his pre-match meal when he became aware something was in the offing.

'I noticed Jim talking to the receptionists, asking "Is that room ready yet?" He was asking for blankets and pillows and that and I was wondering "What's this boy at?"

'He brought us into this big ballroom, a wedding reception room. He switched off the lights and told every man to lie down on the floor and go to sleep. There was thirty of us lying in this big room on the floor, we closed our eyes, and Jim walked around, talking. Some boys had their iPods in and fell asleep, and Jim went around talking about what we were going to do against Cavan, to try and focus in on the early ball. It got a message into our heads.'

While some outside the camp have yet to be convinced about the 'new' Donegal, Rory Gallagher's role within the setup has received a lot of coverage. Characterised as a wandering minstrel, Gallagher's reputation has been trampled and restored down through the years, inside and outside of his home county of Fermanagh. Finally though, people seem to be copping onto the fact that while Gallagher possesses a sharp intellect and a forthright manner, he won't sugarcoat his views in the pursuit of success. He is a bullshit-free zone.

'Rory impresses me. He has a good knowledge of the game. Himself and Jim are always on the phone or else they're meeting up. One night they didn't get home to quarter to two in the morning. You can see him getting more and more into it as the weeks go on.'

Inside the dressing room, Donegal had a secret weapon primed. During the week, McGuinness had thrown a dummy team out to the Ulster Council for their matchday programme and the press. Patrick McBrearty would start instead of Michael Hegarty.

Cassidy has watched with interest how the seventeen-year-old has been blended into the squad.

'Jim's been careful with him. You'd be worried that maybe people might expect too much too early. You get these players who are built up when they're seventeen and eighteen, and they play too much football. He's definitely quality though and when the minors were still in their championship, Patrick would still come up every night but he mightn't do the session, he'd just be around the camp. I think it was a good way to break the man in, get him used to being around the lads, what it takes and that.'

When McBrearty took to the field for the seniors, he was wearing gloves.

Before, he'd never have worn them, choosing instead to smear his hands in hair wax for extra grip of the ball. But for the greater project of Donegal 2011, he would break superstition and habit.

•   •   •

The morning of the match, Val Andrews was lying in bed saying his morning prayers. His thoughts turned to one of his best friends, Kevin Flanagan. Kevin had been his friend back in the days of messing, and he had texted Carmel Andrews the night before, wishing his friend the best of the luck the following day. He would try and get a look at the game but his wife Susan wouldn't be able to.

Susan was seriously ill, in a coma.

'I didn't know it,' says Val. 'I rang him at half-eight on Sunday morning. Here he is, he's in the throes of this and he still sends me a text. Anyway, I called him and she was just after passing away. Kevin would have been with me when I was wild, immature, and irresponsible. There's a special affinity with him. You always remember the fellas who were good to you, when I was a student and I hadn't a penny in my pocket.

'For about half an hour I wasn't right. Coming into a game your emotional state is aroused anyway and I was saddened.'

The day went on. When his Cavan players came through the door of Breffni Park, they were stamped on the arm with a word in Ogham, an early Medieval alphabet that was used to write the old Irish language. It typically appeared on standing stones and on trees, thought to have been a secretive code between druids. The word translated as 'Gaiscioch', meaning 'Warrior'. The idea came from an interest Andrews has in standing stones.

Another motto also carries special meaning for him.

'Their county crest translates as "Manliness and Truth." They were one of the last spots to be colonised by Queen Elizabeth and all the rest of the boys, y'know what I mean? They had difficulty colonising it, so that was the theme that we wanted to get: we fight, and we never give up.'

•   •   •

The Cavan timetable ran smoothly. They were out in time and everything seemed right. Just before the throw-in, Jim McGuinness jogged down the line to warmly shake the hands of his managerial adversaries. Thirteen years ago he was Val's voice on the pitch for Tralee IT; now he's been plotting Val's downfall in front of 9,325 people.

Seanie Johnston opened the scoring with a free in the first minute, then Michael Murphy replied with another free. Within seven minutes, the tone for the day was set when Cassidy put in a monster hit on Cavan's centre back, John McCutcheon.

A minute later, Michael Murphy lines up a sideline ball. It drops short and David Givney catches. Cavan work it through their hands, first to Gearoid McKiernan, to Dane O'Dowd, to Niall Murray. Donegal close down the spaces and make it tight for them. The ball goes to McKiernan again, he gives it onto Ray Cullivan, who transfers it to Givney, but Cavan are still sinking in quicksand, mired deep in their defence. Ryan Bradley gives him a thump that rocks Givney on his heels. Leaning backwards, he puts a fistpass into the air. Cullivan leaps into the air and as he gathers, he descends and sticks out his right foot. It catches Cassidy with all his force on his left shoulder.

Cassidy crumples to the ground. Donegal players react furiously. Bradley is first on the scene as they surround and shove Cullivan. Referee Marty Duffy comes over and sends Cullivan off with a straight red card. Already, Cavan are down a man.

'I don't think he meant it to be honest,' says Cassidy. 'He didn't mean it, but he didn't not mean it, you know that kind of way? When you're up in mid-air, those things happen. You come down and you come down with all your force, but he didn't mean to do any damage.

'Unfortunately it happened right in front of the referee. It was high. Any lower and he would have been grand but he caught me right on the chest.'

After being seen to by the physio, Cassidy was alright to play on. In the days afterwards, the injury would catch him when he lay down at night in bed and he would have the war wounds of stud marks down his chest for another fortnight.

On the line, Andrews could scarcely believe it. 'As soon as it happened, I just said "Fuck!" Terry went green.'

Niall McDermott slotted over a free when the play resumed. It became niggly. Colm McFadden and McKiernan became involved in a little sorting out and Murphy came over to get needlessly involved.

The play went on. Anthony Thompson cut out a Cavan attack and worked it to Cassidy who played a one-two with Ryan Bradley before trying to land the ball into space for Murphy. But he overhit it and it drifted over the sideline. Murphy began back-pedalling when Damien O'Reilly came in to shoulder him off the ball. He went to go again but this time Murphy was ready for him and stuck his shoulder in too. O'Reilly flopped straight to the ground clutching his face as Murphy tripped over his flailing leg. Murphy got straight up and pointed at O'Reilly, telling him to get up. Patrick Carroll came in to shoulder Murphy, a token effort. Referee Duffy consulted with linesman Martin Sludden and astonished the crowd by giving Murphy a straight red card. Fifteen minutes gone and now both sides were a man down.

This time it was Cassidy's turn to disbelieve his eyes. 'It shouldn't have been a sending off, definitely not. But when a team loses a man, the referee often tends to even it up.

'Michael was really revved up for that game and he was getting involved in stuff. We have spoken about it since and it's not what we're looking for but he wasn't going to back down from anything either.'

Murphy suffers from big man complex in football. If he puts in a tackle, it is often blown instantly by the referee unfairly. He may have been in his fourth year of inter-county football but he is still raw and young. As the team's spiritual leader, Cassidy has fought to back up his captain.

Before they faced Antrim in the preliminary round, Jim McGuinness addressed an incident in the Division Two league final against Laois. Murphy became the target for some unsavoury verbals and Cassidy was straight in to sort it out.

'Yer man Billy Sheehan [Laois forward] was doing a lot of mouthing... That's one of the things Jim highlighted; he reckoned me and Michael Murphy just completely lost our focus on the game for five or ten minutes. He said from now on if that happens, we must stay focused. He [Sheehan] started on Murphy first, and then I got involved to get Murphy out of there and get him back on the game.

'I had heard about him [Sheehan] before. When I went into full-back, Neil McGee said to me "Watch that boy, he's full of mouth." For the first ten or fifteen minutes he was a lovely lad, didn't do nothing, and then he started... Jesus Christ! He called me a British bastard! Ah, it wouldn't annoy me at all, but what did annoy me was he got onto Michael about missing the penalty in the All Ireland U-21 final. You know Michael, he's a lovely lad, so that's why I got involved. I wouldn't get riled myself with anything he says to me.'

The match was riding on adrenaline. McCutcheon was launching an attack and he gave the ball on while falling over. As he was getting on his feet, Cassidy came across his path. Bang!

Andrews sprinted up the line to roar at linesman Paul Kneel.

'Cassidy should have went. He knew exactly what he was doing. McCutcheon was getting off the ground and he ran by him and hit him a shoulder into the head just as he was getting up. The minute he had it done he had his hands out, which suggested to me that he meant to do it, because he went for the innocent gesture right away.

'At that particular moment, you'd kill. But it's part of the game, I know it's part

FEELING YOURSELF DISINTEGRATE...
Dick Clerkin gets a red card from referee Cormac Reilly as Monaghan's challenge falters against Tyrone.

SKIRMISH...
Donegal and Cavan players jostle as Kevin Cassidy lies prone on the ground after Ray Cullivan's boot connected with his chest.

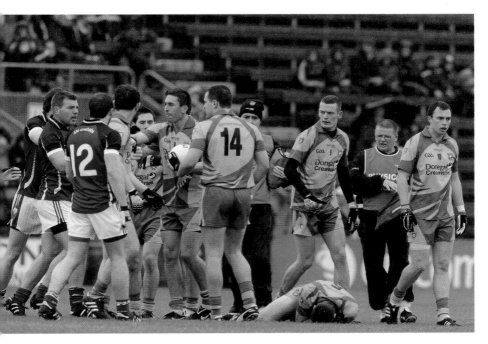

SECOND IS NOWHERE... *John Brennan (above) demanded success a[nd] gained it wherever h[e] went; Left: Antrim coach Liam Bradley [right] watches his s[on] Eoin put on a masterclass in the Ulster semi-final, wi[th] eldest son Paddy [left] absent through injur[y]*

THE SKINNER SHOW... *Another nail is hammered into the Armagh coffin in the Ulster semi-final as Derry's Eoin Bradley thrashes the ball past Paul Hearty's reach.*

AN ALMOST SUNNY DAY IN CLONES...

Tyrone supporters make a day of it with the obligatory matchday feast of tea and sandwiches; (below) Ryan McMenamin makes an attempt to stop Colm McFadden's shot, but it cannons into the net off him; (bottom) Dermot 'Brick' Molloy keeps his cool to seal a place in the Ulster final in the dying moments.

HERE FOR ONE THING ONLY... *(Clockwise from above) The Donegal team prepare to enter Tiernach's Park for the Ulster final; Jim McGuinness finally gets his hands on the Anglo Celt Cup, after losing two finals as a player; 'The Anglo-Celt's for The Hills'; Danny Devlin guesses the right way, the right height, but the force of Michael Murphy's penalty almost rips the net.*

DADDY'S GIRLS... *The washing line in Gaoth Dobhair tells a heartwarming story; [bottom] Kevin with Nia and Sarah with Aoife and the famous old trophy, which [inset] Aoife, (left) and Nia use as their latest toy*

S IS MY HOMELAND... *Kevin Cassidy with his father-in-law, former Donegal player Willie* *'agher and Neil McGee. In the background, Eamon McGee with Thomas McKinley; Below:* *coach Tom Beag Gillespie with the player, Kevin Cassidy the week after the Ulster final; Inset:* *Anglo-Celt makes a visit to the grave of Granny Sally in the spiritual home of Brinlack.*

HAS IT, HE HAS IT... *1 – Kevin Cassidy doesn't even notice how close Emmett Bolton is as he ...es the ball clean with the last shot of the game against Kildare. 2 – He takes a split second to ...ch the flight of the ball before, 3 – leaping with joy at having put Donegal into the All Ireland ...i-final. 4 – Hard work and commitment from Cassidy and Tom Beag Gillespie on the ...ning field, long before he dances under the lights, pays off for them in an emotional moment.*

IN JIM WE TRUST... *Nobody in Gaelic football had attempted the gameplan Donegal broug*
the All Ireland semi-final, but the players never questioned it.

TANGLED UP IN BLUE... *Kevin Cassidy has to burrow his way out of a forest of Dublin defe*

THE GAMECHANGER... *Kevin McManamon punched enough holes in the Donegal defence for Dublin to gain the lead as the game reached its climax.*

FLATTENED... *Neil McGee at the final whistle, lying defeated but spent in a glorious cause.*

ALL OVER... *'Defeat should never be a source of courage, but rather a fresh stimulant.' –
Robert South*

of the game. You might say, why is he trying to get him sent off, but he shouldn't do it. Feck it, yeah I'll roar at the linesmen.'

Cassidy was unapologetic. 'I think it looked worse than what it was. I was going past and he was getting up. I suppose I could have got out of his way but I didn't.'

It was a tinderbox atmosphere. The crowd were baying at Mark McHugh as he prepared to take a sideline kick right beside Hyland. He floated it in and McBrearty used his backside to nudge Dane O'Dowd as he jumped for the ball. The ball fell kindly on the turf and began rolling towards the goal when McBrearty stroked it under Reilly and the net rigging for his first score in senior Championship football at the tender age of seventeen.

Andrews was over at the far touchline after coming on during a break in play. 'I was just coming back over from the far side when they got that goal. I didn't actually see the ball in the net, so I just said "Thanks be to God, he's after missing it."'

Cavan rallied and showed their character, but the defence of Donegal overpowered them again and again. The Cavan players had been given specific instructions on how to play and break down the Donegal blanket defence. They just couldn't do it.

'In one eight-minute spell we went five times up the field. Lost the ball twice in contact, doing things we had spoken about not to do. People ask "What were you trying to do?" We had trained again and again that when we were hit by the wall of Donegal boys, we had to be patient, drag them out gently.

'So if you put it in the corner, they go over that way, you hold the ball for more than twenty, twenty-five seconds and they get tired; it comes back out to what we would term the point guard – Micheál Lyng – they follow him a bit out, then we hit a ball in and work the shot or whatever.

'We don't get the ball and try to go through them. If you get the ball and solo it, they just eat you.'

Donegal turned up the heat. They kept chipping away at Cavan, playing it sensibly, keeping the scoreboard ticking over. After thirty-two minutes, Cassidy got the ball out wide right and let rip with a big shot that sailed over. The practice at Gaoth Dobhair pitch was paying off.

The halftime score was 1-6 to 0-3. Already, Cavan looked a beaten team.

● ● ●

Once they gathered their wits in the Cavan dressing room, they made their switches. Givney would go to full forward and ball was to be rained down on top of him. The coaches urged the players to chase the game; no point waiting for it to happen now that they were six points down.

In the other dressing room, Michael Murphy was hiding his tears in the toilet. Cassidy felt for him.

'We said that he had carried us for long enough, so we would make sure we would get to the semi-final and get a chance to get that red card overturned. We knew right away that we would be appealing it. Even at halftime we knew we would be appealing it.'

The second half began with Cavan fielding a different midfield. Eugene Keating and McKiernan jumped for the throw-in but Donegal won it and drove on for a point. Cavan then put a series of high balls in Givney's direction, but Donegal had the area flooded. There was no space. Cavan players weren't pushing up on their men all over the field. They retreated into their comfort zones and shrivelled.

Ten minutes into the second period, the game was effectively killed. Another high ball from McKiernan towards Givney was broken and Anthony Thompson smuggled it out of the danger area. He handpassed to Cassidy who sprinted twenty yards of turf, before giving it to substitute Michael Hegarty. A further exchange of passes between Rory Kavanagh, Colm McFadden and Ryan Bradley suddenly left Kavanagh clear on goal. He pulled the trigger and put it beyond goalkeeper Reilly. Goal. Even though there were still twenty-five minutes left, this match was over.

• • •

Donegal showed no signs of elation as they made their way to the dressing room. Already they were getting themselves ready for Tyrone.

'There was a good atmosphere,' says Cassidy, 'but everyone was just focusing on the next game. There was some talk about getting Michael's red card rescinded. We had a meal in the Kilmore and Jim told us there would be no beer that night, that we had a recovery session to do the following day.'

Andrews felt he had said enough to the Cavan players, so Hyland addressed them. He told them that feeling sorry for themselves would be the easiest thing in the world to do, but they weren't allowed to feel sorry for themselves. Andrews then told them that he had been here before with a Cavan team, beaten by fifteen points by Derry in his first year.

'Even though you're going to be abused, that's when your character comes out.'

He also told the players to go out and have a night out with each other.

'I know that sounds mad, but we can work on this. Don't be going around with big faces on you, feeling sorry for yourself. Do something about it.'

The team went back to the Kilmore for dinner where Donegal were as well. They managed not to run into each other.

As the Cavan party were sitting down, one person was conspicuous by his absence. So they called Ray Cullivan on his phone.

He was reluctant to come down after what had happened. They spent a bit of time convincing him that they were a family and to stick together. Cullivan is a team player so he put his disappointment aside and joined the squad.

'He would have been absolutely in tatters, y'know what I mean? I said "Lookit, Ray, you're a young man, I'm supposed to be an old fella, you've worked exceptionally hard all year. I don't think you meant to do that." He thought he had let us down, as if we had taken a chance on him and nobody had given him that before. We didn't give him a chance, he earned it. He's a great lad and I hope he's over it now.

'The motto is family. Some day you will have a family and they will annoy you and you have to find forgiveness and say "Look, you're a good lad, look at all the good things you do."'

As they watched the first re-run of the game, Andrews was already forming his opinion on where it all went wrong.

'We scored four points in seventy minutes. That's the damning stat. Never mind the frailties at the back – we still only scored four points. When we went man for man, fourteen on fourteen, perhaps we didn't get the formation right, or the message or whatever. But it certainly didn't happen the way we wanted it to happen in the second half.

'I'm not making excuses, we were just terrible. The managers made mistakes too, let's get that straight.

'The two men I said were to be tightly watched were [Karl] Lacey and Cassidy. We went out and made heroes of both of them. You're asking boys to do a bit of thinking, asking them to come running out in a bit of a spine formation, which is basically four in a straight line. We did it for the first three or four minutes and then I never seen it again. It's very hard to change that back again. But, the responsibility ultimately lies with the manager.'

The Dublin contingent headed back down the road: Andrews, Ger Lyons, the statistician Dave Campbell and his son James. Carmel Andrews would normally hang around for her tea but she went straight down the road. She gets very disappointed with a defeat like that.

'She's extremely supportive, because she would see the amount of work that Ger does, I do, Terry does. And life should be fair, you should get something out of it. She sacrifices huge amounts of my time, so that's her sacrifice too. The criticism would affect the family, more than the protagonists.'

Once he was through the door, he said he wasn't going to watch the game again. But then he watched RTÉ's coverage. And then he watched it twice more. He wrote up his notes on the game, put them into an email, and sent them to himself at 4.30am. Then he turned in for the night.

The following morning he came through the doors of the college and someone started winding him up straight away. He got ate out of it. As fate would have it, RTÉ were calling round to record a snippet for their The Committee Room programme, on the subject of managers taking teams outside their county. What would end up a two and half minute snippet ended up taking two and a half hours to record, forcing Andrews to arrive late for a staff meeting.

In the afternoon, he logged on to the discussion boards to see what they were saying about the team. His team. His players. He knows he shouldn't, he's aware that they're a waste of time, yet he finds himself drawn to them.

'Cavan are very, very comfortable in a quagmire of shit. They love giving out and they love saying people are brutal and useless. Last week they were saying to get rid of all the old fellas. This week they're saying we've gone too far.

'Two years ago after they played Antrim [2009], fourteen lads showed up for training. County board officials were telling me to ring them after training to tell them how we got on [after the next training session]. Now, I didn't know this history thing, right? But basically they were saying, how many of those older fellas did I leave sitting on the bench were going to disappear?

'Then there was a big rumour going around started by that Hogan Stand [website] shite, that "he's no control over the dressing room". That thing has to get closed down! I look at it because lazy journos look at it. And county board officials look at it too. It's part of the propaganda war. This morning I was looking at this and wondering is it time somebody took it up as a cause, and stopped people from being anonymous, or close them down?

'You take Seanie [Johnston]; he was called a primadonna and everything. It's not right, it's just faceless gear. You know in your heart and soul that there are fellas in the camp or close to it that are posting. And that's treachery to me, that's snake-ism. Put your fucking name to it. It's defamation. It's extremely dangerous. I see players now in general acting up about it, and that's a cause waiting to happen. Why can't the GPA say something about that?'

After work, it was on to Westmeath to attend the wake of his friend Susan Flanagan. That house put his thoughts in order.

'It helps then when you think "Well, I have only a football problem, what's the worst that can happen here? They will either sack me, or keep me here."

'That would always be with me since the death of my son. This is football and we can work really hard and we can lose sleep, but at the end of the day it's a loss of a football match. It's not an ineffable loss that you can't touch or you can't go near. You have a bit of control over this.'

CHAPTER TWENTY-FOUR

Shootout!

DERRY v ARMAGH
Semi-final, Clones, June 19

'You have to be a winner in life. You have to walk over people, and be ruthless.'
John Brennan, Derry manager

IN the lead-up to the first Ulster semi-final, the national media were presented with another charismatic case study in Derry's John Brennan.

They found a man who was full of contradictions and surprises, a one-man anecdote factory who toured the country, taking on clubs that had been struck off as a waste of time. He would insert a backbone, help them stick their chests out and win titles. He bred a higher level of self-esteem wherever he went.

There was a caricature of Brennan, breathing fire on referees, linesmen and rivals fans. He wasn't afraid of giving lip to an opposing manager either, or even squaring up to them. When Dungiven beat his Lavey side in the Derry championship in 1997, he came onto the field and struck one of the Dungiven players behind the ear. Occasionally, he struggled with his impulses, but he never hid his authenticity.

Most of all, outsiders looked at a man of sixty-nine years of age and wondered why he had not been county manager before now.

A speed read of the bullet points of Brennan's career would reveal that he was an uncle of Derry's greatest captain, Henry Downey. He, along with his brother Seamus and the McGurks, were the backbone of the great Lavey side of the late '80s and early '90s. On the sideline was Brennan, although suspension prevented him from being in charge in 1991 when they won the All Ireland club championship.

Johnny McGurk once remarked, 'There is absolutely no doubt in my mind that what John Brennan taught us changed our footballing lives.' When pushed on what lessons he taught them, he replied, 'Unadulterated war.' Their manager was a willing and enthusiastic practitioner. He would walk the training fields smashing a fist into his palm, muttering, 'Bone the bastards' as his side approached crucial matches.

When that dream ended he became a travelling miracle worker. He took Slaughneil and Loup in Derry and delivered county titles with odds weighed heavily against them. In Slaughneil, their players still raise a glass to the man they call 'The Beast' at social gatherings, never forgetting the debt they owe him for their one and only club championship.

Antrim club Cargin pleaded with him to take them for the 1999 season. So he did, and brought them to a county title. The following year they retained it. He keeps cattle in west Tyrone and the locals rustled him into taking the Carrickmore job. He obliged and an O'Neill Cup followed.

He wanted the Derry job in 2004 after Mickey Moran stepped down. So did Paddy Crozier. Brennan was fresh from his most impressive coaching job with the Slaughneil success.

They both were interviewed and Brennan was beaten by a single vote. The county board had felt embarrassed in the past when Eamonn Coleman's opinions would sting some administrators. The fallout from Coleman's ousting in the early '90s had scarred Derry football. The more polished Paddy Crozier was appointed instead.

Brennan took the Loup to another county title in 2009 as a reminder that he still had the touch. When the county job came up, his position had hardened. He wouldn't be sitting in front of seventeen interviewers in a farcical situation again. He wouldn't even entertain the notion of doing an interview. Yet county chairman John Keenan was able to unveil him as the new Derry manager in the autumn of 2010.

Football was only part of Brennan. His wife Anne died before her time in 1991, and he used football as his crutch. Being surrounded by young people and working with them over the course of seasons kept him feeling fresh and young. Unusually for a Catholic, he held a high-ranking position for British Telecom but he left that job when Anne passed so that he could bring up his three children, the eldest of whom was only ten at the time.

Unusually again for a northern Catholic, he also played rugby for Ballymena and Rainey Old Boys. In the '80s, he went on a tour with Ballymena to the Bahamas and competed against teams from Canada, America and England. He walked off with the player of the tournament award.

To work and play sport in those circles requires social skills and Brennan compared the job of managing Derry to that of a social worker. Kevin McCloy backed up that claim in a newspaper interview two days before the semi-final when he said, 'It doesn't matter if you're the best or the worst, he'll tell you. It's the first time that I have ever seen one manager pulling with the two Bradleys and who has them eating out of his hand.'

Brennan was a players' man. He understood the spirit of Gaelic football and he never prejudged or assumed anything. When he was with the Loup, they were heading nowhere until he brought Martin McElkennon in to assist with the physical training. They ended that year in the Ulster club championship. Old school or not, he was humble enough to take the advice of others and learn from his mistakes.

• • •

The morning of the match, an article appeared in the *Sunday Independent*. Armagh's much-lauded strength and conditioning coach Mike McGurn had been incensed about a column Joe Brolly had written in *Gaelic Life* in which he had taken the Armagh management to task over what he perceived to be boring football. Brolly had questioned the role of McGurn within the setup and the criticism had stung. Now McGurn was getting his own back.

'We laugh at him,' McGurn said. *'He slated Armagh during the league. He said we're a team of guys who push weights, never train with the ball. There's this photo of us last year before we played Down in the league final in Croke Park. We were stretching and he used the photo and said "There, I've proved my point, not a ball in sight." We were fucking stretching, Joe. And we won that game quite handsomely.'*

It was described in the piece how the Armagh team execute one of their stretches, lying on their backs on the ground, spreading their legs apart and raising their arms up with two fingers raised. He said they call it the 'Joe Brolly Stretch'.

Steven McDonnell had no problem with the article or McGurn. Since McGurn came on board with Armagh he has had a hugely positive influence on McDonnell, so much so that McDonnell had been studying throughout the year to gain qualifications in personal training.

'Mike was totally right in what he did. I don't think you can actively use the ball when you're in the middle of doing stretches. As Mike correctly pointed out, it was a game that we won, playing a good brand of football.

'There's this impression out there that Armagh are a weightlifting team. That certainly isn't the case. Any weights that we do are speed and strength related. Mike McGurn doesn't want to be building us up as macho-men, that's not what his weight sessions are geared towards.

'I'm certainly stronger and a lot of that is down to Mike's training. These pundits should know better because most of them have been in the same situation themselves and they should know what it takes. Sometimes they seem to forget very easily. They shouldn't be talking a load of shite the way they do. They feel that they can write and say what they want about a load of people.'

The Armagh camp were bullish about their chances. They had faced down their neighbours Down and received much praise for their performance.

McDonnell was still being held back with his hip injury, so involvement in training was limited. He would have felt that his sharpness was becoming slightly dulled, but he had Jamie Clarke alongside him and that was enough edge to their attack.

In any case, it wasn't The Stevie and Jamie Show any more. He had forecast that Down would identify that twin threat and mark them extremely closely. The key to victory was the front six to a man driving at the Down defence. Malachy Mackin and Billy Joe Padden sparkled on a night that the Championship caught fire. Micheál O'Rourke was at his creative best. McDonnell may not have scored much, but he didn't need to. The more Armagh battered at the hull, the more water Down let in. In the end, they went down, worn out from bailing so much water.

This was Armagh's chance to get back into an Ulster final. Since their breakthrough in 1999, they had contested eight provincial finals. They simply did not lose in semi-finals.

Derry could hardly say the same. For all their talent, they hadn't featured in an Ulster final since 2000 and had lost seven semi-finals in the interim. Down had proved to be tough opponents for Armagh but they came through that test. Derry had beat nothing but a team of rookies and a divisive manager in Fermanagh.

Twenty minutes before throw-in, McDonnell was at the head of the queue of Armagh players who casually walked out of the Clones tunnel onto the field. The approach was unusual but then again the Cork hurlers had strolled out on the Croke Park pitch for the 2004 All Ireland hurling final which they won. Cork were mindful of wasting too much energy and Diarmuid O'Sullivan had tweaked his hamstring sprinting down the tunnel before the previous year's final.

'It was just something we decided to do. We just felt wanted to keep our energy for just before the game and get ourselves pumped up for it, instead of wasting it all on the run out and the build-up to it.

'If you look at all GAA teams, the first thing they do is sprint out onto the pitch. While it's good for getting adrenaline going, straight away you can feel fatigued within a minute.'

Armagh took their places for the team photographs and then McDonnell brought the ball all the way down to the twenty-metre line at the Clones end and kicked it over the St Michael's Scout Band and the bar. He had plenty of energy for the battle ahead.

● ● ●

When the Derry team bus rolled into Clones, it was a familiar scene for all of them. Not all the panel had played here before in inter-county action, so a week previously, Brennan had managed to convince the Clones authorities to open the gates to the Derry team and let them onto the field. They had a run through of how the game would go seven days later and got to play twenty minutes each way on the surface.

Danny Devlin, the Ballinascreen goalkeeper, had been glad of it. He may be twenty-seven but this was still his first season as the Derry goalie. After Mickey Conlan's quad injury ruled him out of playing the Championship opener against Fermanagh, Devlin grabbed the opportunity and made himself first choice. A couple of impressive saves in the first half had underlined his capabilities and he wasn't going to relinquish his grip on the number one jersey.

Clones was foreign to him. The Derry county team get by with a small but dedicated hardcore of support while the rest of the county subsist on a diet of an ultra-competitive club scene. Any time Derry were playing, Devlin saw it as a weekend freed up from club commitments. That meant staying out late on Saturday night enjoying a few jars, not worrying about cramming into a car and travelling to some far flung place like Clones.

He got to hit kickouts to his midfield targets. The dressing rooms were pretty much what he was expecting but the size of the stands looked daunting when empty. From where he was standing, he was able to watch the Brennan factor at work.

'John was going around different players, getting into their heads, convincing them that they were going to win. You get great confidence from him, just his body language and that. I haven't been involved in previous years so I couldn't talk about them, but it was like a club atmosphere. Everybody gets on well with each other, there are no fallouts, nobody taking huffs and everybody's going in the one direction.'

He knew that with goalsmiths at either end of the field, the kind of performances the goalkeepers would have could be the winning of the game. No bother, he thought, bring it on.

● ● ●

The forward threats were into the game right away. Eoin Bradley got a point from a free. Stevie McDonnell replied in the same way. Another Bradley free, a McDonnell free. Mark Lynch cut back onto his weaker foot and stroked over a point from forty-five metres as if he has been doing it all his life. Conleith Gilligan hit a free and then Bradley jinked one way and went the other before stroking over. One of the great individual performances had just begun and Derry were 0-5 to 0-3 up after the twelve minutes.

Three minutes later, a Ciaran McKeever lineball ended up bouncing into the hands of Jamie Clarke. He laid it off to Billy Joe Padden who dished it to McDonnell. McDonnell had time to think about it but Devlin sprinted from his line to save with his feet. For McDonnell, a goal chance had gone begging, while Devlin had passed his first test.

'You have to hand it to the Derry goalkeeper,' says McDonnell. 'He came off his line very quickly, but I would also say there was an element of luck in that it came off his ankles. I tried to slide the ball underneath him. Maybe, looking back, if I was that wee bit sharper in front of goal, I would have taken the ball around him.'

The ball though was retrieved by Armagh and from a difficult angle Clarke somehow curled it majestically between the posts. Armagh hadn't got their goal but they'd gained some inspiration and were only a point down. On top of that, Derry were forced into making a switch. Brian Óg McAlary had been booked for a foul on Clarke early on so Dermot McBride was moved onto Clarke and McAlary switched onto McDonnell.

At the other end, Armagh had assigned Brendan Donaghy as their man to look after Bradley, but he was booked on twelve minutes. Ciaran McKeever, surprisingly, was moved back on the dangerman.

Bradley instantly added to McKeever's discomfort, taking a pass and toasting the Armagh man before drilling the ball over the bar, but Armagh responded instantly. A ball was kicked into McDonnell who turned inside McAlary. In doing so, McDonnell lost his right boot, yet managed to get up to kick the ball over with his left. It was as if McDonnell and Bradley were having their own private gunfight, before Derry brought on the speedy Ciaran Mullen for McAlary and straight away sent him onto McDonnell.

Armagh made no such adjustments and in the twenty-ninth minute, Bradley shake-and-baked McKeever again to rifle over a point from forty-five yards.

A couple of minutes later, Derry extended their lead to five points, Mark Lynch hungrily seeking possession, breaking tackles before lashing the ball past Paul Hearty into the net. The first goal put Armagh on their heels.

They seemed in total control. Kevin McGuckin was acting as a sweeper in front of Clarke, while Michael Friel, Joe Diver and Enda Muldoon were dominating midfield.

The final act of the half was when Armagh won a free forty-six metres out. McDonnell calmly strolled out, placed it on the ground and kicked his point with an economy of effort.

It was Armagh's first score in sixteen minutes, and as they ran down the tunnel, they trailed 1-8 to 0-5.

●　●　●

In the RTÉ studios in Donnybrook, Joe Brolly and Pat Spillane were getting in some retaliation. Normally, they would be at each other's throats, but Spillane was also criticised in the interview with McGurn when the Armagh trainer said, *'I'll guarantee you one thing. You put Pat Spillane beside the likes of James Kavanagh or Bernard Brogan or Jamie Clarke and they'd blow him away. I'm sure he doesn't want to hear that. But they'd blow him off the pitch.'*

It was an ill-judged remark. Back before medical science was what it is now, Spillane had suffered cruciate ligament injuries and got himself back onto the pitch by making a private hell for himself in his garage of weights. Leaving aside his record of nine All Stars and eight All Ireland medals, he was regarded as one of the strongest players of the great Kerry side of his era, a point Páidí Ó Sé backed up a week later in the same newspaper.

'Jamie Clarke or any of those mentioned could be up on Pat Spillane's back and he wouldn't notice,' wrote Ó Sé. *'I, more than anyone else, know the merits of Spillane because I marked him in training for over ten years and that man, pound for pound, was as strong as anyone on that Kerry team.'*

Paddy O'Rourke did not escape either, as Brolly commented, 'Stevie and Jamie may as well not be there, the ball is not going into them. Paddy O'Rourke is a poor manager. He can't react to things on the day.'

With Brolly in incorrigible form, McDonnell got it too. 'I believe,' said Brolly, 'Stevie McDonnell is a pale shadow of his former self.'

• • •

A matter of seconds upon the resumption, McDonnell would have made Brolly review his theory. From the throw in James Lavery got a fist to the ball as he was falling. Charlie Vernon dived in and kicked it towards the Derry goal. It ended in Padden's hands who quickly scooped it to McDonnell. McDonell in turn spotted Micheál O'Rourke tearing through the middle and gave the perfect pass. O'Rourke drilled it past Devlin. Fourteen seconds into the second half, and now only two points separated the sides.

Derry did not panic. Charlie Kielt lobbed a point over instantly. Gilligan pointed a free. They exerted control over midfield. McDonnell hit another successful free but most of the Armagh players were back in their shell.

Eight minutes into the half, Kevin McGuckin was preparing to take the ball into his chest when McDonnell made a tackle and it popped free. Tony Kernan had a couple of stabs at it before it rolled to O'Rourke. He transferred it over the top to McDonnell who ran clear with a goal on. Instead of shooting, he took a bounce and fisted across goal to the unmarked Jamie Clarke. The pass was overcooked. Clarke stretched to reach but could not control it. The ball hit the post and Charlie Kielt brought it out calmly.

McDonnell knew that Derry had escaped. 'The pass to Jamie was too high. It's one of these things, you need to be ruthless with these opportunities and I wasn't ruthless enough.'

Bradley won another free, and it became apparent that Ciaran McKeever was not the right man to be marking him. He received a yellow card, Gilligan converted it to leave four in it, and Andy Mallon was finally moved onto Bradley.

Two minutes later came the defining moment in the match. McKeever marched out with the ball and hit a long clearance towards Padden which was cut out by Joe Diver. He laid it off to James Kielt who kicked a pass in towards Bradley. Mallon looked likely to collect it but he misjudged it and Bradley had tucked in behind. The Derry man slapped the ball to the ground, soloed once, hopped the ball, drew Hearty closer in and then thrashed the ball high to the roof of the net.

Then, for the full effect, he jumped over Hearty and hung off the crossbar on one hand. Derry were seven points clear and Armagh were drowning.

The score was not only another example of Eoin Bradley's incredible goalscoring talent but it was notable for its genesis. In the days leading up to the semi-final, Brennan had pointed out to Bradley how a lot of the play at Clones was condensed towards the Gerry Arthurs Stand wing, leaving so much room on the opposite wing. When Derry had possession in previous games, the natural thing for Bradley was to break towards his left. Now he was breaking to his right every time and getting constant service.

McDonnell though wasn't going to let this one go easy. With the Derry support still celebrating, McDonnell had another free on the forty-five metre line and once again converted. He followed it up again by making himself available to a quick free from Aaron Kernan, taking it with his right hand and then putting it over with the left foot. Charlie Vernon followed it up straight away. Armagh were still in this game.

In the next sequence of play they had a chance to go ahead. Vernon pumped it long towards McDonnell. With McGuckin tight to him, it broke to Clarke. McDonnell looped his run towards goal and came in on the blindside. Clarke floated it to him and McDonnell once again had just Devlin to beat.

Then he pulled the trigger...

And Devlin saved.

'He hit it good and early. Again I was expecting that he would have brought it on in, maybe even try and take it round me. I was glad to see him hit it from there. Definitely.'

Sean Leo McGoldrick was onto it and moved it on to his brother Barry. It was passed to James Kielt just on the sideline beside the tunnel. He curled it with the outside of his left foot down the line. Lynch beat both Kieran Toner and Donaghy to the ball, with Gilligan left completely unmarked inside. The ball was moved onto him, he soloed twice with his right foot before lacing it with his left, catching Hearty off guard. Derry 3-11, Armagh 1-10 and for the third time this afternoon the Armagh goalkeeper had been beaten with a high shot.

Over the next fifteen minutes Derry would tap over another three points to Armagh's solitary one. Then the whistle sounded. Derry's semi-final hex was finally over. They were finally back in a final while Armagh were gone.

●　　●　　●

After the game John Brennan wore the look of satisfaction. A few gentle questions were lobbed his way about how he broke Derry's dreadful semi-final curse and he compared that theory to an old LP with the needle broken. He was courteous and polite but looked a bit bemused by the scene. After the Fermanagh game he was able to speak to the press while standing on the pitch, but this was like a siege with his back to the concrete wall.

A few minutes earlier he had stood in the middle of a team huddle. Normally, this is a time for a stern talking to from a manager about not letting anything get in their way of focusing on a final. But Brennan was telling his players to make sure they had a decent drink that night, he certainly would be! With a big cheer, the Derry players looked like they were enjoying life and then they answered all media requests with a smile.

That is the power of Brennan. He has this Derry side playing with a smile. Before the season started, he asked two things off Paddy Bradley – that he work hard for the team and cut out the criticism of other players on the field. By the time of his cruel cruciate injury, Paddy was playing the best football of his life and thriving under the new management.

Plenty of Eamonn Coleman comparisons had been made. When Coleman had the team of 1993 flying, he used to individually tell both Joe Brolly and Enda Gormley that they were the best corner-forward in the country, bar none. He played cards with the players on the bus and never put much trust in authority.

There was much to recognise in Brennan. As the year progressed, speculation grew that Fergal Doherty might return to the panel to claim a midfield spot. When Joe Diver became concerned about his role with rumours of a Doherty return, he went to Brennan to ask him about it. Brennan heaped that much praise on Diver that he pleaded with the manager to stop because he was filling up and blushing so hard.

The Derry dressing room was a scene of joy. It was more than beating a team in a semi-final; it was about conquering personal demons and the accusation that they couldn't do it on the big day. Danny Devlin took it all in and radiated in the glow.

'There were a lot of boys that had been beat in five or six semi-finals and there was a sense of huge achievement for them. I was just taking it a game at a time. It would have meant a lot more to them boys but at the same time I'm really looking forward to this Ulster final.'

Once they got changed, the Derry team bus headed to the Four Seasons in Monaghan for a meal. They enjoyed a few pints there and loaded up with a few bottles for the journey back. By the time they left team trainer Conal Sheridan off at a petrol station in Aughnacloy, some were looking for a few refills from the off-licence. Joe Diver led the craic, finally freed from the yoke of failure.

Devlin teamed up with his friends from home and they ended the night in Portglenone at Fergal Doherty's bar. It ended up messy enough but that was alright. Derry were back in the big time.

●　●　●

As team captain, Stevie McDonnell didn't want to hide from reality. He stood outside the dressing room articulating what went wrong for Armagh and how they might put it right for the rest of the Championship. Back in the RTÉ studios, Brolly and Spillane feasted on Armagh's misfortune. The McGurn piece was something they wished to work out of their systems. Spillane said it was fine to have a go at him personally, but 'not after winning one match'. Brolly pronounced the game a 'sideline slaughter' and opined that Armagh 'are a total mess.'

McDonnell felt it was over the top and poor form. 'People like Joe Brolly wouldn't have been aware that I hadn't been able to take part in a training session over the last two months. They base it on me missing the goal chances or whatever yet if I was to turn out in the next game and score 2-5 he'd be the first to jump on the bandwagon.

'What Joe Brolly said about Paddy O'Rourke was totally, totally unjustified. He's never trained under Paddy O'Rourke, he's never played under Paddy O'Rourke, so how can he say how good or how bad a manager Paddy O'Rourke is? They think they can say what they want in front of a national audience and get away with it. Someone in Joe's position should know better than that.'

What's probably the hardest thing for McDonnell is that Armagh are no longer a feared team. During his county career, something has been lost from the Armagh psyche and it cannot be easily retrieved. In years gone by, Armagh would have got the goal they did at the start of the second half and pushed for home. This side were incapable of that.

'The other obvious key turning point was when I was through on goal that time. We were only four down then; twenty seconds later we were seven points down. If that goal chance had gone in, would we have won the match? I'm not so sure. Derry were in total control anyway. Even if we had have won the match, would it have papered over some cracks that we have? Maybe we would have gone on a wee bit further in the Championship and got to a stage where we couldn't have gone back and rectify it. Maybe it's a blessing in disguise that we did get a hammering.'

When McDonnell started down the inter-county road, he looked around the benches of the dressing room and could only see winners. Before they even started winning, they thought like winners. Now McDonnell is thirty-two and hasn't many years left. He knows that the indefinable quality of confidence is no longer there.

'The team that I came onto always believed in themselves. With strong-minded characters like that around you, playing with them week in and week out, you develop that belief no time.

'I'm not too sure whether or not these boys believe or not but I've seen enough of them this year to know that it's there for them if they really want it bad enough. I spent long enough playing with the country's top players in the International Rules to know that what we have in Armagh is no worse than any other county, including the Kerrys and Tyrones.

'There are a number of players in our setup that feel they'll get the better of whoever they're playing: Aaron Kernan, Ciaran McKeever, Brendy Donaghy, Andy Mallon; there's maybe six or seven that every day you know will give a performance.'

But you need more than that.

He thinks of one younger player in particular who came with all the essential ingredients to become one of the most dominant players in Ulster. Yet it has never happened for him.

'He's got everything going for him in relation to physique, skills, power, strength, everything. He's a prime example of what I'm talking about. He could have a super game but then might not have a good game for three games. I think that's down to him not being strong-minded enough to grab it by the horns.'

McDonnell feels that a lack of assertiveness caused the Armagh players to subconsciously abandon the game-plan that served them so well against Down. When players needed to demand and get on the ball during the semi-final, too many retreated into a defensive shell.

'If you have a style of play that the management wants to get across and one player decides he's not going to do it, then the whole thing falls down. I would say not everybody has bought into what Paddy [O'Rourke] is trying to get across.

It's nothing against the manager but individual players are not doing their role being asked of them.

'Against Down we went man for man and everybody knew what their job was and we got a performance and a result. In the Derry match, we went in with the same tactics but I don't believe everybody bought into it. Man for man, against Down around the middle, was totally different than man for man against Derry around the middle.

'If a player doesn't feel he's good enough to go man for man at county level, he shouldn't be there. That's the reality of it. I think when teams play sweeper systems it's passing the buck. I think it's a cop out. Too often players want to pass the buck, to play the sweeper system. They want to invite guys onto them and then pass the buck to the half forward line. You need to be ballsy and stand up and play.'

In the last decade, Armagh had won six Ulster titles. But the only thing remaining from that team is one of their best ever-players and a host of memories.

What probably hurts just as much is that their great rivals Tyrone are still going strong, seeking a third Ulster title in a row.

CHAPTER TWENTY-FIVE

Not Today, Ryan

DONEGAL v TYRONE
Ulster Semi-final, Clones, June 26

NINETEEN days before the Ulster semi-final, Donegal's Kevin Cassidy needed a favour from Mickey Harte. His school in Letterkenny, Little Angels, were looking forward to a prize-giving day and Cassidy thought Harte would be the perfect guest of honour to speak to the children. To get Harte's number, he rattled off a text to Tyrone's Ryan McMenamin. The two have got to know each other from facing each as competitors over the last decade and would occasionally swap texts.

McMenamin replied with the number and some light banter.

Here it is lad don't be giving him bad manners.

So Cassidy returned the ball into McMenamin's court.

I'll save the bad manners for our semi-final in a few weeks' time.

And on it went between the two.

June 13, 8.30am

Cassidy: Comin to get ya, comin to get ya.

McMenamin: Bring it on.

June 23, 8.30pm

Cassidy: Tick tock, tick tock.

McMenamin: Yes, til ure Ulster Championship run comes to an end. Enjoy the next four days.

June 25, 1pm

McMenamin: Enjoy 2day lad.

Cassidy: I will but I'll enjoy tomorrow even better. Tick tock.

As a former teacher himself, Harte accepted Cassidy's invitation. The prize-giving was one of those rewarding days that reminded both men why they were drawn to teaching in the first place. All the pupils received their certificates and the school showed Harte a video of the year's activities. He then spoke to the kids and mentioned how people can help others through their troubles. Nobody knows that quite like him.

Cassidy brought Harte to the staff room where they avoided football talk. Over a cup of tea, some of the other teachers tried to get Harte to chat about the upcoming fixture but he was giving nothing away, fobbing them off nicely. One of them offered an innocent question. How does he continue to do it, how can he keep driving himself after winning so many All Irelands?

'If I didn't have this,' he replied, 'I don't know what I would do.'

• • •

Donegal thought they had ramped up training after the preliminary round match against Antrim but the last fortnight has taught them differently. They sweated hard in various venues: O'Donnell Park in Letterkenny, MacCumhail Park in Ballybofey, St Naul's in Donegal town. The normal training sessions took place on Tuesday and Thursdays but the weekend double sessions on Saturdays and Sundays were the real torture.

This was The One. From his very first meeting with the team the previous winter in Castlefin, Jim McGuinness had targeted Tyrone. As the game got closer, he revealed that everything he had done was based on the belief that they would meet Tyrone in the semi-final. Sometimes if he felt the players weren't getting the message, he would cushion it by saying, 'I don't want to have to keep harping on to youse about Tyrone but they're the benchmark.'

The season has been wonderful so far for Cassidy but there has been strain on the family. Sometimes he has arrived home from training and little Aoife and Nia are upset and still not sleeping. He sees the stress on Sarah's face and repeats the promise he's made so many times now that he's even growing weary of it. 'It's going to be the last time and I'm just going to give it everything I have and hope for the best.'

One of Sarah's best friends was getting married the day before the semi-final. Cassidy promised her he would go along, stay for the meal and then take the children home. Then he had to come home one night from training and tell her that arrangement was off. McGuinness wanted all the players to travel down to Cavan and stay in the Slieve Russell Hotel, leaving on Saturday morning. Another letdown for Sarah, and more guilt for Kevin.

Tyrone usually had Donegal's number, same as Armagh. In previous meetings Donegal would lead with a glass jaw but that's no longer the case. Now, they're coming armed with the right attitude. In training they prepared by playing games of eight-versus-eight, on a forty-metre pitch. The speed of thought had to increase. The tackling had to be precise and it had to be clean. They had to get the ball out of confined spaces before they got bottled up.

'Tyrone bring an unbelievable intensity to the game, and our players maybe down through the years needed space to play, whereas this year we have been focused on trying to play within a confined space.'

Two days before the game, Cassidy sat at home and briefly contemplated defeat. Only briefly. Defeat can hardly be countenanced.

'We feel that this is the biggest game of our lives. If we're beat on Sunday there's going to be a lot of soul-searching done after the amount of effort that has gone into this year. Although Tyrone are an amazing team, we would be confident that we would have young legs all around the field.

'Whatever we have, whatever Jim has and whatever plan we come up with, everybody's going to see it on Sunday, without a doubt.

'This is the game that will make or break us.'

● ● ●

Of all the controllable factors in the game, the most vital to win was the tackle count. In Mickey Harte's first year with Tyrone's senior team, he used a drill where he would line up a corridor of big hitters and instruct players to run down the gauntlet of their challenges. He wanted them to be comfortable with hands in their faces, digs in their ribs and smart comments in their ears.

Ryan McMenamin loved that drill. The sadistic nature of it, torturing flair players that had to go against their instincts, tuck the ball in under their oxter, their chins into their chest, and barrel through to the other side. He flung himself through that corridor and laughed at teammates when he emerged from it.

All of that was nine seasons ago. In the years since, Harte spotted a skill that a goalkeeping coach introduced to his netminders of wrapping the ball up in your arms so you couldn't be dispossessed in the tackle. He asked the coach to demonstrate it to the likes of Peter Canavan and got them to perfect it. Against Tyrone, nobody would get anything cheap.

They knew there was work to do from the Monaghan match but it was better that some areas were highlighted in the video analysis sessions. One was that they gave away far too many frees in scoreable positions for Conor McManus and Paul Finlay to pop over.

'I can't say we've looked too closely at Donegal, to tell you the truth,' says McMenamin. 'We know all their players anyway, the only one we don't is basically [Patrick] McBrearty. We just tend to concentrate on ourselves. Sometimes we change the way we do things because of who we're up against but the conditioned games are geared to the way we want to play the game. Like, if we want the ball in quick, then that's the way the games will be set up. If we want to work on our tackling, the games will be designed around that.'

Tyrone know that Donegal are flexible. In the Antrim game Michael Murphy played a lot of his football deep. Against Cavan, it looked as if they were going to rain down ball on top of his head before he was sent off. In Clones they know that at some stage in the game there'll be a period where that tactic will be utilised.

In their conditioned games, the half forwards have stayed out of the opposition's forty-five metre line. McMenamin, Joe McMahon, Dermot Carlin, Cathal McCarron and Marty Swift were all tried in the full back line against their biggest attackers and the ball was pumped long and high, ball after ball for the defence to clear as soon as possible.

Tyrone are looking forward to getting back to Clones. 'We've had a couple of bad results in Clones but a lot of good ones. We don't really mind where we play but Clones has been good to us and if there's a good crowd there you can get a great atmosphere going.

'I'm sure Donegal are up for it. This is coming to the end of June, start of July. This is when the big games in the Championship start to happen.'

●   ●   ●

At 11am on the Saturday, instead of celebrating matrimony, Kevin Cassidy was boarding a bus in Donegal town bound for the Slieve Russell Hotel. Jim McGuinness's family business is coach hire, and his brother-in-law Kevin McNaney drives the team everywhere.

Once they reached their destination they threw their bags into the bedrooms and came back down to lounge about, keeping an ear open for Fermanagh's qualifier result as they took a beating from London. At 5pm, they went to work, specifically, a two-hour strategy meeting about the following day.

'We've had a hell of a lot of meetings. Hours and hours of dissecting them and how they were going to play and how we were going to play against them. Jim's probably had four talking sessions on Tyrone. He looked at the Dublin game last year, the Monaghan game in the Ulster final, the Monaghan game in the first round this year. He broke down every score Tyrone got. If you look at where they score from, it's from around the 'D'.'

The defence was briefed with clear instructions. They had to trust in the plan and have the mental strength to not fall back to old natural tendencies. If Tyrone had the ball, they were to retreat and set up their cordon, roughly thirty metres out and thirty metres wide, a zone in which Tyrone's attackers were not allowed to shoot. They identified two players, Sean Cavanagh and Brian Dooher; when they had the ball, pressure had to be put on. Otherwise, it was stick to the plan.

It wasn't just tactical matters that were taken into consideration. There was also the crowd that would be at the game, the pressure they would be under and most of all, what they would do when Tyrone cranked things up and got in their faces. Would they steam in and lay down a marker?

That wouldn't work. McGuinness spoke to another brother-in-law, the full-forward Colm McFadden, about it. In the 2007 Ulster semi-final as Donegal were watching the game disappear into the horizon and Tyrone were laying it on thick, a ball was played into McFadden. He was surrounded by five men and Brian Dooher was in talkative mood. McFadden drew back and caught him flush on the chin with a right cross and was sent off.

Rash actions were not going to win them this game. 'Jim said if we were within two or three points of them at halftime, they were going to get nasty, because we're taking this away from them.

'He had a phrase that we all had to say. "Not today." Instead of getting wound up or swearing back and getting abusive, he told every player that this is what we'd say. So if McMenamin would say anything to me, I'd just reply, "Not today, Ryan." Not get caught up in the whole thing. Jim said that even if you think you're not being put off your game saying something like that, he is putting you off your game. But not this day.'

After the meeting, the squad went to the hotel pool for some deep stretching, led by McGuinness himself, of course.

With a background in fitness, coaching and psychology, McGuinness is a multi-faceted coach. When he attended University Ulster Jordanstown, the head of GAA games there, Tommy Joe Farrell, got him involved in coaching the freshers team and was convinced that he was destined for this life. In a way, he has been preparing for this role for the past decade. The U-21 players he brought to an All Ireland final are his keenest students but Cassidy continues to be amazed by one of his oldest friends.

'I like to listen to Jim just before I go out. That's when I really enjoy it, focusing on what you're meant to do. Anybody else would lose the dressing room. Jim could chat for an hour, a straight hour, and not lose anyone's interest. He was always a good speaker. When he used to play with me he used to talk a lot, but then his training in college has helped him. He does a lot of lecturing now and he could speak for an hour and nobody would interrupt him.'

● ● ●

Tyrone kept it simple. They met at Kelly's Inn the day before the game for their video analysis and tactics. It was the same routine as the Monaghan game: in and out in an hour, going through the key points of workrate, the roles they had, and how they were going to play. 'We were confident enough,' says McMenamin, 'that the men we'd matched up against their key men were good enough.'

McMenamin got a cushy number. Tyrone noticed how Mark McHugh would spend most of his time in his own half. They also knew that Martin McElhinney wouldn't be troubling the umpires even though he was lined out as a forward, so that left a spare man at the back. McMenamin would be that free man, with a licence to link defence and attack and push upfield when possible.

• • •

By 9.30am on the Sunday morning, the Donegal squad were beginning to get cabin fever. They knew they could beat Tyrone, it was an exam that they had prepared and revised for, and now they just couldn't wait to get onto the pitch and put their answers down.

They had one last meeting. They stood in a square in a private room and talked about the principles of Tyrone's game. McGuinness compared each side to the walls of Tyrone's game. If they could tear the four walls down, the roof would come crashing in and they'd finally see the light. Everything was about this game.

Just before they left, there was one last clip to watch on the big screen. It was the story of Dick and his son Rick Hoyt. Rick was born in Massachusetts in 1962 and immediately diagnosed as a spastic quadriplegic with cerebral palsy following complications at birth. The doctor's advice to Dick and his wife Judy was simple. Institutionalise your son; without being able to walk or talk, he has no chance of living a conventional life.

Dick and Judy ignored that recommendation, clinging to the fact that Rick's eyes would follow them around the room. His mother taught him the alphabet and at the age of eleven he was equipped with a computer to enable him to receive an education. At fifteen Rick read an article on racing and asked his father if they could take part in a five-mile charity run for a paralysed lacrosse player. Dick was a lieutenant colonel in the Air National Guard and was not a runner, but he pushed his son in a wheelchair. Together, they completed the event. That night Rick told his father, 'Dad, when I'm running, it feels like I'm not handicapped.'

Team Hoyt has become a worldwide phenomenon since. Dick trained by pushing a wheelchair fitted with a bag of cement while Rick was at school, and they progressed to other events. Marathons and triathlons followed. Dick would cycle with Rick fitted in ever more sophisticated vehicles of transport, and during the swimming legs of triathlons, he would pull his son along in a little boat.

Together, they completed over a thousand athletic challenges. In 1992 they cycled and ran across America, crossing 3,735 miles in forty-five days. The next year Rick graduated from Boston University with a degree in special education. He put this to use by working in Boston College in a computer lab, helping to develop systems to aid communication for people with similar disabilities to himself.

McGuinness never explained what the clip was, just told his players to watch it closely. When it finished, two words flashed up on the screen. YOU CAN. Donegal left the room and headed to the team bus in complete silence.

● ● ●

As a curtain-raiser, Tyrone were playing Donegal in the Ulster U-21 shield hurling final. McMenamin and a few other players stayed out to enjoy the fine weather and the match. Once inside the dressing room, the mood was nicely upbeat.

'Out of ten, we felt about an eight or nine going into the game. We go into every match feeling confident, that if we play to the best of our ability, we'll beat any team. It's getting us to play at that ability.'

Unlike most sides, Tyrone don't go to the warmup field across the road from the ground. They get the blood pumping in the dressing room before going onto the field. While they were making the pulses race, a Clones steward knocked on the door and told them that the hurling game had gone to extra time, so they'd be running late with the throw-in for the showpiece.

McMenamin kept the mood light. 'We just took a seat again. I was slagging Mickey, asking him to sing a song, just to pass the time. We've been in that position before and are well used to it, so we just got a bit of craic going, though I stayed away from Mugsy [Owen Mulligan]. He was only a couple of seats down from me but I wasn't going chatting to him the way I was before the Monaghan game!'

Across the corridor, Donegal were mildly agitated. They had the windows open but it was a muggy day and they had spent long enough cooped up. When McGuinness began speaking, a plastic bottle came through the open sash and landed on the floor, some fans having their moment of fun. They got the windows closed again and McGuinness reminded them of the message at the end of the Team Hoyt clip. YOU CAN. Michael Murphy said the last word as captain and then they headed out for their first sunny day of the Championship. D-Day was finally here.

● ● ●

After four minutes, Peter Harte stood over a free. Cassidy had a word with him and the Tyrone forward ended up putting the free wide.

It was all Tyrone though in those early moments. Sean Cavanagh forced Rory Kavanagh into conceding a free and picking up a yellow card. Philip Jordan hoisted a point over from forty-five yards and then Brian Dooher came short to take a free off Sean Cavanagh and kicked it over from distance. With only thirteen minutes on the clock, Donegal were four down.

It took until fifteen minutes for Donegal to gain their first score, coming from seventeen-year-old Patrick McBrearty. A minute later, Cassidy found himself on the end line when he was stripped of the ball by McMenamin. Tyrone worked it down the field and Owen Mulligan hit a poor wide. Then Brian McGuigan kicked wide. Stephen O'Neill had a dig from distance but it fell short.

It was like the early rounds of Muhammad Ali's old rope-a-dope fight in Zaire. They were taking a hammering while inflicting no damage themselves. Michael Murphy was being marshalled superbly by Joe McMahon. Frank McGlynn hung one up but McMahon broke it away from the Donegal captain and McMenamin tidied up the loose ends. A minute later McMahon repeated the trick.

Then at the other end a fistpass from Neil McGee to Michael Hegarty was intercepted by Stephen O'Neill and he stroked over to make it 0-6 to 0-1. On the hill, some Tyrone fans struck up a chant of 'Easy! Easy!'

Not for the first time in the game, McMenamin made a dash in Cassidy's direction, shouting, 'Tick tock, Kevin, tick tock!'

On thirty-two minutes Kevin Rafferty managed to get Donegal's second point. Then Colm McFadden chipped in with a free. Suddenly, for all Tyrone's dominance, Donegal had narrowed the lead to just three.

Then in injury time, Donegal moved the ball up the wing to Michael Hegarty. He played a give and go with Cassidy before passing to McFadden, who was immediately sandwiched between Conor Gormley and Sean Cavanagh hard against the touchline, fifty metres from goal. The ball broke free and Cassidy scooped it up. He avoided the despairing lunge of Cavanagh, had a quick look at the posts before pivoting and booming it over the bar. The Donegal support roared while the Tyrone crowd were noticeably quiet. This wasn't going to be so easy anymore.

Cassidy's point hadn't been either. It was probably the score of the Ulster Championship.

'I'd put in one or two balls into the forward line and we weren't getting any joy because Joe was cleaning up and Gormley was holding McFadden well too. So this time I had a rattle, and as soon as it left my boot I knew it was over. I didn't even have to look once I heard the sound.'

It was the last play of the half. Amazingly, Donegal were going in only two points down. As Cassidy and McMenamin jogged down the tunnel, Cassidy couldn't resist cranking up the pressure, as much as he knew he shouldn't have.

'I went over to him and said "Tick fucking tock now!"

'Normally, when you say something to Ricey, he would have something smart to say or an answer for you, or just smile.

'His face was blank. I could see it on their faces that they knew they were gone.'

• • •

Half-time was a time for cool heads. McGuinness was stressing the importance of concentration, committing to the game-plan and leaving emotion out of the equation. All Tyrone would have listened to, he said, was talk of this fresh, young Donegal side coming to dethrone them. They weren't going to stand aside or let Donegal steamroll them. The second half would be a hell of a fight.

Truth be told, so had the first half. The ferocity of the first quarter in particular had caught Cassidy cold.

'We didn't think it was going to be as severe as it was. But we stuck at it and stuck to the game-plan. It's been like that all year. Even if things are going wrong, don't deviate away from the game-plan. When they went four, five points up, we had no fear. In years gone by we would have thought they were running riot and collapsed, but we were shouting at each other to just get a score, just keep in touch with them.'

Marc Curran read out the stats from the first half. They were getting annihilated in the break ball and kickout count. If they could get a hold around the middle, more chances would follow. Murphy and McFadden were frustrated with their own performances. Then Cassidy took the floor to speak.

'This is what we spoke about for the last two weeks, boys! If we stay within touching distance of these boys going into the last fifteen or twenty minutes… We're right where we want to be! After playing nothing! If it becomes a battle, we know we have the legs for them.'

Somewhere out there in the ground was Cassidy's father, Tommy. He had left a message on Kevin's mobile, asking if he could have a ticket for the game. It was sorted. The last time Kevin and his mother were talking about their family, Anne said she could nearly forgive Tommy for the heartache and the misery. He has enough problems of his own now.

Working in Letterkenny, he's not invisible. Sometimes Kevin will be driving through town and catch a glimpse of him, sitting on the street. For a few seconds they are right beside each other in person, but they live in worlds apart. Sarah asks if that bothers him, but he's being honest when he says it doesn't. There comes a time when you just have to move on in life.

• • •

In the other changing room the defending champions were measured and thoughtful but they wore furrowed brows. What the hell just happened out there?

The bare mathematics of Tony Donnelly's statistics infuriated them.

Donegal had only five attacks yet they'd harvested four points from them. Tyrone had owned the ball. They had bullied Donegal's forwards and had launched eighteen attacks. Eighteen! Yet they'd only scored six times.

They reminded themselves of who they were. They were loaded with experience and that quality meant they were impervious to the kind of panic that freaks out lesser teams.

'We knew ourselves that we didn't get enough scores. We knew it was going to be a tough battle and that Donegal weren't going to play as bad in the second half. At the same time a lot of the boys were expecting more of Donegal, they had been written up as this great team and we were expecting them to be more in our faces.

'In the first half, we were the ones in their faces. We played them in the league and they were aggressive and we thought it would be the same. As Philly Jordan said to me, the first half was the easiest first half he had ever played in his life.'

Brian Dooher and Sean Cavanagh both took to the floor. They emphasised that what had gone before was a hoax, a bluff. The real football and the fighting and hardship would start now. Tyrone had two Ulster titles in a row and wanted three.

Mickey Harte talked then. He said that if Donegal had heart and character, and he was sure they had, then they would come at Tyrone hard. The challenge was to put them back on their arses.

● ● ●

Cassidy led the charge. He robbed Jordan in the first minute of the second half, drove a ball crossfield to Murphy who got a yard away from McMahon. He turned and curled it over. Tyrone 0-6, Donegal 0-5.

Soon after Cavanagh was fouled by Mark McHugh. As Peter Harte stood over it, Cassidy came over and began chatting. He had been doing it from Harte's first free on four minutes that he hit wide. McMenamin came over and had a nibble at Cassidy. The reply came on cue: 'Not today, Ryan.'

McMenamin knew where Cassidy was coming from. Mind games were something he had brought to the next level.

'I did the same once to [Dublin's] Mossy Quinn. Once he missed the first one, you get on to him again about it. Some boys do it all the time but even when Petey was scoring I think Cass was having a word with him about it. I don't think it was bothering Petey but at the same time he wasn't hitting them as sweetly as he would have liked.'

Two minutes later, Cavanagh was awarded another free. Cassidy was again in Harte's ear and as the Tyrone forward began his run-up, Cassidy clapped his hands a couple of times. Harte missed.

'From the first free,' recalls Cassidy, 'I said "You don't have the distance, you don't have the accuracy," and he missed it. He had one from the forty-five metre line then and I kept speaking but he put it over. Fair enough. But I kept at him. Said stuff like "There's number twelve going up on the board there." I wouldn't normally say this shit but now, we have to.'

For that you can blame Brian 'Wolverine' Dawkins.

• • •

In the lead in to the Cavan game, Cassidy felt that while every other aspect of their game was catered for, they needed to get nasty. 'We weren't bad enough. That's not going out and hitting off the ball, but getting in people's faces. That's what the likes of Ricey and them do, get inside people's heads, put people off their game, extra stuff that we weren't doing.'

Martin McElhinney asked Cassidy had he ever seen any clips of Brian 'Wolverine' Dawkins, an American football safety for the Denver Broncos. Cassidy hadn't but looked him up on YouTube before training one Sunday morning. For him it was the missing piece of the Donegal jigsaw.

'It just jumped out at me that this guy was exactly like half of our team, a lovely lad off the field, but an animal on it.

'I asked Maxi to bring the laptop and put it on YouTube. I wondered if there was anything of this that we could tap into because we were too nice. After the DVD, we knew we had to be more ruthless and [Karl] Lacey and Murphy asked Jim if we could introduce something like this.'

McGuinness went away and thought about the issue of mental toughness, before putting his own twist on it. On the journey to the Cavan game, he introduced wristbands for the team and backroom staff to wear, with four elements on them. The Donegal crest is woven on. There is 'GP', which stands for 'Game Plan'. 'MA' stands for 'Mental Attitude' which is the Brian Dawkins element, 'that mental strength,' says Cassidy, 'that mental toughness.'

The last symbol is a number.

'20 is focused on everything we are based on. It represents everything that we're geared towards this year, everything that makes us tick and play. It's what we are, and it's what will make or break us.' For now, it remains a secret.

Everyone keeps their own wristband. Cassidy stores his between games in a side pocket of his kitbag, along with his gumshield and some holy relics. The true meaning of the bands is kept a secret.

'That's the thing about trust in Donegal this year, it won't get out. If it was a few years ago, everybody would know what they mean. It's a symbol of unity. We're in this together and we trust each other.'

• • •

The ebb and flow of the game had changed. Donegal were now having a say in midfield and the intensity dial was turned up. Murphy pointed a free but two minutes later, Stephen O'Neill jinked around the bodies of Cassidy, McGee and Thompson to help himself to a point.

In the same minute, Owen Mulligan was taken off. Donegal never bought into the idea that their opponents had amazing strength in depth and they knew that every substitution was weakening their team.

On fifty-six minutes, Donegal swept upfield and after an exchange of passes, Colm McFadden coolly stepped inside Pascal McConnell before rifling to the net, unusually off his right foot. It hit McMenamin's backside on the way in and suddenly Donegal were ahead, 1-6 to 0-8.

'He finished it well,' says McMenamin. 'I was trying to get back, and I thought he was going to step inside and kick it straight. Instead, he kicked it across me. If I had been a wee bit fatter I might have stopped it.

'That goal came from a turnover. Me and Big Sean were over and the ball was worked in. Cassidy got the turnover for them and it was only a couple of kick passes from our attack to their goal. It was a mistake on our behalf.'

Three minutes later, Dooher won a free that Peter Harte put wide, again after some encouragement from Cassidy. Tyrone were quaking now. Kevin Hughes had been booked for a high tackle on Cassidy on the hour, and a minute later he committed the same offence on Michael Hegarty and was shown a second yellow card.

While all the commotion was going on, Dermot 'Brick' Molloy entered the fray for Leo McLoone, himself a substitute who had put in a dangerous high challenge on Joe McMahon that led to the Tyrone full-back's withdrawal. Bit by bit, Tyrone's All Star cast were being smuggled offstage.

With three minutes left, Peter Harte stood over another free to level it. Cassidy could scarcely believe it. Harte had been fluffing these kicks all day and Cassidy had fully expected Martin Penrose to stroll over and kick it. Once he spotted Harte placing it, he jogged over to put him off.

'I couldn't understand it, why Mickey didn't take him off or let somebody take the responsibility off the young lad. He missed the free but I didn't even want to say anything to him after that one.'

When the ball went wide, Brian Dooher's number went up on the board.

Cassidy remembered that the last time the teams met in Championship, back in 2007, Dooher had been taken off to a standing ovation. There would be no ovation for him today.

In the final minute, McMenamin took matters into his own hands. He carried the ball out of defence, evoking memories of his younger self when he would routinely nick points. He played a return pass with Cavanagh as he made his way into the heart of the Donegal defence. Mark McHugh held him up twenty-five yards out to the left of the post, and though McMenamin managed to get his shot off, he put too much of his instep into it and it flew wide.

'I tried to catch it on the outside of my boot and I didn't catch it enough. As soon as I kicked it, I thought it was over. It went wide and I was a bit shocked. I still thought we had plenty of time though.'

The game was in injury time, with four minutes announced. McMenamin did not hear the stadium announcer and thought they had ten more minutes. It was getting hot, just how Tyrone liked it. They launched another attack. Colm Cavanagh was coming in from the left-half forward position when he hit a loopy handpass to his brother Sean. Paddy McGrath jumped to contest it and the ball broke off both of them and fell kindly for Penrose. He stroked it over to level the game in the seventy-first minute.

The drama continued. Donegal's Frank McGlynn got the ball along the sideline on the Pat McGrane Stand side. Cassidy came in and blocked off the tackle of Tyrone substitute Aidan Cassidy. Tyrone free.

They worked it over to the other side of the pitch. McMenamin was fouled and he kicked it infield to Cassidy, who transferred it to Jordan, but he hit a sloppy pass and left the ball in no-man's land. Tommy McGuigan left it for Penrose but Lacey got there first. Michael Hegarty was onto the break and handpassed to McBrearty on the wing. He stroked the ball towards Michael Murphy, only it favoured Martin Swift who momentarily seemed to have cut it out.

Murphy continued his run though and at the point of contact, Swift dropped it. Dermot Molloy was suddenly through on goal and Murphy seized on the loose ball. Swift and McMenamin dived on Murphy but he was too strong for them. As he was falling, he passed to Molloy.

Molloy took one bounce. Cassidy held his breath.

'I was thinking, "Please, just handpass the ball over the bar!"'

McMenamin was lying on the turf in horror as Molloy drilled the ball. McConnell got his body in place but it hit off his forearm and into the goal.

Cassidy couldn't believe it. 'Where I was standing, I seen the deflection and thought it went away wide. Then the roar came. We knew we were home and dry then.'

McMenamin wasn't panicking. 'I thought there was still plenty of time left.

It wasn't until we were going up the road on the bus that I learned the goal was scored in added time.

'It was unlucky for Swifty, because he had a great game all day, and he came across and intercepted it. We were a man down with a while to go, but any of the back six would tell you that we didn't feel we were being put under any wild pressure. If anything, we felt Donegal went even further back.'

There'd be one last play. Tyrone would work it upfield, but Neil McGee stopped Aidan Cassidy breaking forward, more than willing to take a yellow card. Penrose floated the ball into the area but Donegal mopped it up, kept the ball and ran down the clock. Next thing, the whistle. Tyrone had lost their title. The three-in-a-row bid was over.

For Donegal, there was no fist-pumping or playing to the gallery. A huge battle had been won but hardly the war itself. After the team huddle, some players were intercepted by the media for spot interviews. Colm McFadden stayed out and answered questions but he was the only one. Rory Gallagher appeared from the tunnel, apologised to the reporters and took McFadden back inside. Their plans for the final had to start now.

● ● ●

After they'd talked Kevin Cassidy went for his shower and then sat down after drying off. He fished his mobile phone out of his kitbag and turned it on again. There was a flood of good luck and congratulatory messages but one stood out. It was from Ryan McMenamin.

Well done. Now enjoy the final.

Cassidy replied straight away.

You'll not begrudge us this one. Youse have been the benchmark this past ten years.

Only their time had run out. Tick tock, tick.

CHAPTER TWENTY-SIX

Seven Days Away

AFTER the great Tyrone empire was pitched onto the bonfire, only two teams remained: Derry and Donegal.

Neither side had had it exactly handy. Donegal had to come through the preliminary round. Derry beat what fleetingly looked like a rejuvenated Armagh. The two dominant counties of the era had been taken out and the Ulster Championship would be crowning new winners. A gust of air had blown through the hallowed old competition and the final would be all the richer for it.

The Ulster Championship may have been owned by the duopoly from either side of the River Blackwater for the previous twelve years, but while their achievements were respected, other counties had always got down and dirty with them over the past decade. When Tyrone and Armagh were All Ireland champions, they were particularly vulnerable in their backyard.

There was the sodden day in 2003 when Colm Coyle's lowly Monaghan laid tripwire for Armagh, Paul Finlay announcing himself to the nation with eight points.

Donegal too had their moments. They bumped Tyrone off the tracks in 2004 in a semi-final at Clones and halted Armagh's four-in-a-row Ulster bid in 2007.

Derry humbled Tyrone when they began their defence of their second All Ireland title in 2006, holding them scoreless for the opening half in front of their own fans in Omagh.

The problem was that while they and the rest of Ulster could take one of the big guns out, they could never make it the two of them in the one year. Donegal were losers in three finals to Armagh; Derry couldn't even get as far as the glorious failures tag.

The dominance began on a baking hot day when Armagh broke their seventeen-year absence from the top table with Oisín McConville notching a remarkable 2-7 in the team's humiliation of old rivals Down in the 1999 final. That was a young Armagh side with huge ambition and character.

On Ulster final day twelve months before that game, Tyrone showed their promise for the future when their minor side beat Antrim comfortably. The highlight was a closely-cropped redhead called Owen Mulligan scooping the ball into the path of midfielder Cormac McAnallan who blasted to the net from distance. Mulligan would win three All Irelands since and McAnallan would win one, even briefly captaining his county before his tragic death in 2004.

The main event that day though? Derry and Donegal, the same billing as the 2011 decider. That 1998 clash was a drab affair played out between ageing squads yet also boasted probably the most dramatic finish ever to an Ulster final, Joe Brolly rounding Tony Blake in injury time to strike the decisive goal for Derry. He would celebrate it by infamously blowing kisses to the terraces while that night the whole team would go back to Henry Downey's bar and celebrate 'until,' As Geoffrey McGonigle would put it, 'the birds were singing.'

Among their number was a skinny beanpole with mesmerising skills, Enda Muldoon. He remains the only player in Ulster medallist outside Tyrone and Armagh still playing inter-county football and he's dropped hints that this is probably his last year.

It's time for a new name on the cup.

• • •

Dean McGlinchey Park, the home of St Colm's GAC, Ballinascreen, is discreetly hidden in the back end of Draperstown village, up a narrow side road along St Columba's Church.

The ground is an uneasy mix of old and new. A hi-tech two-storey clubhouse looks out onto the pitch. To the left of it is an expanse of concrete standing room. In the corner is an old-fashioned 'gents', a roofless box of concrete with bare walls and troughs that have served their purpose for many years.

At noon on Sunday, July 10, the Derry team are loitering around the outside of the dressing rooms. Some are already in their rigs but some, like the laid-back Muldoon, are in no great rush to get togged out for the training session that will replicate what they aim to do a week later in the biggest game of their lives.

As the minutes roll on, they emerge in their training gear: black tops, grey shorts. It's July, but in name only. The last week was a long one for them. Media requests for interviews were turned down politely and everywhere they went they were faced with that tiresome question. 'Will you win?' Of course they'll win. Why else would you dedicate your year to it if you weren't going to win?

Eoin Bradley is hanging about with the two Kielt brothers, Charlie and James. That triumvirate form the central line that Derry need to penetrate the Donegal defensive code. Charlie is the centre-back who loves to push up and hit points. James is the centre forward whose talent and skill led to offers of playing Australian Rules. He could have been named man of the match in the Ulster semi final, only for Bradley's stunning return of 1-5. It seems that almost every year one of Bradley's goals is in contention for Goal of the Year. The one he got in the second half against Armagh would make any shortlist.

His talent has never been disputed but he's carried baggage. In the 2010 Derry club championship, he clashed with referee Declan O'Connor after his team Glenullin were defeated by Ballinascreen. He was handed a forty-eight-week suspension that was halved on appeal. A succession of Derry managers failed to cure his enigmatic nature but he could still produce moments of such reckless skill to thrill all fans of the sport.

Even against Armagh when the game as a contest was over, he couldn't resist a bit of mischief. He went to retrieve a ball when Armagh were awarded a free, only to blast it off Andy Mallon's shins. It was a pointless act and led to Mallon gripping Bradley's throat in a rage. Soon after, John Brennan wisely took Bradley off.

In the absence of his supremely-skilful brother Paddy, he has taken on the mantle of the go-to-guy. Almost everyone agrees he has flourished under the wing of Brennan.

Brennan understands that Bradleys are rare talents but that they've had to contend with the label of being troublesome within a camp. Brennan came in and instantly felt the vibe. It suits some to paint the two brothers as being arrogant or brusque, but they are also young men who are programmed to demand the best of themselves. When others in their stratosphere fall short of those exacting standards, then difficulties arise. Even in the macho environment of Ulster football, an arm around the shoulder can work with the most unlikely individuals.

These boys are the sons of Liam 'Baker' Bradley. They're cut from the same granite as him: perfectly personable and friendly but ruthless competitors. It shouldn't be held against them.

• • •

Along with the two Kielts, Bradley makes his way onto the pitch. Some have already begun the tradition of killing time by taking shots for points. A sign at the back of the other goal reassures us that this is another Prunty pitch.

At 12.30, Derry trainer Conal Sheridan blows his whistle to begin the warmup. The players jog in and briskly handpass the ball in a grid. Joe Diver, the giant midfielder, receives a pass delivered low which hits him in the groin, and he half-laughs, half-winces with the pain that is the preserve of males. 'Oh! That'll waken me up!'

Sheridan tells the players to work the ball through their legs, calling 'Figure eights!' All the players lift one leg after another and get their stretches done without noticing, apart from Conleith Gilligan, who is joking and showing the rest of them how it is done in Harlem, weaving and bouncing the ball basketball-style through their legs.

Within five minutes of the session starting, John Brennan appears. Without anything being said, frivolity ceases. He has that effect. He pauses his walk on the field to have a word with his captain, Barry McGoldrick.

The players spread across the pitch to aim kicks at each other from a distance of forty yards. Gilligan and Mark Lynch are pinging it into each other's chest. Sheridan calls out the next instruction, to get a bit more distance into the kicks and ensure that the ball bounces once before the receiver collects.

Liam Óg Hinphey is also there. The half-back was brought into the squad a week before the semi-final and his aggression is welcome in the setup. The family name is synonymous with hurling in the county but Liam Óg and his brother Kevin are also notable footballers with the Dungiven club. Across the family table, the discussions are riveting, with Liam senior a natural raconteur. Hurling was always his first love and he managed his two sons a couple of years back with the county hurling squad. It was he who coined an immortal phrase when asked his views on modern-day football. 'It's a bit like homosexuality,' he proclaimed, 'alright between consenting adults, but not something to be encouraged among the youth.'

The practice moves into contact drills. One man holds the ball while his partner tries to dispossess him. Over by the stand, Brian Óg McAlary bobs and turns, while PJ McCloskey is the aggressor. McAlary is caught with a stray tackling hand around the face, and he squats down to recover from it. McCloskey shows some concern. 'Are you alright? Sorry about that, Brian.' McAlary temporarily stops training and heads inside the dressing room for five minutes.

Brennan keeps his distance while the session continues. Sheridan's voice is the dominant one. Bibs are handed out and two teams make their way to a narrow strip of the pitch along the sideline that has small goals fifty yards apart. The aim of this game is to be comfortable in narrow spaces while keeping the ball.

While this is ongoing, another drill utilises the main goals. Two attackers face two defenders. The attackers begin their move when the first whistle is sounded, and have to keep it until the second whistle is blown, whereupon they get off a shot.

At 12.57 the whistle blows again and the players run in to take water on board. Brennan enters the circle and begins to speak over at the far end of the pitch from the stand, out of earshot of the interested onlookers that have gathered around the fence to get a look. Six minutes later, the players go into the two dressing rooms while Brennan stays out on the field in conversation with Sheridan.

A referee emerges from his dressing room.

At 1.10, players come out of one dressing room wearing the kit of the Glen Watty Grahams, predominantly green but with a gold hoop, close enough to the

Donegal colours. Another team, this time in the Derry strip, depart their dressing rooms two minutes later.

At 1.13, the referee throws the ball in to begin the game. Two minutes in, Eoin Bradley peels to his right and loses his marker, Kevin McCloy. He barely touches the ball before he puts it straight over the bar. Conleith Gilligan follows it up with a massive point from forty-five yards.

There is resistance from 'Donegal'. Gerard O'Kane is playing with the second string and looks to be flying. He breaks a tackle and takes his own shot on to take a point back.

A couple of plays later, Joe Diver lays a ball off and goes for the return. Liam Óg Hinphey blocks his way and the two players have a small wrestling match. Players are playing for places here and the opposition for 'Derry' are not allowing themselves to be patsies.

'Donegal' grab a goal on eleven minutes. Strong foraging from Hinphey placed Marty Donaghy in a good position and he slots it beyond Danny Devlin.

James Kielt has a free and plays a neat little one-two before letting the ball into Bradley who turns to kick another point. 'Derry' have withdrawn their half forward line and are leaving as much room as possible in front of Bradley for him to exploit. A minute later, Kielt adds a beautiful point of his own.

Gilligan is another player who is buzzing around. He takes a pass from Michael Bateson and beats two men before pointing. Emmet McGuckin replies for Donegal with some sharp attacking. He's one man who will definitely see action on Ulster final day.

Declan Mullan is playing a sweeper role for Donegal and while his athleticism is impressive, he seems unsure of the role. Could his stationing here be mimicking the work of Karl Lacey?

Bradley is by a distance the most impressive player on show. He gets another ball as the half draws to a close, out wide on the right. Despite having a couple of men shadowing him, he breaks free and curls a magnificent point between the sticks. The referee calls for the ball and the players go into a circle.

At 1.44, the second half of the game begins. It is only one minute old when Bradley helps himself to his fourth point. From the next kickout he adds his fifth. He is in phenomenal form but is undoubtedly helped by the fact that the team playing in Glen jerseys resemble Donegal in colours only.

Would Donegal leave so much room for him to operate in? Could Jim McGuinness leave one marker isolated on Bradley? The problem with trying to replicate another team's performance is when players remain in trial match mode: taking an extra solo out of the ball to look good, pushing up to join in the attack when the real Donegal defence would sit back. Every man is still bidding for a starting jersey or minutes on the field.

PJ McCloskey replies for Donegal with two points in two minutes before Bradley lands another monster from distance.

Two minutes later then, Bradley is running into space to collect a pass when there's a moment's hesitation. His body crumples and he goes down roaring with pain, holding his knee.

The physio and team doctor rush onto the pitch. Hush comes over the ground. Conal Sheridan gathers the remaining players over by the far end of the pitch and they go through a series of light aerobic exercises to keep warm.

A stretcher is brought out from the clubhouse. Bradley refuses it and gets to his feet with some help. He is carried off the field with his arms on the shoulders of medical staff. Halfway to the dressing rooms, they pause as he attempts to put some weight on his limping leg. It's no good. This session is over for him and he hobbles off the field in pain.

'You knew he was gone straight away,' recalls Danny Devlin. 'I was down the far end of the pitch and most of the lads came down there. A few of the lads said they heard a crack so at that stage I thought it might have been the leg, but it was the knee. Gutted for him. It couldn't have happened at a worse time.'

After tending to Bradley, Brennan sets off in the direction of everyone else. He has a quick conference with other management and they go further to the players who immediately circle up in a huddle.

'John came over and said the same as all year. People get injured and one man's misfortune is another man's fortune. At this stage there would be a space up for grabs the following week. That's been John's attitude all year round, whether we lost James Conway, Paddy or Eoin.

'It didn't take long for news to filter out. A couple of lads were watching it. Some of the players said that nobody needs to know but you weren't going to keep that quiet. Plenty of the ones watching knew it was serious.'

The teams line out again. Cailean O'Boyle takes the place of Bradley on the 'Derry' side. They go to it again. Joe Diver seems agitated with a few of the challenges, calling out, 'You didn't see that, ref?' All the time Brennan maintains a distance from the other members of the management team.

A few more points are added on from both sides but the urgency has evaporated. At 2.28 the players are called in and go through their stretches. Brennan talks to them animatedly before they return to the dressing room. He stops on the forty-five metre mark to pause and talk with Kevin McCloy. They begin to walk off before stopping again on the twenty-one yard line and continue their chat.

A selection of players pose behind a banner advertising 'Cairde Catherine', an upcoming charity match in memory of the late Catherine Quinn, wife of former Derry legend Danny.

With that taken care of, Conleith Gilligan picks up a stray hurl and brings a sliotar out to the '45. He strikes the first one over, hits the second one wide, and tops the third and final attempt.

Some time when the game resumed and Bradley left the field, he put a call through to his brother Paddy, asking him to come up and collect him from the pitch. Paddy enquired what was up and Eoin said, 'I think I've done my cruciate.'

A victim of the same injury himself this spring, Paddy immediately began crying from his wee brother.

At 2.45, Eoin exits the dressing room on crutches with ice strapped to his knee. Paddy arrives through the gates in his car and emerges, limping himself and carrying a Derry kitbag. He shakes his head ruefully when he sees his brother.

His cruciate is gone. Their dream is gone.

CHAPTER TWENTY-SEVEN

Breaking Into Heaven

DONEGAL v DERRY
Ulster Final, Clones, July 17

News of Eoin Bradley's injury was hoovered up by GAA websites and spread everywhere within hours. Neil McGee had been the man psyching himself up to face the Derry man in seven days' time when a text popped into his inbox. He forwarded it to his clubmate Kevin Cassidy: Skinner out for Sunday.

Cassidy wasn't convinced. He would occasionally swap texts with Paddy Bradley, so he fired one off to him: Any truth in the rumour about Skinner? Bradley texted back that it was indeed true. Cassidy asked Paddy for Eoin's mobile number and when it came, he forwarded his sympathies. Later in the evening, Paddy texted Cassidy with the message: I want a proper final next year, with us two men back.

The injury swung the pendulum in Donegal's favour. They knew it.

Club championship took centre-stage after the semi-final and the panel was cut loose for a week. Leo McLoone's cheekbone was then broken in a melee in the closing stages of the Naomh Conaill defeat to Glenswilly. After publicly calling for the matches to be postponed, Jim McGuinness was disgusted with the turn of events. He had appealed through a Highland radio broadcast after the Ulster semi-final for the postponement of these games. The position the Donegal competitions control committee took was that they'd received no official request.

Tensions still simmer between McGuinness and a few administrators. Some of them sat on the interview panel when he went for the management job before. They didn't comply with his requests for equipment for the interview and looked down at their shoes throughout his presentation.

'There are people now just waiting for Jim to fall,' says Cassidy. 'That's a horrible thing to say but it's true. I don't know if it's down to club rivalries or what, but that's what's happening at the minute.

'Had Jim not won Ulster with the 21s, he would not have got the senior job. Few of the players would know much about all that though because he doesn't want any negativity seeping in.'

Eight days after the Tyrone game, the panel met for an evaluation. There was no back-slapping. They looked at it coolly and then broke off into groups of five to rate their scores in tackling, scoring situations and other areas. From all the games they had played, going back to the McKenna Cup, it was the worst implementation of the game-plan.

Even in that, the evening contained an epiphany for Cassidy. 'I sat there thinking how it was a sign of how far we have come. To reflect on beating Tyrone and be almost unhappy about it.'

They were glad to be rid of Tyrone and all the head space they and their aura had occupied. Derry would be a different challenge, a different message. They attacked the Tuesday night session hard.

The two-hundred metre runs are the hardest drill they do. Back in January when they were running through snow in Castlefin and emptying their stomachs over barbed wire fences, Cassidy would just about get home in less than forty seconds. Now, the entire squad is able to do them in twenty-five seconds. Between the front and the rear, there is a two seconds gap.

The minimum amount of runs they do is six, but any time they ask how many runs they are doing, McGuinness adds a couple.

'Before, we would have asked him how many we were going to do, so he would put us through our runs, stop it, and say "Okay, Kevin asked us how many we were going to do, so we'll do two more, Kevin."

'Tuesday was horrendous. I was in the toilet after, puking. Every man was sprawled out over the park in Letterkenny. I couldn't eat anything after either. It was tough but hopefully it'll work out. I'd say this is the best shape all the boys have ever been in.'

For the players, the most enjoyable aspect is the series of seven-minute matches. One team turns their training tops inside out to become 'whites', the others keep their black shirts on. McGuinness shortens the field to work in a tighter space and they go at it. The moment a ball goes out of play, there is another put in. If a free is awarded, it is taken instantly. If there is a foul, nobody stops to enquire how the injured man is. Once the seven minutes are up, players have four minutes exactly for recovery, timed on Jim's watch. The losers of each match have to drop and do seventy press-ups.

'You could do seven games a night so if you lose seven games you end up doing 490 press-ups. Every one of them is counted, there's no token effort. It's serious stuff! At the start you didn't really mind, but once you've been down a couple of times... The intensity is unbelievable. There are sparks every night, boys coming off each other, getting really upset.'

If a player makes a mistake and a teammate curses at him, McGuinness blows the whistle and everybody gets down for a hundred press-ups. He is big on respect. Players respect the management, management respect players, everyone respects each other.

'That's happened since January. Nobody goes out to try and make a mistake. There are some nights when one side are just flying, and you're safely looking at doing five hundred press-ups. Then you know that after that you'll have to do your two-hundred metre runs then.'

But they also know this blue-collar approach is working for them.

●　●　●

The final would have many interesting subplots, most notably the contrast in managerial styles. Derry's John Brennan was the oldest manager in Ulster at sixty-nine, and nationwide, only second to Mick O'Dwyer. When he revealed his interests in a newspaper Q&A slot, one of his pastimes was reading through a collection of old newspapers he keeps. He enjoys the music of Rod Stewart and Bob Dylan. And his favourite method of relaxing? A barbecue in the company of friends and family, including his grandchildren.

Donegal's management were from the other end of the spectrum. Only for a nasty leg break, Jim McGuinness would still be playing club football. Rory Gallagher was only a year out of county football and won an All Ireland club title with St Gall's in 2010. They were probably the first inter-county management team to have a fondness for house music and reaching for the lasers.

During the Derry press night at their Owenbeg training complex, a reporter questioned Brennan on what was termed the 'super-slick' Donegal management. He had a line on his lips that drew laughter; 'I can use a laptop too, you know.'

He continued on the theme. 'They may be slick. They might be all that. But I have come across these people before.

'We played Sligo in a challenge match for the opening of Ballinascreen's new pitch. There was a black pot along the sideline. It was a beautiful day. I thought someone was setting up a barbecue. I thought we were going to get burgers. But it was a heart monitor machine which Sligo had brought with them for a challenge game in Ballinascreen. I thought to myself "There is something going haywire here."'

The line earned him some further raucous laughter and he underpinned it by continuing.

'Jim McGuinness may have ideas. But this year Derry have encountered Mickey Harte and Kieran McGeeney and we managed to come out on the right side of the result. I'm about long enough. I don't fear anyone. I respect my own intelligence and my ability to make changes and adapt when necessary. I have no doubt about my own capabilities on the line.

'I am a modern manager. People say I do it the old way. But I go home and I think and I draw plans up for the game. We will see who comes out the winner in twelve days' time.'

The last line angered Jim McGuinness. He had already fought Donegal's corner after the Cavan match on how The Sunday Game pundits scoffed at the Donegal performance against Antrim. The derisory way Ryan Bradley was picked out as man of the match hurt him. By now, he had enough of people disrespecting Donegal. He pointed out the comments to his players and asked them, 'If he's that arrogant, what are the rest of his team like?'

'That thing that Brennan said about beating the Mickey Hartes and the Kieran McGeeneys,' recalled Cassidy, 'well, we've beaten Tyrone twice this year and gone up to Celtic Park and hammered Derry. Jim said he never made any reference to that.'

Whenever a team meeting was required, McGuinness never notified his players beforehand. He would normally come into the dressing room after a session and just say, 'Right boys, let's go in here.' After all the information they had to absorb for the Tyrone match, there wasn't the same level of detail on Derry. Players got home early and weren't complaining. McGuinness held off until the Thursday night before the final before he went into detail.

'It was all focused on us for the final. He felt that against Tyrone we had played within ourselves, given them too much respect. Tyrone came out and played with their chests out in the first fifteen minutes and had intimidated us.

'We knew that we were going to be away for the weekend and he would do most of his talking then, but he never even named the team. I don't know if that was because they didn't want the team to get out to Derry or he didn't want the players thinking too much about it. He's not big into naming teams anyway, but you might think for an Ulster final he may have.'

Eoin Bradley was the recipient of the Ulster GAA Writer's Monthly Merit Award for June. In the accompanying reports alongside the presentation photograph, Bradley was modest in his achievement, brushing off its significance and praising the contribution of the players around him and the service he was provided with as a forward. It was another morsel that McGuinness latched onto.

'Jim took both of those things and said to us "They're giving us their game-plan there, boys. They're going to win midfield and kick direct ball to the inside men."'

Donegal would go on the road again and stay in the Slieve Russell the night before the final. The county board were unwilling to pay for it but McGuinness managed to find a way around it when Tony McFadden, a London-based owner of a construction company and native of Falcarragh, footed the bill.

Once Cassidy mounted the steps of the bus, he would be entering another world where nothing existed except Derry and Donegal. It's what he had come back for.

'When I was going to work the day after the Tyrone game, it finally hit me that we had a chance here of doing something. It won't be about the big day or the crowd or anything like that; it'll be about performing on the day, ensuring you give your best and hopefully trying to achieve that instead of another hard luck story. We'll do anything we can to win it.

'The medal is irrelevant to you when you finish up, it's what you've done in your career. It would be nice to finish off thinking that you played for so many years and finished off with an Ulster title in 2011. That would be an unbelievable achievement. The amount of work we have put in this year... That would give me more satisfaction, knowing that we worked so hard and to thank God we'd got a prize at the end of it.'

• • •

There was a comforting familiarity to things when Donegal boarded the team bus on the Saturday morning in Donegal town. The vibe was relaxed. They made the journey down to Cavan in their familiar positions, the older hands on the back seat, Cassidy stretching out on his own seat, clearing his head.

They got into the hotel and left their bags up to the rooms. After stretching in the pool, there was a brief meeting. They examined where Danny Devlin put his kickouts in previous games, where the ball was broken to and who was coming in to scavenge for loose ball. It was wrapped up fairly quickly and players were ordered to bed.

Cassidy rooms with Ryan Bradley and as the big Buncrana man drifted off to sleep, Cassidy couldn't stop his mind from wandering. Staying in hotel rooms can do that to him. Before the Cork game in 2009, Donegal were staying in Malahide and he found himself down at the pier the night before the game at 4am, staring at the boats. He knew that lying on would only make it worse, so this time he jumped out of bed at 1.30am and went for a walk with the iPod plugged in.

The walk cleared his head and he slept like a baby. In the morning the team went into a private room for a team meeting. They watched a video of Donegal playing in the previous Championship games, scoring points, defending well, with a musical soundtrack.

They gathered in for the huddle. 'Everybody was just bouncing, ready to get out the door. Jim went around and thanked everybody for committing themselves for the year. He said he was there for two Championships – Ulster; win or lose, whenever you get out that's it over. And then you move onto the All Ireland. He said we were good lads, we had good times, but now that we were in the final we would have to make it count. Everyone was just mad to get out the door.'

Once on the bus, Cassidy turned on his iPod and continued a tradition he had from the Antrim game. He watched a few minutes of the RTÉ documentary

'Galvinised', on Kerry's Paul Galvin. The prospect of facing Galvin has been his inspiration all year long.

'Every single day I think of Paul Galvin. I think he's the best wing forward in the country, and if we get to the All Ireland final, I hope we get them. I take a lot of pride in my own personal performance and I want to come up against him. Every single day, I think of him.

'If I'm at training and things are not going well enough for me, or even if I'm training on my own and I want to get another few runs, I just think of him. I've marked him twice before in the league and I would never be in good shape during the league. I want to stay with him. I have the engine for him and it's the great challenge keeping me going.'

Something else happened that came out of the blue on that journey to Clones.

'The phone vibrated in my pocket and I wouldn't normally look at it, but it kept vibrating so I looked at it. It was mum calling. She would never, ever ring before a game, even for a couple of days before. Whenever I leave Gaoth Dobhair that's normally it until I come back.

'I thought there was maybe something wrong so I answered it and mum started crying. She wished me good luck and said my granny would be proud of me.'

Granny Sally had passed away in 2004, having fulfilled her dream of returning to Donegal. She bought every paper her grandchildren appeared in and she was their connection to the area.

'I thought that was a wee omen that we were going to do it. Even though you believed anyway you were going to win, when something like that happens and it's never happened before, you take it as a sign.'

●　●　●

On the radio station Newstalk's live coverage of the event, their correspondent Ciaran Murphy was describing the crowd in the Gerry Arthurs Stand as 'a real who's who of Ulster football.' In any section, there could be representatives from all nine Ulster counties. There is something about the psyche of the northern Gael that keeps them coming back to Clones, to the annual football festival, no matter who is playing.

Cassidy was the first Donegal player through the gates, keeping his head down and earphones plugged in. He acknowledged the well wishers with a quick wave but never broke his stride to the dressing room.

Derry had already arrived. Conleith Gilligan came through the gates sharing a joke with Michael Friel. By 2.15pm, they had left the dressing room to go and do their warmup in the pitch across the road.

Ten minutes later, Donegal marched out to do the same. When they got to the pitch, Derry were in the middle of a drill at the bottom corner. Rather than walk around them, Cassidy ran straight through it towards the bottom end of the field. Everyone followed through the gap he created. He was here for one thing only and it was a marker laid down.

Back in the dressing room, Donegal were primed. Another huddle. McGuinness walked inside it with a sheaf of printouts in his hand. He held up the first one, a picture of Henry Downey with the Anglo-Celt after Derry beat Donegal in the 1993 final.

'He said to Ryan Bradley "Look at that there, Ryan!" And Ryan was just nodding away "Aye, aye, aye." Jim asked him "Who's that there?" Ryan hadn't a clue! But he just kept looking at Jim. "Who the fuck's that there, Ryan? Who's that there?"

'One thing about Jim is that if you don't know the answer, you just shut up and say nothing. We all knew, and it wasn't a case that we would start laughing at him but we knew Ryan hadn't a clue!

'Jim obviously copped on, so he said "That's Henry Downey!" and he threw the sheet on the floor.'

He showed his players the picture of Kieran McKeever after the '98 final. Threw it to the floor. The same for Kieran McGeeney in 2002, McGeeney and Paul McGrane together lifting the cup in 2004, then the injured John Toal helping the pair of them lift it again in 2006.

On the floor lay five sheets, each of the five finals that Donegal had been in since 1992 and had left empty-handed. Those sheets, vowed McGuinness, would lie there until Donegal had a cup to set on top of them.

The cup was outside at that point, having ribbons tied on to its handles by Ulster council officials Stephen McGeechan and Martin McAviney. The St Michael's Scout Band were on the pitch playing 'Sean South'. A piper appeared in various locations of the ground and in an unfussy way, got through 'The Hills of Donegal' to massive cheers. The Hill was filling up and the town was emptying as fans made their way to the Coliseum of GAA in the province.

Ulster final day was here and it was beautiful.

● ● ●

It began nervously. Michael Murphy hit a shot towards the O'Duffy Terrace that appeared to slice inside the posts but was waved wide. Cailean O'Boyle hooked an effort wide for Derry and Patrick McBrearty was also off target in the opening three minutes.

There were a couple of points on the board before Derry launched an attack in the tenth minute. It was frustrated and held up by Donegal and the first vivid example of how their defensive system would work. Anthony Thompson strolled upfield and got a point, bookended by wides from Conleith Gilligan and Michael Hegarty. Gilligan, Joe Diver and Enda Muldoon also all hit efforts wide as Derry were forced to shoot from distance, unable to break the cordon.

A run from Ryan Bradley through the heart of defence exposed Derry's Charlie Kielt and he put Donegal ahead by 0-4 to 0-2 on twenty minutes.

Derry's frustrations begin to manifest themselves. While they hunted for a way to punch holes through the Donegal wall, a ball was played wide for Michael Bateson but the bounce deceived him and the ball flew over his leap. Mark McHugh was operating deep and came across to tidy it up. Once he released the ball Bateson hit him late along the touchline.

Derry needed inspiration and they got it from Charlie Kielt, who swept the ball over from wide right with a lovely arching effort. Just after a wide from Sean Leo McGoldrick, Gilligan converted a free to leave the minimum in it.

The sprightly Marty Donaghy was introduced for Bateson. He took the ball wide on the right side of the attack and laid it off. It was worked through Mark Lynch, Gilligan, O'Boyle and presented back to Donaghy who popped up on the other wing to level the game.

Joe Diver was getting animated. He started shouting to his teammates, 'They don't have it! They don't have it on the big day!'

Cassidy was standing nearby and responded to Diver. 'We have you exactly where we want you.'

Donaghy was becoming a problem. He got another ball in the corner and laced it across the face of the goal in the direction of Sean Leo McGoldrick, but Durcan got a touch to deflect it from his path. Derry were now having their period of dominance. Lynch kicked a wide before they were presented with a '45 which Muldoon spurned. On the sideline, John Brennan shook his head ruefully and checked his watch.

Halftime seemed to come too soon for Derry. They were now causing Donegal problems, learning when and how to get a shot off and that the ball had to be worked from wing to wing until an opening presented itself. But already they'd eight wides chalked up.

Jim McGuinness was happy. Like Cassidy had told Diver, they had them where they wanted them. Their target before the game was to be within two or three points of Derry at halftime. They fully believed that they couldn't be beaten. The sheets depicting all the winning captains against Donegal in Ulster final lay on the concrete as they awaited the knock on the door for the second half. Their time had come, this was the end game.

Two minutes in, Neil Gallagher was fouled in midfield and Michael Hegarty took the ball from him. He hung it up in the air and the wind carried it towards goal like a riptide. Danny Devlin was concerned about the clouds parting. 'It was the only time in the whole game the sun came out! I reached for the cap a minute before. Your man hit it with the outside of the boot and it swerved. It was going well wide of the far post and it came back across. I had the cap on and lost it a bit.'

Michael Murphy watched the flight of the ball as it danced in the stratosphere. His reading wasn't bad and just as it fell to earth, he was on the right side of his man and got his fingers to it. It happened so quickly that Devlin never glimpsed him.

'I thought I was getting there and I didn't see him coming. I knew they were coming across me, but I had my eyes on the ball. I thought it was coming straight to my chest but he just got his fingers to it.'

Devlin slid in but upended Murphy who crashed to the ground. Maurice Deegan sounded his whistle and ran to the scene of the collision. On arrival, he spread his arms wide to signify a penalty. The crowd groaned and cheered in stereo.

Barry McGoldrick, Dermot McBride, Kevin McGuckin and Devlin surrounded Deegan and protested the decision. Murphy went to retrieve the ball for the penalty. Devlin stood on the penalty spot while other Derry players talked to umpire Pat O'Sullivan, pleading with him to give his view to the referee who had been positioned poorly to make the call. Deegan walked in and spoke to O'Sullivan but he was adamant. The penalty would stand.

Murphy put the ball down and Devlin stood two yards in front of him with his hands on his hips, trying to spook the Donegal captain. Murphy never looked in his direction. The ball was slightly in front of the penalty spot and Devlin spoke to Deegan about it, who told Murphy to put it back onto the spot. Devlin backpedalled to the line and Murphy took his steps back.

Devlin stood on the line with his arms straight in the air, jumping up and down. The duel was on.

This was the truest test of character that Murphy could be put through. The previous year in the All Ireland U-21 final against Dublin he'd crashed a last-minute penalty against the crossbar. As recently as this year's league final he had to live with the taunts of Billy Sheehan among others about it. Now here he was, in a bigger game again, charged with the captaincy and all the responsibility.

His opponent was no novice. In his first couple of appearances for Derry in the McKenna Cup, Devlin showed what he was capable of when facing a penalty. Against Queen's, his Derry teammate James Kielt stepped up. A left-footer, he kicked to Devlin's left and Devlin saved. Another time, he stared down Paul Finlay of Monaghan. Finlay kicked to the keeper's left and again, it was stopped.

'This last year or two I would have worked a bit on the penalties with Johnny Kelly [Derry's goalkeeping coach], looking to see what way a player is shaping just before he kicks it. With the spot being in a bit further now, you need to commit a wee bit to going earlier. Especially if it's a good penalty, you need a good stretch before it's hit. This last year or two I've been getting closer to penalties, getting better at reading them.'

Murphy started his run-up, and while he did so, Devlin crept off his line. 'I was out a couple of yards off the line. I thought he was panicking a bit, and felt he was going to just put the foot through it and to that side. I wanted to get a few steps out and close it a bit.'

The ball was struck true and fierce.

Devlin had guessed the right way and even had the right height but the shot was a bullet.

'It went straight through my hands. I got a wee bit of a touch to it and was disappointed that I didn't keep it out.'

The net billowed and Murphy celebrated with a roar that started in his boots. From the moment the penalty was awarded until it was taken, two minutes sixteen seconds had elapsed, with the pressure sucking the oxygen out of the ground. Cassidy knew Murphy was the man for the job.

'If there was one person you wanted in that situation, it was Michael Murphy. Anybody else would be pushing boys out of the way but he just went over to get the ball back. He's so laidback. There was no way he was going to miss.'

Now Donegal were a goal up. Ciaran Mullan shouldered into Murphy as he celebrated. Fifteen yards away, McBrearty and Dermot McBride were niggling at each other. McBride loosely threw his arm back and McBrearty went down. Murphy went over to his teammate but Derry captain Barry McGoldrick came in and hauled McBrearty's body off the turf by his jersey. A fracas ensued. Diver jumped in to become involved but Neil Gallagher shoved him to the floor. Derry were unravelling. Emotion was overriding clear thinking.

Cassidy began pulling men away from the scene, exhorting them to concentrate on the match. He knew that given the reaction to the penalty, the referee might be tempted to dismiss a Donegal player.

Between the penalty and the subsequent row, seven minutes of the game were eaten up. The game was close to the final quarter yet little action had occurred.

From the next kickout, Derry brought the ball upfield but after probing an age for an opening, they couldn't find it. Eventually Diver charged through a corridor of defenders but Frank McGlynn got a hand in. The ball was flicked to Mark McHugh who charged out and popped it to Martin McElhinney. A long ball was sent in which Michael Murphy fielded and laid off to the onrushing McFadden. He swept it over the bar. Donegal 1-6, Derry 0-5.

The next kickout after, Karl Lacey got a hand to the break. Hegarty played another direct ball to Murphy, continued his run and got the return pass to point. Derry were being flattened and their lack of a sweeper meant Murphy owned everything that came within his reach. Kevin McCloy was sent on for Mullen to stem the tide.

James Kielt hit two points to drag the difference back to a goal but McFadden and Murphy restored the margin to five as both sides freshened their teams for the final push. Emmet McGuckin came on for Gilligan and PJ McCloskey replaced Muldoon. Derry's big name players were not going to close this one out.

With seven minutes left, Derry substitute Ger O'Kane tapped a free to James Kielt. He put it in high and Emmet McGuckin touched it above Paddy McGrath. He couldn't hold on but got his hands to it when Neil McGee came in with a challenge. Both men were twisting at the time and McGuckin was floored. The ball was worked out but play was halted when Michael Friel stopped David Walsh with an enormous hit.

Penalty! roared a posse of Derry players.

Deegan didn't blow for it.

When play resumed, Donegal worked it to Neil Gallagher on halfway. A series of passes ended with Hegarty on the opposite wing under the Gerry Arthurs Stand wrestling off a Friel challenge before cutting inside and pointing. The movement had taken fifty-four seconds and fifteen passes, involving nine different players, starting on Derry's thirteen-metre line. It was a monument to calmness and composure and more importantly had put six points between the sides.

Devlin knew the game was up.

'Whenever they were adding on two minutes of injury time at that stage... It was "How do I get out of here?" as soon as the whistle went. Some people get emotional about it but if we had won I wouldn't have been in tears of joy about it either. It wouldn't be the way I would react to it.'

Cassidy was now stationed in the full back line. Derry tried to find a combination to carry a goal threat but the ball wasn't being provided. The sting was out of the game.

In the second minute of injury time, Murphy was again onto a ball forward in and he laid off to McFadden who kicked a monster point.

Jim McGuinness remained inscrutable on the line.

Beside him, Rory Gallagher punched the air.

On the pitch, Cassidy punched Neil Gallagher a playful dig in the ribs.

Gallagher admonished him.

'Cut that shit out. The game's not over!'

But then it was.

• • •

This was it. This was the moment.

Players lay on top of each other, sprawled on the turf in bearhugs. They were joined by men and women. The stadium announcer appealed for fans to stay off the pitch, but in the battle between civic obedience and the release of nineteen years of frustration, there could only be one winner and within moments the field in St Tiernach's Park was bathed in green and gold. Strangers threw themselves at players like they were long-parted family. Gleeful supporters sprinted past the vanquished Derry players who hunched or lay on the ground in devastation.

Kevin Cassidy, the man who retired in Crossmaglen thirteen months earlier, looked out at all the beautiful madness. Finally, Donegal had their Ulster Championship. Finally, he had his Ulster Championship medal. The BBC's Thomas Kane had run onto the field on the whistle and asked him for an interview, so he was pulled into the tunnel, in dreamlike ecstasy.

Kane asked how he was feeling. Cassidy's eyes were watery and his voice wavered as he responded.

'It's just unbelievable, hi. We've waited so long for this. A lot of hard work has gone into this. It's relief more than anything else. Had we been beaten here today... We've turned our lives upside down this year to win this Ulster title and it's just brilliant.'

He answered another question, but his heart was elsewhere. He was on autopilot talking about assessing the game the following day when emotion got the better of him and he excused himself, saying, 'I have to go out to the boys here, okay?'

The stewards created a manmade cordon and players squeezed their way inside. Michael Murphy climbed the steps to the podium and unfolded his speech. He looked out across the Clones pitch and surveyed the scene. Green and gold flags, jerseys, teddy bears, hats and headbands. His people. People that he would live amongst and represent; people who shared his defeats and celebrate his victories. To them, at this moment he is their chieftain, the fifth Donegal man to lift the Anglo-Celt.

He hoists the cup and the crowd roars. This is glory.

A microphone is put in his hand and the crowd can almost hear his heartbeat. He acknowledges the players on the steps. 'The effort, the sacrifice that each of these players made, right throughout the year up until now, has been nothing short of unbelievable. I just want everyone to show their appreciation for them.'

He then went through the backroom team, mentioning each by name. Maxi Curran, Laurence McMullan, Michael McMenamin, Pat Shovlin, Adam Spiers, Eugene Ivers, Finian McClafferty, Gavin Ward and Paul Fisher.

Then, the medical team. Dr Charlie McManus, Dr Kevin Moran, JD McGrenahan, Shane Collins and Tommy Kerr: 'to all, a big thank you.'

The sponsors, Donegal Creameries and Azzurri. The food caterers, Jimmy McGlynn, and McGuinness Buses. 'And the county board; thanks for doing everything in your power to make this happen.

'To the men themselves, Jim McGuinness and Rory Gallagher. For the players and the people of Donegal. I just want to give you boys a big, big thank you for giving me the opportunity here today.'

He bid three cheers to Derry and thanked the fans. He lifted the cup again with one hand and playing on Anthony Molloy's immortal line from 1992, called out, 'The Anglo-Celt's for the Hills!'

● ● ●

John Brennan took the loss badly.

Radio Ulster asked him if he would mind giving them an interview and he told them where to go. A group of reporters waited for him around the Derry dressing room, but once he got there, he marched past them and ignored their questions. After some sweet-talking from the press to county chairman John Keenan, Brennan eventually reappeared, looking agitated. The interview would be a terse encounter.

Paddy Heaney of *The Irish News* opened the questioning.

Paddy Heaney: *The penalty was the turning point of the game…*

John Brennan: *If you say so, Paddy.*

Paddy Heaney: *Do you think it was the turning point?*

John Brennan: *Well, if you say so. People probably had a better view than I had. I had a better view than the referee, he decided it was a penalty.*

He'd meander on then for a couple of more minutes, finally agreeing it was 'the turning point of the game' and that Deegan should have consulted his umpires but he didn't. 'I don't care if people think I'm being wrong, or breaking GAA rules; that is wrong, what he did today.'

Brennan was then asked about his team's capacity to turn around within six days and play a qualifier. For the previous ten years no beaten provincial finalist had been able to manage such a turnaround in such a timeframe.

Colm Keys [Irish Independent]: *Can you pick yourselves up from this, John, in the short term?*

John Brennan: *Absolutely. I, you know Orla, [to Irish Daily Mirror reporter, Orla Bannon], they might have a slick management. They might have…*

John Fogarty [Irish Examiner]: *Will you look for an extra day…*

John Brennan: *…But you know…I beg your pardon. They might have a slick* *management, but you know, if you look, there's implication, insinuation, that slick means they're better than us. I don't know what the implication or insinuation was. I didn't like it. I don't know whether Paddy [Heaney] it was a friend of yours in The Irish News, a co-reporter, has said that I referred to the Donegal management as slick. I didn't. It was put to me how I would deal with it, and my answer was, similar to other managers.*

But there's another meaning to being so-called slick. You read the full Oxford dictionary [definition] of the word slick; there's also an insulting part in it as well.

Orla Bannon: *You're digressing here, John, em...*

John Brennan: *Ah, you digress. You could use some other word, Orla. And if you weren't female, I would use it.*

Orla Bannon: *Anyway, that's maybe a smokescreen...*

John Brennan: *I'm disappointed in you, Orla, I'm disappointed in you.*

Orla Bannon: *I'm really not sure what you're getting at, at all...*

John Brennan: *Oh, do you not? Right, well...*

Orla Bannon: *Maybe we can chat about this at a later point. I'm sure everybody else here would maybe like a few explanations from you as regards why the team were only able to score eight points today. Was the loss of Eoin Bradley too much to overcome really?*

John Brennan: *Orla, I'm not answering that. That is a ridiculous question. Eoin Bradley wasn't on the pitch!*

Orla Bannon: *You talked about that before. I'm just asking was that a factor why you were only able to score eight points?*

John Brennan: *We didn't get enough ball in. Okay, we had three possibilities in the first half, which I think we should have hit the target with. But Eoin Bradley wasn't there... The other two of the inside forwards, it wasn't their day. I feel sorry for the fellas, they didn't go out there deliberately to do that. I'm not talking about Eoin Bradley. Eoin Bradley's a good fella... but don't bring up a man who didn't even start there today!*

● ● ●

The Donegal players got back to the dressing room. They sat in dizzy thought, drinking in their achievement. The day had gone to plan and they sat, quietly talking among themselves, getting used to the new parameters of being champions, for once. The A4 print outs of the victorious captains against Donegal remained on the floor, forgotten about. They no longer had any relevance. Instead, there was a gleaming cup in the middle of the room.

McGuinness said that the time was right for the players to go out and meet their loved ones at the back of the stand. Kevin met Sarah and when she started beaming he saw her tears softly falling with relief and happiness.

Only the previous morning she had asked how he was feeling as he was getting ready to leave the house. He said he felt good and she warned him, 'Do not come back into this house saying "I couldn't get into the game." If the ball is not coming to you, you go and get it.'

Now, he had done it. Together, they had made it happen because without her encouragement and selflessness, he wouldn't have made it back.

The Derry team were showered and changed, trying to kill time outside until the bus lifted them. After enduring a hellish seventy minutes, this was like torture. They envied the happy faces and the easy way of the Donegal players. They felt terrible and they wanted out fast.

Danny Devlin felt every second go by. 'It was ridiculous how long we were sitting waiting. If there had have been someone I knew in the car park I would have been away. It's not the place you want to be.

'Nobody had contemplated defeat; it was hard to get your head around it. John came in and tried to get us roused. We knew we had to play a game the following Saturday but it was the only time in the year when you didn't tune in and take in what people were saying. We just wanted to get down the road.'

Back in the dressing room, It was party time for Donegal. 'The Hills' got an airing, along with all the other party songs. After a shower, the players had a post-match meal in the old dressing rooms in Clones.

They returned to the bus and were awaiting their departure when McGuinness came on and asked everybody off it again.

He wanted to get a picture of the entire squad, management, and support team together, with the cup, in the deserted ground, on the turf where they had made history.

Then it was time to roll.

After a few miles, the bus pulled over. There was no announcement; McGuinness and his brother-in-law Kevin McNaney just got out with the cup.

The whispers working their way up through the players confirmed that this was *the* spot. This was the spot where McGuinness and his brother Mark were travelling shortly after the Ulster final of 1998 when their car hit a dump truck, killing Mark and putting Jim in intensive care for a spell.

A cross marks the spot. McGuinness crouched over it, untied the green and gold ribbons from the handles of the Anglo-Celt and wove them onto the cross. Even in his greatest triumph, Mark was there with him.

The players sat in silence on the bus, watching the act in reverential awe. They asked each other should they applaud him back onto the bus, but McGuinness hadn't made a big fuss over the act, so they felt it was best to leave it private.

There was somebody Cassidy was remembering at that point too: Adrian

Hanlon, the young county panellist from Dungloe and boyfriend of Cassidy's sister, Carol Ann. He went out for a few drinks on the Monday after the Antrim game but it was a few drinks too many for the management. They cut him loose from the squad.

Hanlon's clubmate and former Donegal selector Tony Boyle, had texted Cassidy his congratulations, but asked would he drop Hanlon a line as he was feeling low. Cassidy and a few others had already remembered Hanlon in the middle of the euphoria.

'He never went to the game or anything; he couldn't face it. He'll be back next year but he's missed out on an awful lot. So I rang him on the bus to check on him, and in fairness all the boys were asking about him. I told him to come and join us in Donegal town. He didn't want to come out but I told him all the boys were asking after him.'

The bus crossed the border from Fermanagh into Donegal at Pettigo. The last time Cassidy had been in the village with a Donegal team was that cringeworthy episode in 2003 before the defeat to Fermanagh. Now, they were happy to be placed on a stage to the musical accompaniment of a duo belting out the same song: 'Walking Tall in Donegal', by Margo. The trailer swayed with the weight of numbers as the players were introduced by name before they made their way into a local bar to watch The Sunday Game's take on the final.

Back on the bus, the musical talents of Dara Gallagher and Dermot Molloy were coming in useful. They play in a band together and rattled out a few of their standards. Christy Toye took the spotlight for a rendition of 'Wonderwall'.

When they reached Donegal town, McGuinness made it clear that these players were representing their county and there would be children there at the celebrations. They were to keep professional at all times, with no alcohol in sight. A silver band led them into the town and when they turned the corner into the diamond, Murphy shared the cup carrying with Donegal town's Four Masters representatives Paul Durcan and Karl Lacey. The cheer bounced back off the sky.

A route was cordoned off for the team to make their way to the stage over at the far end. Walking through it, Cassidy recognised the faces of so many club players he has done battle with, applauding him on. He stopped for a word with Tony Boyle and they promised to meet for a drink later on.

Murphy was introduced first onto the stage, with Durcan and Lacey following. The trio lifted the cup together and the crowd went crazy.

On the stage there was the usual mix of public representatives, town mayors and others who lend their support. Cassidy had already gone through his party piece on the bus journey but was asked to do it again for the benefit of the crowd present.

He took the microphone and like an old pro, worked the crowd.

'As Jim McGuinness said, we want to thank you fans, you've been absolutely terrific. I want one more help with a song, alright?'

And then he started into it, his take on an old Depeche Mode classic from thirty years earlier.

'When I'm with you Donegal,
I go out of my head,
And I just can't get enough!
And I just can't get enough!
All the things you do to me,
And everything you said,
I just can't get enough,
I just can't get enough!
We slip and slide as we fall in love,
And I just can't seem to get enough of,
Duh-Duh Duh-Duh-Duh-Duh-Duh....

All the while singing it, Cassidy was hopping, which was only right because all of Donegal was hopping too. Every bar was overflowing with crowds but eventually the Donegal squad would have the ballroom of the Abbey Hotel to themselves. Friends and relatives were brought in by players at their request, with bouncers stationed at the doors.

It was the first chance that players had an opportunity to mix freely and for wives and partners to be able to meet each other. Cassidy took pleasure in meeting the likes of Ryan Bradley's parents and many others. By the time the disco started, it was already gone 4am. At 7.30am, Kevin and Sarah called it a night.

• • •

On the analysis for the BBC covering the final, Martin McHugh had said after the game that the team were set for a recovery session on Monday morning at Murvagh beach.

Leaning up against a bar at Monday lunchtime, reflecting on the haze of the night before, Rory Gallagher turned to Cassidy. 'You're not for this beach, are you?'

'Nah, there'll be no beach today for me, Rory.'

Nor would there be for anyone else in the bar either. A few were already trying to fight off hangovers with cold beers. Gallagher called over to McGuinness. They were on the beer for the day. The partners had already left at this point and all that remained were the players and backroom staff for an intimate few hours.

A bus was arranged by McGuinness for the entourage to head over Letterkenny direction to Michael Naughton's Clanree Hotel. They had food laid on, a big screen was arranged to watch the game, and the craic started.

As the evening wore on, McGuinness gathered his players. He told them that they had had their few pints, and to go on drinking now would only be drinking for the sake of it. He had buses coming that would be leaving people back to their own villages and towns. Nobody would be able to have it that the Donegal players were falling over each other like drowsy cattle, full to the gills of pints.

Jim McGuinness. Always thinking.

Cassidy went straight to Mickeys, his local in Gaoth Dobhair and stayed until 11pm, before boarding taxis with the McGee brothers, Christy Toye, Martin McElhinney, Tom McKinley and Michael Boyle for the festival in Burtonpoint. At 3.30am, the party was over and he was brought home by his sister Carol Anne and Adrian Hanlon.

● ● ●

He dreaded the Tuesday training. Everyone did. McGuinness seemed in foul form. A whisper went round the players that the doctors had warned him off doing a hard running session because of the dangers of dehydration and muscle fatigue, given the couple of days they just had. He pulled them in and put them in mind of the next goal. 'Well done, you had your few drinks and whatever. Everyone was well-behaved and there were no incidents which was great. We'll get back to it tonight with a light session.'

It may have been a 'light' session but they still worked plenty of badness from their systems. After training Cassidy felt as if he was alive again, but a wicked craving gripped him. Since the Ulster final he hadn't had a proper big feed, existing instead on bits of breakfast, sandwiches and finger food. He mentioned it to the brothers McGee who knew exactly what to do.

And that's how two days after winning the Ulster title, three Gaoth Dobhair men sat in a car park of the Letterkenny Kentucky Fried Chicken shop, with a family bucket of chicken each in their laps. Each bucket contained twenty pieces of chicken and they dropped the bones back into the bucket before lifting more out.

There was hardly a word spoken, only the sucking of chicken off bone and slurping of cartons of coke as the car windows steamed up. Anything that was said was along the lines of 'Jesus, thon's some feeding boys.'

McGuinness would have hell waiting for them on the Thursday but that night, in that moment, life was bliss.

CHAPTER TWENTY-EIGHT

Creeping Out The Backdoor

FOR teams that are knocked out of their provincial Championship, the qualifying series – commonly known as 'the backdoor' – grants a lifeline. The curious thing about it is not every team is hugely enthused about taking it.

For Ulster teams in particular, the qualifiers can be hugely anti-climatic. In its early years the backdoor offered novelty and adventure but after a while when teams still finished up with only memories but no silverware to show for their extended campaigns, it seemed to lose some of its appeal. With each county in the province having featured in an Ulster final over the past decade, the Anglo-Celt feels attainable to them. Indeed for most of them, the Anglo-Celt is the Holy Grail; anything else can seem almost secondary.

The introduction of the qualifying system in 2001 was devised with counties like Fermanagh in mind. No longer would the footballers of the county have to train for ten months to be beaten in a first-round game.

They took a couple of years to find their feet and then attacked it wholeheartedly. In the 2003 qualifiers, they sprang a considerable shock with a six-point defeat of Meath who had contested the All Ireland final only two years earlier. Then Fermanagh travelled to Sligo and beat Mayo in a monsoon to book their ticket to August football with a quarter-final in Croke Park.

Despite retirements the following year they beat Meath again, crushed Billy Morgan's Cork, found a way past Donegal in a dogfight in Clones before their greatest-ever victory in beating Armagh in the All Ireland quarter-final. They took Mayo to a replay in the semi-final but probably missed the boat on the first day.

Barry Owens won an All Star for his performances off the back of that glorious run. Now, seven years on, the Fermanagh side he was captaining weren't just beaten by London but were blown off the field, lucky to keep the margin to six points.

London hadn't won a Championship game since 1977, long before Owens was born. In Championship football, losing to London was as low as you could get. True, the dream of an Ulster Championship had died some time ago, but this was bottoming out and it was especially brutal for Owens.

He never saw it coming. Mayo might have got the fright of their lives against London in the Connacht Championship but the exiles hadn't a track record of getting it together for the backdoor. The tradition was that half the team would walk and a second string would valiantly bow out.

Poor preparation couldn't be used as an excuse either. The Fermanagh squad flew over on the Friday and went over to Ruislip for a kickabout and to familiarise themselves with the surroundings. They had watched videos of games from London and knew that there would be Country and Wobbly music blaring from the speakers. Nothing they encountered visually or aurally would have come as a surprise.

London drove at Fermanagh with remorseless intensity. By halftime they were 0-9 to 0-1 in front.

In the sanctity of the Fermanagh dressing room, a beleaguered John O'Neill addressed his side. 'He gave us a complete bollocking for doing what we were not supposed to do,' recalls Owens. 'Lads were running into the tackle and losing the ball. We knew they were going to be bigger than us physically. Any points they got were through everyone running forward at us. There was no tracking back.'

For the second half Fermanagh had to just go for it. A comeback was launched and with fifteen minutes to go they were back to within four points. London tacked on a couple of points to relieve the pressure and Owens knew Fermanagh were gone. Then Derek Fahy blew the final whistle.

'They went buck mad. Bananas just. You could see how much it meant to them. It was the first time for a lot of them to win a Championship match because for a lot of them they might not have played Championship with their own county. Plus, I think each of them had £200 on themselves. That was doing the rounds.'

London's star player Paul Geraghty came over and swapped jerseys with Owens. The former All Star made the exchange a quick one and ran for the dressing rooms and never stopped to pause until he got into the showers.

O'Neill thanked everyone for sticking around to the end of a turbulent year and said he hoped that they would all be back for the next season. Owens was next to address the room.

'I just thanked them all for giving their best for the year and thanked John and them. I said "Hopefully we will be here for many years to come. We shouldn't be in Division Four, we have good enough footballers to be out of it, so it's up to ourselves to learn from our mistakes that were made today and over the last couple of days."'

After the post-match meal and a few drinks, it began to sink in. 'It probably was the lowest I've been with the team. I know the lads are capable of so much better. That's the biggest disappointment.'

It capped a haunting year for the county and a measure of Owens' sympathies lay with the manager. He knew that the politics of the situation would probably drag on and pointed towards the split in the county that had existed from the moment O'Neill was installed as manager.

'I think that the county board will probably wait about for a few months instead of sorting it out straight away. I'd say they'll get rid of John, if I'm being honest. There are a couple of lads that never wanted him there. It's a bad sign whenever you know of county board members wanting their own county to lose so that they can get rid of the manager. I think it's a total disgrace what's going on at the minute.

'They haven't wanted him there from the start. They've been putting stuff out in the media that has been totally untrue, that has been proven untrue. I don't even think it [the stories and rumours] were coming from the boys who left. It was more deep-rooted than that. All year, as soon as John was announced as manager, there was a vendetta against him.

'I feel sorry for John. It hit him hard. It wasn't fair on him or his family. He was only trying to do his best for Fermanagh. He wasn't getting anything out of it.'

With the embarrassment of the result, the likely outcome was that O'Neill would be removed. Former players were also exerting pressure. A couple of days after the London result, Owens opened a text message from one of the men who left the panel during the league campaign.

Please say you gonna stand with us. Management must go! We have a few years left with the best 30 players we can achieve something.

That message sickened Owens.

'That's just basically saying that they think they are better than the lads that were there. I don't know why he sent it to me. I didn't reply. It would piss me off. It would just make you disheartened over the whole fucking thing. How can you play with those lads you can't trust now? I wouldn't be able to trust them. Why would I put my body on the line for lads who are going to cry over a bit of food, a bit of money, that sort of thing?'

During the dispute, none of the disaffected approached Owens or his clubmate Hughie Brady to join the protest.

'They know I wouldn't have stood for it, that myself and Hughie don't give a shite. We just want to do our best for Fermanagh and hopefully Fermanagh will do their best. We don't need whatever they were getting, for years before, to turn out for the county.

'Could anyone tell me exactly what the players' problems were? Because I don't know. If I'd thought things were wrong I wouldn't have been there. I know people were complaining about the training but the training was the best.

'I'm twenty-nine now and another year wouldn't be that appealing at the minute, after all that's gone on. There's been days when you come home in horrid bad humour, and there's been times when I wouldn't speak for two days over the whole craic. There's only so much you can take. What's to say they won't get another manager in next year and they'll do the same?'

When the imperial forces of Tyrone and Armagh had a vice-like grip on the Anglo-Celt for over a decade, Fermanagh were probably the pluckiest and most noble members of the resistance, driven by a dream that one day, yes, they could win Ulster.

Now they're a joke. The revolution appears over. The dream is dead.

●　　●　　●

Other first-round exits weren't quite as dramatic. Cavan met neighbours Longford at home and were wiped out, 2-16 to 0-11. The final indignity for them was that the game was hosted as the undercard to the potentially explosive Louth-Meath tie, a repeat of the infamous Leinster final of 2010. Playing landlords to another drama was a stark pointer to exactly where Cavan were left at the end of the season.

Val and Terry remember the devastation of their first year in Cavan over a decade ago, but by year three they were leading an Ulster final. Changes have already been made – Terry has stepped down to selector and chief talent-spotter again, John Morrison has replaced Ger Lyons as coach, and they are going back to their belief in 'honest gasúns'.

After the Tyrone game, Dick Clerkin appealed against his sending off and had it rescinded. A rash of club games in Monaghan left the county team without any challenge games to blow the dirty fumes out of the engine. Waiting for them were Offaly.

The midlanders' motivation was stoked by comments made on radio by former hurling All Ireland medallist Michael Duignan. In a conversation that was rooted in complaints about the hurling team experiencing problems in training facilities, he took a swipe at the footballers, saying, 'They don't want to train, they have no pride in their jersey, they're going on the beer and all that sort of thing.'

Clerkin knew there'd be a backlash. 'I wasn't surprised with their intensity. I was surprised at our lack of it when the questions were asked. It was a shocking performance.'

Nobody in the setup emerged with any credit as they were knocked out on a scoreline of 1-18 to 1-10. Clerkin was taken off at halftime and the stats on his first Championship season as captain would cut him deeply. Two games, two losses. Sent off in one game, taken off in the other.

'I hadn't been playing well. My man scored three points and a couple of them were from individual errors on my part. On another day you'd have taken him to the cleaners but he played well and everything I did went wrong. The harder I tried, the worse it got. It would have been better off if I hadn't been looking for the ball to make amends. It was just one of those nightmare halves of football.

Physically, I felt poor. For whatever reason I felt jaded and tired. I couldn't get my second wind, I felt leggy. Whether it was a mental thing from playing poorly, I don't know what it was, I couldn't put my finger on it and felt exhausted at halftime.

'Speaking to Eamonn after about it, he thought there might have been something wrong physically to affect my performance. That was one of the reasons in his mind for taking me off. He can be forgiven for thinking that. There might have been something in it. As the year went on I didn't feel as fresh as I had earlier.'

Clerkin went along to the Ulster final with his mother and auntie for company. He looked on as Donegal claimed the title but refused to let his mind make grand promises to himself.

'I didn't feel bitter or indifferent. I was reflective in terms of where Monaghan stand. We know we are better than them when we want to be. We have done it and we have proved that. We would have had question marks over whether we were good enough for Tyrone because we hadn't proved that we were.'

The first year of captaincy wasn't a delight but he still feels that good times might be around the corner, with the right mindset. 'When you still have something to offer you owe it to yourself and the people who have given you the opportunity to make the most out of it. I mean, when you see the likes of [Kevin] Cassidy and [Rory] Kavanagh and these boys... Cassidy had retired and look at where he is now. It just shows you, if you're good enough for long enough, things will go your way eventually.'

By late-September, Clerkin was checking in for regular sessions with a personal trainer. He was going to give every bead of sweat as Monaghan captain in 2012.

The dream lives on in at least one household in Monaghan.

● ● ●

Sitting inside his Lamh Dhearg clubrooms before the Westmeath qualifier, Paddy Cunningham's mobile phone buzzed with a message from Liam Bradley.

Speak to you outside.

The Antrim team had been watching the highlights reel from The Sunday Game featuring the opposition they would meet in a couple of hours. Cunningham stood up and walked out.

'I went out and he said that he wasn't starting me, that they would wait until the game opened up a bit and put me in late on. I was in complete and utter shock.

I had always started for Antrim in Championship matches since I made my debut, or any match as long as I was fit to play. I just said "Right, dead on.'"

Antrim were much too good for Westmeath and Cunningham played the last ten minutes, managing to score a decent point. He went back to training and vowed to get the head down and regain his spot for the next game against Carlow. He didn't start but came on at halftime and hit four crucial points to help Antrim edge home by the minimum.

That evening another message came through from his manager.

That's the Paddy Cunningham of two years ago, well played.

He won his place back as Down came to Casement Park for the next round. In the stands, Down supporters outnumbered the home fans four to one. The Antrim bandwagon had yet to catch on that their side were one game away from a possible Croke Park date.

Down pushed ahead with four unanswered points in the opening quarter and while Antrim would claw it back and even go into the lead for a spell, three brilliant Down goals in the second half would end Antrim's season. Cunningham was almost relieved when the end came. His mood has darkened and football with Antrim had ceased being a pleasure long before this game. He's not the most optimistic either about 2012.

'We're miles off compared to where we were two years ago. I know Kevin Niblock's away to university in England, and from speaking to other lads, there are a few that might not be there next year for one reason or another. I think Antrim needs everybody to be involved to be able to compete. Liam's staying on but the backroom team needs changing. Things would need to change on every front if we're going to compete at all.

'I just didn't enjoy the year. The setup, the atmosphere... That was the first time that happened and it's a terrible thing to say. But if you aren't enjoying it, it's reflected in your performances as well.'

●　●　●

Six days after the Ulster final, Derry had to face Kildare in Croke Park. It was always going to be a stretch and the outcome of the game was preordained by the lack of recovery time allied to the abilities of a battle-hardened Kildare side.

Mickey C never made it back. His torn thigh was only the end product of his injury woes. It was initially thought his quads were weakened by osteitis pubis, but when he received a pain–killing injection for that, they discovered he had a hernia that was the underlying problem.

Derry referred him to a specialist who confirmed it. In the meantime, he made a brief comeback for Ballinderry but broke down injured again. 'My season went from starting out as Derry's number one to not getting any football, even with the club. Ach well, these things are sent to try us. Hopefully next year I'll be a different person.'

Next year. Of course there's next year for Mickey C, exactly as he told a disbelieving Adrian McGuckin coming back from the 2010 county final. He feels he owes it to his county.

'I wouldn't rule out getting the opportunity to play for Derry next year, especially if they're putting me through my hernia operation, I'd like the chance to prove myself again. If they're sorting me out, I feel I have to repay them.

'This whole year I've been playing with all these problems, and maybe I should have had them all looked at before, but I was trying to come through as a county keeper.'

Even though he never got a chance to march behind a band on Championship Sunday, he took himself out of his comfort zone and learned life lessons by dreaming big. Twelve months ago he was on the bread run. Now, he is out on his own in business, running personal fitness classes himself with a growing number of clients.

'I'm in a very positive frame of mind at the minute. It's taking off well and I am going to concentrate on it and expand it. It's off my own bat, using the house and the Ballinderry facilities. It's turned out a lot better than I expected.

'I'm lucky and I want to work hard at it and make a real go at it. That's what I've enthusiasm for and you are as good as you want to be. If you want to do your research, get yourself well qualified, get people results and make it enjoyable; that's what I have an enthusiasm for and so far, it's working for me.

'When things are at their worst but you look at them positively, that's often when things work out best. So do I regret giving up the job to play county football? Not in the slightest.

'Leaving that job gave me the opportunity to follow my dream. Sometimes those are the things you do to follow your dream.'

● ● ●

Minutes after Derry were dumped out of the Championship by Kildare in Croke Park, Down would face Cork there in the main event and a repeat of the previous year's All Ireland final.

Aidan Carr was granted a few minutes at the end of the Leitrim game, came on for Benny Coulter in the last five minutes against Antrim, but never got on to face Cork. He ended the season just as he had started it, committed to the Down cause, devoted to the team, but completely unsure of where he was in the pecking order.

He has suffered but made gains from that too. Nor does he want sympathy either. 'I'm not the model player. The model player would not go through the motions in training, but it happens. But I didn't throw the head up and cause a scene or anything like that.

'I learned how much it meant to me. It's probably something you can take for granted. When you're fit, ready and available and you're a sub, it's not a nice feeling.'

All he ever wanted to do was play for Down, so he will pick himself up and go again. His name is Carr. A Down team without one just doesn't look right.

• • •

As the evenings got longer, Stevie McDonnell put his personal training studies to one side and vowed to devote more energy to them once all the football was out of the way. He was targeting an intermediate championship with Killeavey as well as fighting against the tide with Armagh.

Supporting him as ever was his wife Lisa. She has always been behind him through his career but he has a few other motivations to keep going: his children Cliona, Caolan and Ryan. Caolan is five now but Stevie brought him to play his first Under-8 match recently with Killeavey. Every morning when he wakes he throws on a jersey of one of his father's teams; Killeavey, Armagh, the Irish International Rules and, of course, Liverpool.

Recently, Caolan's coach told his daddy that he was coming on well and is already well capable of playing with boys older than him. While McDonnell was glad to hear it, he wasn't putting too much importance on it. His own father never pushed him into football and he won't be doing the same with Caolan. The only advice he ever gives to his son when they are out kicking around the park at home is to practise with both feet.

'Coming home from matches this year, even if we lost, for them to say they were there gives me great pleasure and satisfaction that they have the opportunity to watch me play. All of Cliona's friends would talk about it. She is nine years old and sometimes gets a wee bit embarrassed about the whole thing, but it's great. Even the youngest fella now, Ryan, he's only three but is getting more involved in football, kicking around the place.'

In their first game in the qualifiers, Wicklow came up to Armagh and shot out of the traps, going 0-9 to 0-2 ahead. There were raised voices at halftime.

'Of course there was anger there. The thing about Armagh is that there are a number of leaders in the team. It's not one or two players that make the calls; I feel there's maybe eight or nine players that can step up to the mark. That was the case at halftime. We were angry with our performance at halftime. We knew we'd let Wicklow come up to Armagh and dictate to us.'

The second half went to plan and they were two points up entering the final stages when a Leighton Glynn penalty put Wicklow one point up. Gavin McParland stepped up to bring the game to extra time but Armagh couldn't put them away on the night. They had a tricky replay in Aughrim, a graveyard for many Ulster teams in the backdoor, but they got through thanks to two Jamie Clarke goals, setting up a tasty tie against Tyrone in Omagh.

'My first reaction was that I was happy about it because we were going to find out where we were as a team. If we were good enough to go on in the Championship we'd beat Tyrone; if we weren't, at least we were being put out of our misery at an early stage.'

Playing at centre forward, McDonnell orchestrated everything good about Armagh going forward. Ryan McMenamin had been detailed to mark him but struggled and eventually had to be switched before being taken off. At one point the two men had a clash that threatened to turn ugly. They squared up to each other and there was a bit of grappling before the referee had a word and booked McMenamin.

Things were going good for Armagh and they held the lead before Paul Hearty fluffed his clearance and Tyrone stole in for a very cheap goal. The body blow left Armagh on their knees. Towards the end, with Armagh eight points down, McDonnell took a shot that was blocked by Joe McMahon's foot. Penalty.

McDonnell stepped up to take it and break his duck for the Championship. Conor Gormley was in his ear all the way but that was hardly unexpected.

'I decided I was going to go for power all the way. The worst thing for a penalty taker is to change your mind. Even when Conor was talking away to me I had it in my mind that I was going to go for pace and power. But I struck it too good and it went over the bar.

'I don't think the goal would have got us back into the game, to be totally honest. It would have thrown us a lifeline for a short period of time, but I feel Tyrone would always have had enough to pick it up a level or two.'

Armagh lost and for the first time in his inter-county career McDonnell had gone a season without hitting the net.

'I don't mind that. It's guys like Jamie that have maybe taken over the mantle of goalscoring. I used to be the top goalscorer for Armagh for ten or eleven years but you can't always expect to be that.

'I probably wasn't getting in the positions this year that I would have liked to. Maybe I'm not as sharp in front of goals as I used to be. The Derry match was the one game where I had three opportunities and took the wrong decision three times. I didn't take them but I wouldn't worry too much about them.'

Over the next couple of days he thought he would get the head down and concentrate on the club, but that was disturbed by a phonecall he took from a journalist wanting to know if McMenamin had 'fish-hooked' McDonnell in their brief encounter.

'I didn't comment on it whatsoever, especially as we were knocked out of the Championship. You want to move on, to concentrate on something else.'

A story appeared in the *Irish Examiner* concerning a possible probe into the incident. A friend emailed a weblink to McMenamin at work, showing him that it had been lifted and put up on the Hogan Stand website. McMenamin immediately called the paper and asked where they'd got their information from.

After learning the author of the piece, McMenamin was shocked. 'It was a fella who'd I'd given an interview to the week before. I tried to get him a couple of times but eventually I got him and it became a right heated argument. He said he was standing by his piece. He said he was going by a photograph with a hand on his [Stevie's] face or something.

'I'd been on to my solicitor about it. He'd read it and was happy enough that the article was misleading, that there'd been no fish-hook and that there'd be no probe into it.'

McDonnell was abroad on business but he texted McMenamin, explaining that he had nothing to do with it.

'I didn't want to see anybody missing out on the opportunity of representing their county in Croke Park; it doesn't make a difference who it is. You want to see all the best players playing the game and Ricey's been a top player over the last ten years, regardless of what people's opinions are of him. I sent a text to tell him I had nothing to do with the piece in the paper and if the GAA were going to do anything about it I would stand up for him as best as possible. There was no malice in the thing at all.'

McMenamin was delighted that he had the support of his old rival. But he wasn't going to let the issue lie. 'I phoned my solicitor and he had a letter written for me and emailed it to the editor. They had their retraction in the next day.

'It was decent of Stevie. He's a great fella. The two of us have been marking each other on and off for about ten years now and I would have good respect for him. We would have been away on All Star trips and I would have got on well with him then. On the field, the two of us would have respect for each other. As he said, it was only really horseplay what went on that time.'

Once the controversy died down, McDonnell was happy to pick up the pieces back at the club and become a bit more involved in their 125th anniversary celebrations. In 2012 though, he will be back with Armagh for more. Providing the flesh is willing, his wife will insist on it.

'If it was Lisa's decision, I would be back with Armagh next year and I'd have no say in it.'

He'll get that next goal of his yet.

CHAPTER TWENTY-NINE

Falling Off The Face Of The Earth

WITHIN the Tyrone squad they call it 'The Talk.' It normally comes just before you take the field for a Thursday night training session, when Mickey Harte approaches and requests a quiet word.

It wasn't wholly unexpected for Ryan McMenamin in the lead up to the All Ireland quarter-final against Dublin. He had been taken off in the previous two games against Armagh and Roscommon.

'When you've been around as long as I have, you sense these things. It wasn't too big a shock when he told me. He apologised, he said he didn't want to do it, but he had to do it for the good of the team.'

Harte patiently explained that with the height of the Dublin attack, he felt he needed the presence of Justin McMahon at the edge of the square. McMenamin responded, saying he understood where Harte was coming from. This would be Harte's fifty-fifth Championship game in charge of Tyrone and McMenamin had been virtually ever-present. Such a demotion could put a player off through the session that would follow but not McMenamin.

'It was Mickey's call and I have nothing but the utmost of respect for him. Of course you're annoyed you're not starting, but I'm a firm believer that the manager is the boss. If I started questioning why he was dropping me, it could have had a ripple effect through the squad.

'I was thinking of the bigger picture. I could have thrown the head and not done the training after he'd told me, but at the end of the day, I'm not going to question Mickey Harte. If I got dropped for Dromore or taken off for Dromore, I wouldn't question Paul McIver [Dromore manager]. Training wasn't the place to question him either. Mickey's open enough that you can give him a call and he would always tell you where you're going wrong or right.'

One of McMenamin's greatest qualities has been his unflinching desire to play for Tyrone. Now that his starting jersey was taken away, he also displayed admirable maturity and loyalty to Harte.

His house is being built but more than once his father John and cousin Kevin Donnelly have chased him off the site and away to training. Then there's the upcoming wedding to Maura in December in Ballybofey. There are other places he could be and other things he could be doing but McMenamin is happy to make the sacrifice for the sake of Tyrone and their manager.

'If I was dropped and started throwing the head, then you're throwing away all the loyalty that Mickey showed to me. You have to weigh up the two things – he's been loyal to me so I have to be loyal back to him.'

Others weren't so patient or as content. During the league, Philip Jordan skipped a night's training. He wasn't enjoying it and wanted some time out, but it broke in the newspapers and became a story. After a talk with the manager, Jordan came back into the fold.

During the Championship then, Owen Mulligan took a spell away. There was an attempt to cover up the situation but the perils of social media caught up with him when a photograph of him partying hard mid-Championship in a local nightclub was posted on a Facebook page.

He too was coaxed back. When he returned, McMenamin tore him to bits in the dressing room banter stakes. 'I reckon it was a call for help and I said I would get him back on the straight and narrow. Hub [Kevin Hughes] reckoned that he had no steady girlfriend and he needed to settle down, so he's going to come in and live with me for a while.'

After contemplating the situation, Joe McMahon began comparing the possible scenario with the film 'You, Me and Dupree', where Owen Wilson plays a gooseberry friend of Matt Dillon who spoils the glow of newly-married life with his wife, played by Kate Hudson. With Mulligan growing his hair out and keeping it dyed a Californian blonde, it was the perfect fit. For a few weeks he became known as nothing but Dupree.

Frustrated by his lack of opportunity, young Niall McKenna also quit before returning. The older hands ribbed him about not milking it like Dupree had.

With all the temporary retirements, it became a topic of fun rather than something to fret about. 'It's been eventful with all the boys coming and leaving, it's given us plenty of craic. We're actually taking bets on who's leaving this week, and if Mickey Moynagh [team logistics man] left, you get all bets refunded, like a Paddy Power special.'

And yet, for all that, they were convinced they were on the right path. The Thursday night before they played Armagh, they performed a familiar handpassing drill devised by trainer Fergal McCann. The most passes they had managed in the allotted time was around the mid-forties; this time they broke the fifty mark. The prospect of Armagh coming to town had electrified them. After an initial spell of discomfort, they slapped Armagh to the ground and kept a knee on their backs.

The show rolled on towards Croke Park and they stayed overnight in familiar haunt, Carton House. Tom Herron is a new addition to the backroom team this year whose main role is encouraging new breathing techniques through the nose, but he's also become a fulcrum of joviality. When he vacated his room before the Roscommon game, some unnamed players crept in with a pair of scissors and made ribbons out of his jacket. He was left with not much more than a body warmer.

Before matchday, they were reminded of their horrific recent past. Tyrone were back in Croke Park, big news again. RTÉ would want to talk to Mickey Harte after the game but he would refuse to do so. The escalation of the dispute was as unseemly as it was avoidable. After his initial protest following the Monaghan game at the perceived treatment the national broadcaster had inflicted upon his personal friend Brian Carthy, the following morning's John Murray Show featured a crass sketch using voice recordings of Harte, and finished up by playing 'Pretty Little Girl From Omagh'. Given the recent personal history of the Harte family, it disturbed many that such crude humour could be passed as fit for broadcast.

Harte spoke to his players before they travelled to Croke Park, explaining his stance and that he would not be speaking to any radio or television from RTÉ and asked his players not to either. That was fine by McMenamin.

'Even with RTÉ Radio, he asked us not to. We backed him 100 percent. In our eyes it [the Murray Show skit] was tasteless. Once you start going into his life and taking things out of it, especially after the six or seven months that he's had, boys need to take a good look at themselves.'

Tyrone beat Roscommon, needing Sean Cavanagh to evoke memories of Jack O'Shea with a powerful run and goal in the first half to keep them at bay. Senan Kilbride and Donie Shine served notice that Tyrone were porous in defence and Cathal Cregg caused McMenamin enough bother for him to be substituted.

Tyrone though felt they had only a few glitches in the system.

Then along came the Dubs.

● ● ●

DUBLIN 0-22 v TYRONE 0-15
All Ireland Quarter-final, Croke Park, August 6

Just like that, it was finished. McMenamin had to watch the entire episode unfold as Diarmuid Connolly had a career-defining game and Tyrone were obliterated all over the park. Dublin missed a stream of goal chances in the second half kicking in towards Hill 16 where the blue hordes were baying for blood. For them, this was payback for 2008 when the same scoreboard read Dublin 1-8, Tyrone 3-14.

The end wasn't quite as gruesome for Tyrone as it could have been. Warriors like Conor Gormley, Brian Dooher and Stephen O'Neill kept pushing to the last and kept the scoreline reasonably respectable but it was still a bitter end.

Back in the dressing room there was the realisation that this time, they were nowhere near what was required. They had looked at Championship defeats in the last three years against Cork, Dublin and Donegal and placed their tally of wides on the scales against the margin of defeat. Each time, they came away feeling that if they had shown a little bit more composure they would have tipped the balance.

They couldn't wrap themselves in that comfort. Not now.

As they sat in the cool dressing room with steam rising from their bodies, there was also 'that other thing': the unsaid pact between the players and backroom that Mickey Harte had given so much to them and now they wanted to win something back for him. For Michaela. Now that chance was gone.

'It was tough but we never made a crusade of it and Mickey never made a crusade of it that this is what we had to do. Just the boys put the head down and once we didn't do it, all the players felt bad. We wanted to do something for him.

'When you get beat in any Championship game, you're gutted. With what we wanted to achieve for Mickey, it was ten times worse. There were a lot of sad men in the changing rooms.

'Mickey left us for a while to let it sink in a bit. But then he came in and addressed us, spoke well, saying it wasn't the plan and that you never know what could happen next year. He thanked us for our effort through the year, but at the end of the day we came up short.'

For the first time under Mickey Harte, Tyrone had been played off the park in a Championship match. For such a proud side, it cut deep. County chairman Ciaran McLaughlin spoke in the dressing room. He asked anyone considering retirement to give it a lot of thought and to speak to Mickey before making any decisions. They were to do it the right way; as McLaughlin called it, 'the Tyrone way'.

McMenamin hadn't seen the defeat coming at all. 'Going down, I thought we definitely had a good chance of beating them. I thought it was going to be a close match but in fairness to Dublin their game-plan worked well, they got bodies back into the defence, they had a lot of space for the Brogans and Connolly to cause damage. Everything went right for them on the day.'

That evening, McMenamin and Peter Harte exited the stadium together, two members of Tyrone's present but whose careers span different eras. Harte was meeting his family while McMenamin was meeting his soon-to-be-wife. They met up with another couple and went for a few drinks in Gill's before continuing onto McGowan's in Phibsboro. A few Dubs supporters called over to him and he had a bit of craic with them.

'I suppose it's the best thing to do when you're beaten by the better team. You have to be gracious about it. They were real football people.'

Now, a rebuilding job awaits Tyrone. The cornerstone of the team went in late

September when Brian Dooher walked away for good. McMenamin reckons about three further retirements might occur, but he wouldn't be confident of naming them.

He won't be making any decision on his own future until Dromore's championship run ends. When Paul McIver spoke to him at the start of the year, he told McMenamin to concentrate on Tyrone and give everything to his county. Now he is giving everything to the club.

For him, the season would roll into the autumn.

CHAPTER THIRTY

I Just Can't Get Enough

IT'S not like he'd thought it would be. He spent years chasing a Championship, thinking the final whistle would be a ticket to the greatest out-of-body experience possible.

Not so.

Don't get him wrong, it was still one of the biggest moments of his football career and indeed of his life, but when he watched other sides collapse on the finishing line and lie victorious, their faces marred with dust and sweat and blood, their glee would be what would push him out the door to train on a January night, or drive hours across Ulster on a midweek night to play a second string of rookie county players.

This thing, this joy, this entire experience must be a slow burner, he thought.

What was foremost on his mind was the fact that he hadn't truly needed to strain every last sinew. Derry were a beaten docket with a quarter of an hour left in the match. He wanted to exert himself, to nick the win or else charge to the finish with a late scoring splurge. That would have been fitting. That was the way he fantasised it in the past.

The past's failures led to fantasy. The reality was days like Crossmaglen, or conceding 1-27 to Cork, or scoring only six points against Fermanagh after a rainy morning signing autographs in Pettigo. That was the past and this was the present and future. This was success. And yet it was oddly weird.

The day after the first training session back, followed by the supper of Kentucky Fried Chicken, Kevin Cassidy reached for his diary.

Wednesday, July 20
Not happy at the way I'm playing and realise that I need a big game in the quarter-final. Ring Tom Beag to ask for some help.

Tom Beag Gillespie was an old school manager when they won a county title with the club in 2002 and was involved again when they won it in 2006. His devotion to coaching had led to him attending multiple conferences and keeping up with the latest developments. He moved with the times but he never lost his belief of mastering the skills. Nothing gives you confidence like practicing. It's something he always tells the underage teams that he's bringing through in Gaoth Dobhair.

Cassidy called Jim McGuinness. He wanted to be excused from the following night's training session so he could do some work on his own. It took an age convincing him, but he managed it.

'I felt I needed to do it, more for my head than anything else. I wasn't playing the way I wanted to be playing, even in training leading up to the Ulster final. I know I was physically in really good shape, but you need to be doing things like breaking tackles, being on the end of moves, and it just wasn't coming for me. Even though I was delighted that we won Ulster and was delighted with the celebrations, when I woke up the Monday after the night before, it was still eating at me that I hadn't been flat out and I wasn't going the way I wanted to go.'

On the Thursday morning he met Tom Beag at the gates, waiting for him with his stopwatch. There was nobody about, just as they liked it. 'We did two-hundred metre runs, one-hundred metre runs, forty-five metre runs. It ended up with me on my knees, puking. I wanted to work with Tom. He's been there since I started and we'd have a good relationship. He just knows how I should be moving.'

After the running, they dedicated themselves to the art and science of shooting. 'He stands in the goals and have twelve balls at a time. Normally, in a shooting drill you would steady yourself up, but his take on things is that in balls ten, eleven and twelve you're tired, and you're going to be tired in games, so he'll bang twelve balls out at me, high, low, either wing, and I have to run onto them and bang them over the bar. The '45 on this pitch isn't realistic, it's too short, so I'll stand a bit back from it. He kicks them out and then my break is the time it takes for him to gather the balls up again.

'If I don't get eight or nine, we'd be really unhappy. I go into Tom Beag and ask him what he thinks the problem was. He tells me then if I lifted my head, or the follow-through wasn't good, if my leg was coming across the body, something like that. To finish up, if I get ten out of twelve, then we leave it at that.

'Then we do another one, where I have it in midfield, give the ball to him, come through and he'll pop it up to me, shouting right or left and I have to hit it with the outside of the boot to get it over. In all, our little workout normally takes an hour.'

The pitch is his place where the world stops. Close by is a long, steep dune and when Cassidy feels he needs to do some power work, he will sprint up it twenty-five times. Just beyond that is the pier where he jumps in for a swim and bathes in the ocean water.

By Saturday, he was back with the team. They trained in Donegal town and McGuinness drove them like slaves. The following morning they checked in at Letterkenny and he annihilated them, but in a huddle after one of their short games, he urged them to trust him and patiently explained to them that what they were undergoing was a process of hyper-exertion. Their bodies might have been broken now since the Derry game, but with the right rest and food, they would be fitter than ever before for Croke Park.

Vomit covered patches of the field and there were calls for a hose to at least take the bad look off it. The smell was overpowering. Cassidy had missed the worst punishment on the Thursday night. Marty Boyle had to be physically carried off the field even though he's a teetotaller from the Glenties and had hardly abused his body after the Ulster final. Michael Hegarty had said he thought he was going to suffer a heart attack.

'Jim's warmups are unbelievable,' says Cassidy. 'You feel like dying in the middle of them. We might have warmed up with the ball for half an hour. Then we go into our sprints, eighty-metre sprints, one hundred-metre sprints, shuttle runs, cones on twenty yards either side of you and you have to sprint to the cones and back again. You have four men in a line, and if there is any more than a second or two seconds difference between the four men, you go again. There is no slacking off, there is no way out. It's the hardest I've ever trained in my life.

'We got to a ball drill but it's basically a hundred metre run after you do the kicking. He wants good, quality ball into the forwards, so once you kick the ball you run after it. If you're not running hard after it he just stops the training and goes back to only runs.

'Another drill is with three cones in a line. They will be one hundred metres apart and we have to absolutely hammer the ball at each other on the ground. If he's not happy that it is kicked hard enough then he will stop the drill and do press ups. Once you hammer the ball the other person has to get it up in one touch and hammer it on to the next man. If it's a half jog, he stops and punishes us until we get it right.'

Cassidy has shaved time off his personal best in the two hundred-metre sprints. He now makes it home in 21.6 seconds, almost half of what it was on those snowy days in Castlefin, though he still has a bit to go to catch Mark McHugh who is down to 20.4 seconds.

●　●　●

The Sunday evening was a sacred one for Cassidy. He took the cup home with him after training. It only visited a few selected places and the first was the grave of his Granny Sally in Brinlack. He placed it on the grave and took a photograph, knowing it was sentimental and the right thing to do.

When he married Sarah, his friend Hugh McGinley did the honours as best man. He brought it over to the grave of Hugh's father, Sean. The grave is connected to St Colmcille's Chapel and he also paid his dues to Father McGettigan, the founder of the GAA in Gaoth Dobhair who lies buried in front of the church.

Naturally, it also visited Tom Beag to let him hoist it up and let a cheer out of him. It went from there to Teach Mhici, the local watering hole that is the home of football and sean nós singing in the parish.

After a while, he became wary of being the man who was parading the cup around the country, so he brought it home where it stayed in the kitchen for a couple of days. The first morning it was in the house, he came down from the stairs in the morning and had to do a long double-take. It was surreal.

Little Aoife and Nia loved it. It was another toy for them and they crawled all over it and sat inside the chalice.

He draws strength from these people, these places. Around the road towards Falcarragh is one of the most spectacular sights in this isolated island off the west coast of Europe: Bloody Foreland. In the long summer evenings, the sun gives a reddish hue to the banks and during autumn the ferns glow a reddish brown.

Before each game he plays, he visits Granny's grave and then drives down to the foot of Bloody Foreland. He gets out and walks over to the rocks, sits down and looks out to Tory Island, listening to the Atlantic lap up against the shore. It opens his lungs and his heart. No place quite like it.

● ● ●

Donegal were drawn against Kildare. Cassidy had watched the draw on TV at the house of John Mór Diver, a former full-back whose sons are friends and clubmates. In his diary he noted: *I'm happy because I know it won't be easy, but we can beat them.*

Before he could face them though, there was something else he needed to do to get an edge. He got a number for John Morrison, his Donegal coach in 2002.

'I hadn't spoken to John since 2003 but in a minute I was feeling much better about myself. The man's a genius. I told him the story, that I wasn't happy with the Ulster final. He said to me, "If your mother goes to the shop and asks you to scrub the floor, you can do it and be happy with yourself about it. Your mother might come back and not be happy with the job you did. It's all about perceptions. You were asked to do a job but you must express yourself within that job."'

Morrison also told him to write down his strengths, what he wanted to get out of the Kildare game, his targets, and to give him a phonecall later when he had the time. On the coach down, Cassidy had written, 'Keep my man scoreless, be involved in three Donegal scores, one good catch, two good turnovers.'

He put the call through. 'I told him that even though the year was going well for me, there were times when I was questioning myself. Do I really have the stomach and the fight for this? To go the whole distance? That might sound strange after winning the Ulster final and getting to where we are, but I was in a couple of training sessions wondering was this the right place for me, should I be here? It wasn't that I wasn't able to do the training or not able to compete at that level, but more did I even want to?

'John said that there are over twenty-five other counties that would love to be in the exact same position as we are. Every club player in the country would love to be where we are. Every Armagh player would love to be in a hotel that day, facing into a game like this. He said "I'm going to tell you now, youse are going to beat Kildare. Youse are too good for them. Just believe in yourself, go out and express yourself, play to your strengths."

'What he was saying might have been very simple but I found it very good for me. I love playing in Croke Park anyway and the bigger the day, the better for me.

'Up to now I would have been talking more and trying to gee men up before games. But from when I got off the bus for the Kildare game I had a smile on my face. I just knew I was in the right place and there to play a game of football. Win, lose or draw, it was going to be a great occasion.'

● ● ●

During the journey down on the Friday evening, Jim McGuinness stood up in the coach, took the microphone and told the players to listen up.

'There was a story,' says Cassidy, 'about to break in the newspapers in the morning. He'd just got a call from a journalist, saying that the Kildare camp had contacted the newspaper seeing if they would run this story to put pressure on the referee.

'He said just in case we would read it in the morning, that we were to go out and play our normal game and not to change it for anybody. Jim flipped it all on its head, saying that Kieran McGeeney must be worried if he had to do this the night before a game, that he mustn't have much confidence in his players that they could see off the job by themselves.'

Friday night rolled into Saturday morning. Sure enough, a story outlining Kildare's concerns on how the referee would deal with the occasion appeared in the *Irish Independent*, with Niall Carew, a member of their backroom, quoted as saying, 'If he lets Donegal continue with the cynical fouling of the opposition half-back line in particular, then yes, they will be hard to break down. If he punishes them and hands out yellow cards when they are merited, then we'll have a chance.'

The players never passed any remarks, concerned instead with their own game. With Morrison's reassurance providing the balm Cassidy needed, he slept soundly through the night. Before the match he had a meal of a bowl of soup, a scoop of spuds and a couple of sandwiches. Then it was time for the huddle.

'Jim went around the circle and touched every man. He told us that regardless of what happened in this game he was absolutely delighted with us and thanked everyone for the effort that they have gave all year and that he was really proud of us. But now, the real business started with a massive game today. He told us that we were going to win the game, how we were going to win it, and by how many points.

'After that, Maxi had a wee video clip that was focused on our tackling. Rather than show us scores that we have hit all year, it was all the tackling. Rory Gallagher had told us he hears this song by Lady Gaga that applies to us, 'On the Edge of Glory', and that was playing over the footage. At that stage, then there was no more talking because the time for talking was over.'

●　　●　　●

From the moment the ball was thrown in, Michael Hegarty clashed with Kildare's John Doyle. Both men got up with limps.

Kildare were presented with a close in free after two minutes. Doyle hobbled over to it and the crowd urged him on. It was time for the mind games to commence. Irish rugby fly-half Ronan O'Gara had been in the Kildare camp offering his advice to their freetakers, but news also came back to Donegal that Hugh Campbell, a sports psychologist who had previously leant his expertise to Armagh in 2002, had been working with Doyle.

'I don't know how Rory Gallagher found out, but any time myself and [Rory] Kavanagh were walking past Doyle, we would say "Hugh's not happy with your kicking", or "McGeeney doesn't have much faith in you." We had heard that McGeeney was lining up another freetaker that week too.

'He kicked two balls, but he didn't want to know about frees after that. I found it strange because my memories of Johnny Doyle were of a top class freetaker down through the years.'

On seven minutes Cassidy burst forward to set up Paddy McBrearty for a point. He was already involved in a score; one of his targets was underway. Eoghan O'Flaherty had to take over the place kicking duties and speared one over, before following it with another from play.

The game took an age to take shape. Donegal were faltering in attack but McGuinness had Michael Murphy in reserve. He had suffered a hamstring tear in training, but now he was sent on after twenty-six minutes along with Eamon McGee. Eamon Callaghan stretched Kildare's lead to three points but Mark McHugh brilliantly kept in a ball from Michael Hegarty that had been drifting wide and exchanged passes with Anthony Thompson to clip it over. That made it Kildare 0-5, Donegal 0-3 at the break.

The second half was just as tight. Kildare had the ball in the net but Tomás O'Connor was controversially deemed to be in the square and it was ruled out. Substitutes Dermot Molloy and Alan Smith traded scores before Cassidy drove forward and kicked a point to tie the game at seven points each. He'd now been involved in two scores.

Eight minutes later, Christy Toye was sent on and wasn't picked up by a marker. From the Kildare kickout, Donegal worked it in and found Toye unmarked in front of goal. He held his nerve and drilled it home calmly. Donegal were now up a goal with twelve minutes on the clock.

Anthony Thompson had a chance to put four in it, but his relatively straightforward chance hit the post and went wide. Eoghan O'Flaherty sent one over before James Kavanagh took possession under the Cusack Stand and floated a massive kick over the bar.

There was only sixty seconds of normal time left. Donegal were a point up.

Panic gripped the leaders. Paul Durcan punted the kickout and Kildare took possession once again, going down the barrel and exerting the pressure. Rory Kavanagh fouled but Kildare wasted the free. Donegal brought it up the field and a ball sent towards Michael Murphy was overcooked and drifted out over the endline.

The board went up on the sideline. Agonisingly for Donegal there would be four minutes of time added on.

Shane Connolly kicked it short and Kildare worked it up the field. Rob Kelly was in possession but Karl Lacey ripped it from his grasp and began the counter attack. Rory Kavanagh gave a fist pass to Toye in midfield but he waited too long for it and it was knocked away. Nothing was sticking for them.

Emmet Bolton took it into the heart of the Donegal defence, drew Anthony Thompson close and shoved him down. He kicked across the body with his left foot and dragged it too much. Wide! Only one minute of the extra time was up.

Durcan kicked out. Again Kildare won it and worked it upfield. Again James Kavanagh swung a high ball in from the Hogan Stand sideline. It hung in the air before dropping towards the small square and Mark McHugh climbed high to palm it back to Durcan. He looked to return the pass but McHugh turned his back on him for a split second and the ball went loose again.

Emmet Bolton picked up the break. It was passed and defended and overturned and lost again three times in ten seconds. The ball was like a gold bar that players flung themselves at. Morgan O'Flaherty got his hands on it and just at that point, Rory Kavanagh came in to tackle. Contact was made, O'Flaherty went to ground and David Coldrick blew his whistle. Free in!

Donegal players protested long and hard. Eoghan O'Flaherty stood over the free and television commentators began ruminating that Kildare's conditioning would see them dominate the extra-time period.

O'Flaherty drilled the ball over the bar.

Durcan kicked out. Again Kildare won it. Hugh McGrillen played a ball into Sweeney but it bounced wide. Durcan kicked out once more and full time was blown. It would take another twenty minutes to separate the two teams.

Cassidy walked past Coldrick. He told him he felt that Kildare had been given a soft free at the end.

● ● ●

The game had become a contest of wills and resolve. The strict game-plans that both sides had stuck rigidly to for the first hour had dissolved into sheer graft and flashes of talent as the finish line approached.

In the Donegal huddle, Cassidy's attitude was defiant. 'Going into extra-time we didn't feel we would lose. Everyone was the same, adrenaline was driving us on and there was no way you were going to put up your hand and ask to come off.'

Rain came down over Dublin as the Croke Park floodlights were fired up, giving the evening a heightened sense of the drama unfolding. The tension hung thick in the air until a streaker took it in his own hands to provide a bit of light relief as the teams lined up for the first half of extra-time.

It took five minutes for the first point, from Kildare's Ronan Sweeney.

Then Kildare sub Gary White pointed a free. In time added on Alan Smith added another point from play. Donegal were three down. They looked exhausted and spent.

They worked the ball up to the captain Michael Murphy who fisted it to Lacey. He made no mistake. Yet again Donegal had stolen in for a crucial point just on the stroke of halftime. The score was now Donegal 1-8, Kildare 0-13.

Normally, teams would turn straight around and instantly play the second period of extra time. Instead Coldrick and the authorities told each team to take a break, so cramp could be massaged out of players' legs and they could sufficiently hydrate. It was a sensible move that also had the effect of cranking the tension up another notch. All around the stadium, nobody could take their eyes off the two team huddles with two of the brightest young coaches in the game exhorting their players and willing them on.

It wasn't looking promising for Donegal. They needed three points to win and they had taken eighty-five minutes to accrue 1-8. With fatigue kicking in, victory looked unlikely.

Their task was made all the more difficult when Bolton landed a beautiful point in the first minute.

Donegal countered immediately. The unlikely figure of Frank McGlynn popped up at corner forward and sent it out to Murphy who stroked it over.

Donegal attacked again and won a free. Murphy came out and played it across to Bradley who was in front of goal but fifty yards out. He was hauled down to the ground by John Doyle. Murphy stood over the free with the crowd wincing for his hamstring. He nailed it with the ball flying over with yards to spare. Donegal were back within a point and Cassidy roared at his teammates to keep the effort up.

The closing stages would all be about heart and desire.

'The game had gone crazy. I started on Pádraig O'Neill but I don't know what system they were using or whether it was to confuse us or what, but after every ball that went wide they would have a new man on me. They must have been rotating. I was on Morgan O'Flaherty, Mikey Conway...

'By extra time, both teams just had a policy of picking up the nearest man. That's what it came down to. There was no man to man, apart from the full back line, but out the field it was a case of just picking up whoever was closest to you.'

Connolly hit his kickout long and high. Kildare launched their attack and Conway kicked wide as the contest entered the last five minutes. Kildare's Rob Kelly had to be replaced with cramp while McGuinness made a final gamble by sending Paddy McBrearty back on.

The play tilted back and forth like a game of pinball. Bradley was once again taken down to the ground when he took possession, this time by Brian Flanagan who received a ticking. Kildare were doing everything in their power to wind down the clock and try and close it out, even if it meant resorting to blatant cynicism.

Rory Kavanagh got the ball in the corner. He passed to Dermot Molloy, the late hero of the Ulster semi-final, but he put too much slice on the shot and it bounced wide. Donegal were still a point behind and time was running out.

The kickout came. Cassidy climbed and broke the ball. Rory Kavanagh collected and drove through a thicket of bodies, getting a pass off to McHugh. He turned outside and Donegal recycled to David Walsh who laid off to Murphy. The captain kicked it further out to Cassidy, who ran into space forty-five metres out, steadied himself and pulled his kick wide. Another miss.

A minute was on the clock.

Connolly went long and high with the kick. Eamon McGee palmed it down and Cassidy latched onto it. Walsh kicked it over the sideline.

Kildare played the percentages in the build-up. They kicked upfield and lost it just as the stadium announcer said there would be two minutes of time added on. Thompson took a pass from McGlynn and kicked a high ball to Murphy. It broke and fell to Toye. A jink and a shot off the left later and Donegal were level.

LEVEL!

The crowd were on their feet screaming and roaring and although Croke Park was only half full, the place was rocking.

Kildare got a free from a push in the back when the kickout was dropping. Hugh McGrillen played a pass in and Karl Lacey cut it out. It ran to Eamon McGee who was falling but managed to handpass to Neil Gallagher. As he picked it up he was fouled. Donegal had the ball and there would be one last, final play in this epic.

Cassidy made himself available. An opponent was trying to cut down the space but collapsed with cramp. Cassidy cut back inside and delivered to Gallagher, and onto Toye.

Toye kicked a pass towards the sideline. Murphy beat two men to the ball but if he tried a traditional pick-up he would have been smothered. Instead, he chipped it up into his chest and burrowed a hole through the gap between the two men.

It came to Gallagher who fisted to Walsh who fed it to Kavanagh and onto Toye. Cassidy was lurking.

'We'd worked on situations like this in our training sessions all the time, where the ball is worked to a certain area and you nearly always get a wee pop shot in and around that area. I just drifted in there. I thought Toye lost it but he got his toe to it and I was just standing beside him.'

Toye could not gather the ball, but he stuck the tip of his boot out to the break and guided it to the full-back Neil McGee who had been pushing up. McGee did a quick scan of his surroundings, turned back and saw Cassidy appealing for the ball, sitting in the pocket like a fly-half.

The ball found its way to Cassidy. He already knew where it was going.

He was fifty-three metres out from the goals at the Hill 16 end but in his mind he was home with Tom Beag in the Gaoth Dobhair pitch.

The ball is popped to him and he goes with the left.

The player catches it flush and it leaves his boot, creating an arc like a rainbow.

There was no spin, no swerve or curl. Cassidy got his head down, concentrated on the ball and kicked through it. David Walsh was hunched over with his hands on his knees gazing at the flight as it climbed further and higher. Cassidy turned and leapt in the air. Kildare's Shane Connolly was already looking for a ball to restart the game.

It sails over the bar. The stadium is in delirium. In the commentary box, Kevin McStay screams, 'HE HAS IT! HE HAS IT!' A rumble began in the Lower Hogan Stand and became a thunderous cheer throughout the stadium. In world sport that weekend, there would be nothing to match the drama being played out right here.

'As soon as I hit it, I knew. Those pictures of me in the air, the ball isn't even over the bar at that stage. I leaped up and I turned away from goal and for a horrible moment started to think that it wasn't over. You can see David Walsh watching it go over as I was jumping. I remember coming down and being relieved because I would have been some clown to be jumping about like that if I had missed! But once I connected, I just knew it was over.'

He knew he had to go for it. The miss a few minutes earlier meant nothing. He'd put in too much groundwork in to doubt himself.

'A lot of people have been saying to me "Jesus, anybody else would have passed that on!" But you don't train all year to get in those positions and pass. You train all year and you have to back yourself.'

He'd met his target as outlined to Morrison. He'd been involved in three scores.

The game wasn't over. He vowed to himself that if he could get near one Kildare player on the ball, he was taking him down.

He didn't have to as Coldrick blew the whistle.

The lights, the football, the tension, the emotion all made a heady mix. The emotive 'May We Never Have To Say Goodbye' began playing over the speakers. Donegal remained on the field, accepting the standing ovation. Maxi Curran ran on and wrapped Cassidy up. Michael Murphy cradled Cassidy's head in his hands in disbelief.

Kieran McGeeney stood there letting this latest crushing blow take effect. His players were littered all over the pitch, some in floods of tears, all of them inconsolable. They had been outdone by another squareball decision by an umpire and it was too much.

For one night, Cassidy had lit up the city and the country. There were many topics of conversation but this was the main one. It had a beautiful poetry attached to it, the aesthetic quality of the shot contrasting with the brutal warfare that the game developed into. The following day he would fade into the background of Irish life, taking his family for a day in Dublin Zoo, away from the din, away from the crowds, the lads and the football. But for now, he was a hero.

Cassidy began trotting down the tunnel but was called back. Gaoth Dobhair's Mairtín O'Fearraigh is the county secretary and he had spotted some faces in the crowd. He told Cassidy they were waiting for him. He jogged back out, leaned across the barriers and swallowed Tom Beag Gillespie up in the tightest bearhug his body could give.

They had done it together, the coach and the player. On the following night's Sunday Game, presenter Des Cahill would pose the question that if Kevin

Cassidy took ten balls down to his local pitch, how many of those shots he would get? If only he knew...

Sarah's uncle Frank was there again too; Rory Kavanagh's sister Alma, and Declan Curran. They all told him he was the greatest Donegal man ever.

He got into the dressing room. They went into a huddle and Jim McGuinness was holding a towel to his nose. An over-exuberant photographer had shoved his lens in his face, trying to get the perfect snap. He spoke to the group. 'I suppose I have to congratulate Cass, but if he had missed that one, he wouldn't ever be getting another jersey again!'

Cassidy changed without fuss. Sarah was waiting outside with Aoife and Nia. He slipped out the backdoor of Croke Park and into a taxi to the Skylon Hotel. He horsed recovery drinks and water into him and fired off a text to John Morrison.

Thanks very much for everything, it really helped.

Morrison replied: If you want, we could have a meeting before the semi-final.

Cassidy smiled. I'd love that.

Inside the bowels of the stadium, a dozen reporters stared glumly at the coach and twitching nervously when the dressing room door opened, waiting in a futile effort to get a few quotes from the matchwinner.

The rest of the Donegal team boarded the team bus, exhausted and emotional but Cassidy had other plans. With a babysitter sorted, he and Sarah caught a taxi to the Harcourt Hotel where his brother Stephen had arranged for a few Irish Rebel bands to play and coincide with the visit of Celtic to Dublin for the pre-season Super Cup tournament played on the other side of the city that day. There he met his Glasgow cousins and settled down for a night of partying and release.

His game was back, Donegal were in the All Ireland semi-final and it was largely down to him.

After a diversion to Copper Face Jacks, they returned to the sing song at the Harcourt. Naturally, the most famous man in Ireland on that night was pressed into action. He cleared his throat and gave a lusty rendition of 'Home To Donegal.'

'This is my homeland, the place I was born in,
No matter where I roam it's in my soul,
My feet may wander a thousand places,
But my heart will lead me back home, to my Donegal'

They wanted an encore.

He was up for it.

It could only be one song.

'When I'm with you Donegal, I go out of my head...'

All That You Can't Leave Behind

IT wasn't their fault. They were just some lads from home who probably felt awkward and had a few drinks, standing making nervous chit-chat with him.

But at that time, Kevin Cassidy didn't want to talk.

He made his excuses and slipped through the side door. He found Sarah inside, sitting with some friends and having a drink. He asked her for the keys to the bedroom upstairs. He could feel the lump brewing in his throat. He knew it was coming and he was never the type to hold back.

Sarah read the situation and went with him. The lift doors opened. They stepped inside. The doors closed and he collapsed into heaving, racking sobs.

It set off Sarah too who started crying in sympathy for him. After everything, all the nights when he would leave her with two little girls crying on the kitchen floor and ring back home to apologise for having to do it, it was over. Donegal's season was over.

They got to the room and he found it hard to breathe with the dull ache in his heart. He had never, ever been like this over a football match. Sure, he could feel down, but somewhere at the back of mind he always had that little nag – you didn't really give it everything. That wasn't the case now. In 2011, he had given it everything. His heart, body and soul.

He wanted to hide away for the night. Didn't want the crowds, the bustle and the clink of the pint glasses and the claps on the back. Couldn't stomach somebody coming up and telling him how proud everyone was of them. He just lay there until Sarah asked him what the worst thing was about his pain. He described how he had been spending the last while putting everything into playing in an All Ireland final. When he closed his eyes at night, he dreamt of running out of the tunnel on All Ireland final day. But now it was over.

'Well Kevin,' said Sarah, 'it's going to be very hard to walk away from that now.'

● ● ●

Donegal had stuck to their routine for the weekend. They stayed in the Ashbourne Hotel, watched a bit of soccer on television on Saturday night, did a bit of light stretching in the pool. Absolutely nobody knew who was or wasn't starting. Even by Jim McGuinness standards, this was extremely cloak and dagger.

Three hours before the ball was due to be thrown in for the All Ireland semi-final against Dublin, McGuinness gathered all his players in the meeting room. The entire backroom team, including physios, doctors and the bus driver Kevin McNaney had to be there as well.

There, his first command was that everybody should take out their mobile phones out and turn them off.

He took out his own phone, turned it off and popped it into a bag.

He collected around fifty phones, zipped them in the bag as well. And then he said it.

'Right, this is the team and this is the way we're going to beat Dublin.'

It was no wonder he had waited so long to unveil his masterplan. If it had been revealed any earlier word of it might have filtered out of the camp. Its greatest value, Donegal's greatest asset now, was its shock value, the element of surprise.

It was radical. It was bold. It was brilliant.

Donegal wouldn't be playing nine men behind the ball, ten men, even eleven. Fourteen. They'd be playing fourteen men behind the ball.

Colm McFadden was going to be up there by himself, doing the best he could.

Michael Murphy would drop back to wing forward and everyone else was to filter back.

The team's personnel would be different to the one released during the week. Eamon McGee was in as was injury doubt Paddy McGrath. Ryan Bradley was in midfield along with Rory Kavanagh. Frank McGlynn, a back by trade, was named at wing-forward, Christy Toye was at centre-forward, with Mark McHugh on the other wing, but both McGlynn and McHugh were to come straight back at the throw-in.

Dublin could have all the possession they wanted in their backline, but once they crossed the halfway line, it was to be an all-out war of attrition. There to meet them would be a defensive blockade right across the field, the long great wall of Donegal. Then when Dublin would be repelled and have the ball stripped off them, the invaders from the north would attack up the field as quickly as possible.

The temerity of it would later astonish a nation but in that room everyone just nodded.

'You never, ever question Jim. Nobody was looking at each other or anything like that; it was a case that we had believed in him all year and we were going to go with this too with everything we had.

'He told us "This is the way it's going to go. This game could end up four-three, doesn't matter. As long as we're on the right end of the result, that's all that matters. The longer we keep them without scoring their first-half goal, without getting their big run for ten or fifteen minutes at the start of the game, the pressure will be all on them. They'll start kicking crazy wides, the Brogans are going to shoot from anywhere. They're going to get frustrated and they won't be able to understand why they can't break you down. Diarmuid Connolly is not going to get a kick on goal. And every time they hit a wide, they'll be reminded that they're not playing against Tyrone now."'

Cassidy reached into the side pouch of his kitbag and pulled out his Donegal wristband. He looked at the symbols and considered them. 'MA' meaning Mental Attitude. 'GP' standing for Game Plan, and '20'. 20 was the number of aspects of a game that players could control, such as their workrate, their shooting, the break balls, the kickouts. McGuinness told them of it but never committed it to print. They were to control everything in their power. If they managed that, victory was theirs.

Since the Kildare game, Cassidy had squeezed in five kicking practices with Tom Beag and had spoken with John Morrison in person when he came up to Ardara to take a coaching session. Now it was time to shine.

• • •

The lineout raised not just eyebrows but blood temperatures. After twenty minutes, the teams were tied on one point each. Every time Donegal launched an attack and began to pass laterally on the halfway line, the crowd howled with boos. This was football with the only objective of winning.

At halftime, Donegal were in front, 0-4 to 0-2. They enjoyed the break. The last time they had played Dublin here, back in 2002, there was tea and biscuits left in the dressing rooms for the teams at halftime. Now, it was all sports drinks and energy gels.

Cassidy was pleased.

'All I kept thinking was "This is going the way we want it to." We held the ball, switched it over, went back, went forward. That was the way we were told, keep possession, find an opening, don't panic, don't think that you have to launch a shot because you've had it for so long. Just keep it until you have an opening.

'In the first half we were getting the scores but Jim had said that it was going to take a goal for us to win this.'

The chance arrived in the first minute of the second half. Michael Murphy handpassed to Colm McFadden, who threw a shimmy that beat his man and went through on goal. He put his head down, struck the ball fiercely, but it went inches over the bar. McFadden got up with a pained expression. That was the goal chance and there was no guarantee that another one would come along.

After hitting two frees wide, the Dublin goalkeeper Stephen Cluxton found his range with a point. McFadden replied but Cluxton converted another on fifty-four minutes to leave one point in it. Dublin had a goal disallowed a minute later and Donegal were hanging on with their fingertips.

Just two minutes later, Diarmuid Connolly got caught in possession and a jostling match developed. Substitute Marty Boyle got up in Connolly's face and an agitated Connolly shoved his palm into Boyle's face.

Linesman Rory Hickey had seen the incident and Cassidy immediately told him and referee Maurice Deegan that Connolly would have to be red-carded.

Cassidy would later be heavily criticised for urging a fellow player to be sent off but all those years of losing to more ruthless and cynical teams had now brought out a colder, hardened side in him.

'I didn't see Marty being struck but I saw him hitting the deck. I was straight onto the referee, to be honest.

'I never used to be a player that would have done that, until this year. You do whatever it takes and it was a chance to get rid of one of their boys. The game was in the melting pot then and I make no bones about it, I saw it as a ticket to the All Ireland final. I just said "He hit him, he hit him, he has to go" and I said it to the linesman as well.'

Donegal were one point and one man up with twelve minutes on the clock. Twelve minutes away from an All Ireland final against Kerry – and Paul Galvin. Cassidy's dream was coming true.

And then, for the first time all year, it didn't go to plan.

Dublin's Kevin McManamon, Bryan Cullen and Bernard Brogan all hit points. Donegal could no longer control the controllables. They tried a few futile high balls in. Maurice Deegan blew for the last time. It was all over.

Cassidy lingered on the pitch, his eyes glassy. He didn't want to let this feeling go. Himself and Philip McMahon had been at each other all game with verbal jibes but now McMahon was over to him, saying, 'Ye're a credit to your county and don't listen to any bullshit that people say.'

McMahon asked him if he would swap shirts but Cassidy asked if he could keep his own as it would be worth too much sentimental value. McMahon understood.

He sat on his hindquarters for a while trying to take it in, and then trudged back to the dressing room alongside Rory Gallagher.

Inside, it was deathly quiet. Cassidy looked round the room at all the players and his mind was on those snowy days in Castlefin.

'You're looking around thinking that it's gone for another year, it's all over and there's no chance of rectifying it.

'We got into a huddle. Jim said he was proud of us and there was no point any of us going around with our heads down. I wouldn't normally be that emotional after a game to this extent, but this time I knew we were good enough to go the whole way. We left an All Ireland medal behind us because I know that Kerry would have struggled with us. Definitely. If we brought our system past Dublin we would have learned how to go a bit more offensive while still minding the house.

'Jim said it was a great year, and he reminded us of what he said in our first meeting – it would be two years before this group of players would get any respect from anybody outside Donegal and this was still only year one. We had come a long way, delivered the first Ulster title in years, we were in Division One of the league, up with the big teams. "Next year starts now, when we leave this dressing room," he told us. "It's as simple as that."'

Cassidy stripped off in silence, Anthony Thompson and Paul Durcan either side of him. He stood in the showers dazed with defeat, got dried off, changed and then climbed onto the team bus.

When it was ready to go, they emerged from the darkness of the stadium into late summer sunshine. The bus turned left off Jones Road onto Clonliffe Road. When they got as far as Quinn's pub, hundreds of Donegal fans applauded their heroes. Cassidy couldn't escape this feeling of failure, burning in his stomach like acid. They continued up to the Skylon Hotel where the only person Kevin wanted to see was Sarah.

●   ●   ●

They didn't know how long they had spent up in the room. Could have been thirty minutes, could have been two hours. They decided to go down and have a drink. Kevin Cassidy met up with his Donegal teammates and recognised his emotions in their eyes. After a couple of drinks, the pain began to subside.

It was time for the team to leave, to return to the Hills for the winter, with the Anglo-Celt to warm the homes of Donegal.

Kevin had to go and tell Jim McGuinness that he was staying down in Dublin for the night.

'See you next year, so,' said McGuinness.

And Kevin Cassidy, the man who had retired in Crossmaglen in 2010, the man who had promised himself and his wife all through the year that 2011 would be his last, could only say one thing to that.

'Without a shadow of a doubt, Jim.'

APPENDIX

Ali, Muhammad *210*
Anderson, Willie *117*
Andrews, Carmel *89, 90, 100, 184, 189*
Andrews, Joseph *89, 90*
Andrews, Val *10, 11, 87-89, 91-101, 129-131, 178, 180-182, 184, 185, 187-190*
Austin, Liam *11, 92*
Bannon, Orla *236, 237*
Bateson, Michael *221, 231*
Beckenbauer, Franz *154*
Bellew, Francie *31*
Blake, Tony *69, 218*
Bogue, Niall *31, 79, 80, 81, 82*
Bolton, Emmet *265*
Bonner, Kevin *49*
Bonner, Packie *115*
Boylan, Anne *144*
Boylan, Sean *155*
Boyle, Brendan *26*
Boyle, Marty *259, 272*
Boyle, Michael *241*
Boyle, Tony *25, 239*
Bradley, Eoin *149, 150, 192, 195, 196, 198, 218, 219, 221-227, 237*
Bradley, Liam 'Baker' *84, 110-115, 135, 137, 138, 140, 219*
Bradley, Paddy *117, 119, 192, 199, 219, 222-224*
Bradley, Rosemary *152*
Bradley, Ryan *185, 188, 227, 228, 230, 231, 240, 270*
Bradley, Simon *81, 82*
Brady, Hughie *150, 244*
Brady, Kevin *112*
Brady, Paul *69*
Brannigan, Aidan *102*
Bray, Stephen *19*
Breen, Chris *13, 150*
Brennan, Anne *192*
Brennan, John *12, 36, 37, 65, 66, 116-119, 145, 147, 149, 191, 192, 194, 195, 198, 199, 219, 220, 222, 226, 227, 231, 236, 237, 238*
Brennan, Mark *98*
Brennan, Michael *98*
Brewster, Paul *79, 177*
Brewster, Tom *12*
Brogan, Bernard *197, 272*
Brolly, Joe *40, 193, 196, 197, 199, 200, 218*
Burke, Sean *136*
Burns, Jarlath *55*
Byrne, Declan *98*
Cadogan, Eoin *121*

Cahill, Des *267*
Cahill, Fintan *116*
Callaghan, Eamon *262*
Campbell, Dave *189*
Campbell, Hugh *262*
Campbell, James *189*
Canavan, Brian *151*
Canavan, Peter *48, 107, 152, 162, 165, 205*
Carew, Niall *261*
Carolan, Ronan *131*
Carlin, Dermot *173, 206*
Carr, Aidan *14, 15, 55, 57, 59, 102, 103, 152-162, 164, 248*
Carr, Aidan (snr) *152, 153*
Carr, Ann *66, 67*
Carr, Barney *151, 152, 153*
Carr, Ellen *66*
Carr, Fionnuala *15, 156*
Carr, Gerry *152*
Carr, Hugh *152*
Carr, Mary *66*
Carr, Mickey *66*
Carr, Mickey Jr. *66*
Carr, Ross *14, 54, 59, 123, 151, 152, 153, 154, 155, 156*
Carr, Sarah-Louise *156*
Carr, Theresa *157*
Carr, Tommy *10*
Carroll, Patrick *185*
Carthy, Brian *254*
Cassidy, Aidan *171, 215, 216*
Cassidy, Aisling *67*
Cassidy, Anne *211*
Cassidy, Aoife *9, 24, 204, 268*
Cassidy, Carol-Ann *67, 239*
Cassidy, Cealain *67*
Cassidy, Damian *11, 12, 40*
Gerald Cassidy *62, 65*
Cassidy, Kevin *6, 9, 20, 22-30, 41, 66-69, 71, 74-78, 133, 134, 136-141, 182, 183, 185-189, 203-206, 209-216, 224, 225, 227-231, 233-235, 238-241, 246, 257-262, 264-273*
Cassidy, Nia *9, 24, 204, 268*
Cassidy, Sarah *9, 24, 25, 27, 30, 74, 76, 132, 204, 211, 238, 268, 269, 273*
Cassidy, Siobhán *67*
Cassidy, Stephen *67, 71, 74, 182, 268*
Cassidy, Tommy *66, 67, 77, 211*
Castro, Fidel *17*
Cavanagh, Colm *20, 215*
Cavanagh, Sean *25, 168, 170-173, 206, 209,*

274